CHE GUEVARA, PAULO FREIRE, AND THE PEDAGOGY OF REVOLUTION

Peter McLaren

Foreword by Ana Maria Araújo Freire

ROWMAN & LITTLEFIELD PUBLISHERS, INC.
Lanham • Boulder • New York • Oxford

ROWMAN & LITTLEFIELD PUBLISHERS, INC.

Published in the United States of America
by Rowman & Littlefield Publishers, Inc.
4720 Boston Way, Lanham, Maryland 20706
http://www.rowmanlittlefield.com

12 Hid's Copse Road
Cumnor Hill, Oxford OX2 9JJ, England

British Library Cataloguing in Publication Information Available

Library of Congress Cataloging-in-Publication Data

McLaren, Peter, 1948–
    Che Guevara, Paulo Freire, and the pedagogy of revolution / Peter McLaren.
       p.   cm.
    Includes the bibliographical references (p.) and index.
    ISBN 0-8476-9532-8 (cloth : alk paper). — ISBN 0-8476-9533-6
(paper : alk paper)
      1. Critical pedagogy.   2. Guevara, Ernesto, 1928–1967.   3. Freire, Paulo, 1921– .
I. Title.
LC196.M29 2000
370.11'5—dc21   99-32890
                                                CIP

Printed in the United States of America

♾ ™The paper used in this publication meets the minimum requirements of American National Standard for Information Sciences—Permanence of Paper for Printed Library Materials, ANSI/NISO Z39.48—1992.

This book is dedicated to Jennifer McLaren,
in unyielding devotion.

CONTENTS

PETER McLAREN: THE POET LAUREATE OF THE EDUCATIONAL LEFT

Joe L. Kincheloe

The beginning of the twenty-first century—especially as it coincides with the publication of this book—is probably a good time to proclaim Peter McLaren the poet laureate of the educational left. No one operating in critical education has Peter's capacity to turn a phrase, to focus our attention on the relationship between pedagogy and injustice, or to make us chuckle while moving us to see anew. I am pleased to be privy to Peter's critical humor, unparalleled phraseology, and brilliant insights into the world of the political, cultural, and the pedagogical. These qualities are present throughout this volume—maybe Peter's best work ever.

Only Peter could conjure the following McLarenisms:

The Shroud of Turin: "From the days in 1855 when Sir John Bowrigg, the Victorian bureaucrat, proclaimed 'Free Trade is Jesus Christ and Jesus Christ is Free Trade' to the current era where Christian fundamentalists such as the Reverend Jerry Falwell proclaim capitalism, democracy, and Jesus to be as seamlessly connected as the Shroud of Turin and equally as mystical, there has been a willful ignorance surrounding the paralyzing effects that the victorious embrace of capitalism has had on the powerless and destitute of the world."

Bargain-basement capitalism: "Enduring imbalances in the 'globalitarian world'—the worldwide problem of overcapacity, the random destruction of the ecosystem by unregulated markets accompanying the new bargain-basement capitalism, the imposition of exchange values upon all productions of value, the creation of a uniform culture of pure consumption or Wal-Martization of global culture, the vampirism of Western carpetbaggers sucking the lifeblood from the open veins of South America, opportunistic politicians, assaults on diasporic cultures, and new waves of xenophobia—have brought about a serious political inertia within the United States Left in general, and within the educational Left in particular."

No-fault apostasy: "And why now, at a time when the marketplace has trans-formed itself into a *deus ex machina* ordained to rescue humankind from eco-nomic disaster, and when voguish theories imported from France and Germany can abundantly supply North American radicals with veritable plantations of no-risk, no-fault, knock-off rebellion? Why should North American educators take seriously two men who were propelled to international fame for their devotion to the downtrodden of South America and Africa?"

Sunday School proselytizing: "The conceptual net known as critical pedagogy has been cast so wide and at times so cavalierly that it has come to be associated with anything dragged up out of the troubled and infested waters of educational prac-tice, from classroom furniture organized in a 'dialogue-friendly' circle to 'feel-good' curricula designed to increase students' self-image. It has become, in other words, repatriated by liberal humanism and been transformed to a combination of mid-dle-brow, town-hall meeting entrepreneurship and Sunday School proselytizing."

These, of course, are only a few examples—there are countless more through-out the book—of what we have come to expect from Peter. He is undoubtedly one of a kind, as Nita Freire illustrates so profoundly in her tender comments printed here. When Natalie Merchant and her Ten Thousand Maniacs sing about Jack, Alan, Bobby, and the rest of the beat boys howling at night, they can now add a new verse about Peter. Perhaps the funny and loving stories Jenny McLaren can tell about his howl. Nita understands Peter, focusing on his pas-sionate identification with Paulo Freire and Che Guevara and their ability to love. Always devoted to the work and now the memories of Freire and Guevara, Peter, like Nita, recognizes the magical possibilities such a radical love open up for those exposed to it. I have learned enough from Paulo to understand that the critical revolutionary is directed by an irrepressible radical love. Peter makes this point time and again in this work.

The fusing of reason and emotion and the necessity of teaching the mind and heart evoke Peter's passion for Che Guevara and Paulo Freire. In their lives he finds the conceptual ore that transports him to the next evolutionary stage of crit-ical pedagogy. The Freire and Guevara that Peter presents speak to us from beyond the grave about a type of love that serves as a generator of critical action. As an inspired hermeneutic medium, Peter interprets their messages in a vari-ety of ways. Using verbal pictures of Guevara's martyred, rough, and severed hands and Paulo's tender and bold ones, to their shared visions of what the world could become, Peter analyzes the contemporary meanings of their lives. The insight of Peter's comparisons of Freire to Martin Luther King and Guevara to Malcom X adds new dimensions to our understanding of the man with the long gray beard and the man in the black beret. The dialectical interplay between Freire and Guevara along with these images of them can no doubt help us for-mulate both new ways of understanding twenty-first century globalization and fresh methods of resisting its socioeconomic cancers.

Here emerges the central question, the purpose of the book: Why should we take Freire and Guevara so seriously now? Another question is for North American readers: Why should gringos pay such close attention to these two men who worked so hard for the oppressed of South America and Africa? Peter uses these queries to fashion the following pages, as he struggles to make sense of the world these visionaries left behind. In this context Peter encounters something that I believe will play a central role in twenty-first century pedagogies and politics of social justice: a radical ontology. Freire and Guevara not only help us understand and change the world, but they provide insights into new ways of being and becoming human. My own work is profoundly influenced by the spirit of human possibility that Freire, Guevara, and Peter offer us here.

New ways of being, however, cannot be separated from the socioeconomic and the political—as Peter well knows and as many in the educational and psychological avant garde have forgotten. The world Freire and Guevara left behind is a frightening place. Salaries for executives explode in the transnational corporations while worker wages are driven down as companies find cheaper labor in poor nations. Indeed, it is fascinating to watch the U.S. stock market fall whenever there is the slightest rise of wages for the poorest workers in the American economy. In Freire and Guevara's beloved Latin America and Africa, the news is not good, as poverty continues to expand into the twenty-first century.

Monitoring these trends, Peter describes the globalitarian world with its unacceptable and increasing disparity of wealth. In this context he documents the economic and environmental effects of NAFTA on the Mexican people—disease, birth defects, and an intensification of poverty. All of this is occurring at the same time that many political and educational leaders are proclaiming the virtues and victory of the unfettered free market. In the name of freedom they demand that the peoples of the world submit to the demands of the market. As the U.S. government provides grants of public money to corporations, budget cuts gut programs designed to help the victims of unregulated capital. As Freire and Guevara so well understood, such a reality cannot continue indefinitely without some type of violent explosion. We all pray that it will not take a major human tragedy to awaken citizens of the United States to the horror that current policies are producing among the "have nots" at home and around the globe.

Peter admonishes those academics who, in the name of transgression, promote trendy social theories while ignoring the suffering of the lived world. Taking his cue from Freire, Peter points out the ways that some social theory labeled as postmodern often ignores the brute realities many working people face around the world. As Paulo often maintained, reconceptualizing the categories employed to analyze the world has value only when such efforts are part of a larger struggle to change the world. With this in mind, Peter delineates a pedagogy in which students confront knowledge that is not only contemplative but sensual. In one of the book's most powerful passages, Peter calls for critical educators to engage students in the lives of the poor. As he puts it: "Opportunities must be made for students to work in communities where they can spend time with ethnically diverse populations in the context of community activism and participation in progressive social movements. Students need to move beyond simply knowing about critical, multicultural practice. They must also move toward an embodied and corporeal understanding of such practice and an effective investment in such practice at the level of everyday life such that they are able to deflect the invasive power of capital and the defrauding, ideologically self-interested reporting on national and international events by the mainstream U.S. media, a reporting that serves to protect through its journalistic-industrial complex the corporate interests of the state. As such, critical pedagogy should put ideology-critique at its center of gravity."

Peter fights to prevent Freire and Guevara's legacy from being so diluted that they appear merely a warm and fuzzy teacher with creative methods (Freire) and a depoliticized cartoon action figure (Guevara). We must never allow the world to forget what Freire and Guevara's struggle was for and the ways the mainstream reacted to them during their lives. Freire's evisceration shows up time and time again in my own attempts to teach and write about him and the issues for which he fought. I recently finished a book on teaching that was conceptually founded on the struggle for social justice, the act of problematizing the knowledge of schooling, and other Freirean principles. My editor was not happy with the book, asserting that in no way could a general audience understand issues of epistemology, ideology, hegemony, discursive analyses and their relation to the teaching act.

In order to "save" my book, he directed me to follow the lead of an author who had just written a book on a critical Freirean pedagogy for the editor's company. I dutifully read the manuscript, hoping to pick up hints that would help me make my book more readable—a goal I work to achieve in all my writing. Before I was halfway through the text, I began to sense something quite strange about it. Not once in my reading had the political dimension of a critical education or of Freire's work been referenced. With this realization, I began to flip through the rest of the manuscript, searching for just one political reference. There was none to be found.

Once again, my cognitive limitations confronted me. What my editor wanted was for me simply to delete those uncomfortable, unnecessary, and complex references to the ways that power operates and reproduces itself in the educational and social domain. For better sales he fancied a Freire-inspired text without Freire's raison d'etre, his driving passion, the motivational force behind his call to teaching. Peter McLaren refuses to give us a sterilized, depolicized Freire or Guevara. His Freire and Guevara do not surrender to a liberal humanist comfort zone. They call us to the type of action that is necessary if we wish to avoid the tragedy that awaits us. Along with my co-editor, Henry Giroux, and former Rowman & Littlefield editor Jill Rothenberg, I am proud to welcome Peter's book into our series.

FOREWORD

Ana Maria Araújo Freire

What makes a blond man of the "North," a respected professor and intellectual, want to write about two men from the "South," accustomed to and engaged in the centuries-old, daily round of oppression and exclusion of the people of Latin America; two men united by similar aspects of courage and daring in historical time but, principally, in the space of solidarity, generosity, and humility?

What, I repeat, would make Peter McLaren lean toward a Brazilian and an Argentinian with a Cuban soul? Is it mere, though justifiable, epistemological curiosity? Let me put the question another way: what is the common identity between Paulo Freire and Che Guevara, each of whom offered his life to make the world more beautiful and just, and the author of this book?

Paulo and Che went off to battle to subvert the unjust order of a reality so different from the antiseptic world of the then adolescent Peter. They departed from the ugliness of the miseries of hunger and disease, of illiteracy and prostitution, of not being able to say or do anything because you have been chained for hundreds of years by every kind of oppression and exploitation, on a common undertaking—although they had never seen or spoken with each other. What brought this young man close to revolutionaries of liberation and revolutionary pedagogy since, in the 1950s and 1960s, he must have only been reading about themes that the "banking" curricula demanded, especially as educators and politicians in the "First World" believed themselves to be free of problems existing only in Latin America and Africa? What justifies the *leit-motiv* of Peter's journey, as a man and as an intellectual, of his "pursuit" of the political educator Paulo Freire and the educative statesman Ernesto Guevara? Why, for years, has he been so preoccupied with the pain and injustice of the oppressed, from an epistemological and affective viewpoint, within this world that initially was not his?

Paulo and Che fought for their convictions until their deaths, because they had given themselves, lucid and engaged, to the political tasks of liberation: educative praxis and armed revolution. Why, then, this choice of Peter's, a man born in the frigid hemisphere that continues to dominate the hot world peopled only by lazy good-for-nothings whom the dominators want to believe were born only to serve them? Would it not have been enough to acritically and simply peruse the "worldly readings" the two made about the lives of the ragged and ruined men and women of their world; whether they were pronounced in universities, or in culture circles, or even in the "sierras maestras?" No. He studied them and understood them rationally and passionately. He engaged himself in them. He felt them as part of his very being that ponders the world. He identified with the feeling common to both Paulo and Che, which is also very much his: the ability to love. A feeling that, when deep and true in human beings, is not wasted on itself but opens possibilities for those who live it radically, both for reflections in the political and epistemological field and everyday, ethical and generous, praxes.

I met Peter McLaren in the late 1980s in Los Angeles during one of the trips on which I accompanied Paulo in his work as "pilgrim of the obvious"—there he was, trying to hide behind the hair falling over his face and his frank, boyish smile and soft speech, this marvelous gift that some people have in a very deep and special way: that of loving men and women independently of their social, ethnic, religious, gender, or chronological condition. Peter's choice was surely born in admitting that he admired Paulo and Che above all because they had created the pedagogy of love.

In the "era of cynical reason"—as Peter has so aptly characterized the times in which we live, in what Paulo saw as the new, purified, and perverse version of capitalism—it is very difficult to truly love. The examples of this human possibility must not die with the deaths of Paulo and Che—and so many other men and women scattered about the world; we have to take them as Peter does, with the intention of concretizing a more just and human world order. We must dedicate our best political, pedagogical, and epistemological efforts to making ourselves available to every like-minded man and woman in the struggle to realize a democratic utopia.

Men and women invent technologies through their capacity to think and to create their own survival in the construction of their histories. All these inventions are up-to-the-moment products of their times, advances never before seen. Plantation, irrigation, the wheel, writing and reading, the printing press, the compass, navigation, commerce, the steam engine, modern industry, trains, electric light, the telephone, radio, automobiles, airplanes, television and videotape, and so on, have brought us to the "communication age." Recently, computers, space ships and the conquest of sidereal space, artificial satellites placed in the cosmos for telecommunications, and the internet and fax temporarily complete the list of instruments said to be at the service of humanity.

Really, the facility with which we speak on the telephone with a friend or relative, or send by fax messages of the most diverse kinds (written in our own words!) to other distant people, or travel in a few hours to anywhere in the world in planes that become faster and safer every day, makes the human need for communication explicit.

In the meantime, this human creative capacity is being distorted, in a generalized and contradictory way, in acts and actions that negate the ethicality we have to have inside us to guide and prescribe our social behavior. True communication, which would widen contacts and knowledge indispensable for the progress and equality of the different peoples and social segments of the world, is being transformed into a mere extension, using Freirean categories, in the service of the globalization of the economy that is holding us all hostage to a few "world bosses." The communication age is actually becoming the era of borders, of frontiers more sharply delineated than ever by human incommunicability, in a vast field of lovelessness.

Consequently, it is an age that denies authentic communication, which has at its essence the I—THOU dialogue. A dialogue that ought to involve, in a single amorous act, the subjects with an object that can and wants to be known but, above all, an authentic communication that must be established between knowledgeable subjects. Never in history has there been so great a distance as today between scholastic education and social practice as dictated by the sophisticated technologies created to serve the dominant economic and ideological interests. Like the sounds of a magic flute, these technologies and ideologies enthrall almost all men and women, making reality opaque and alienating people, severing the possibility for loving dialogue. This devastation by chaos of the legitimate interests and aspirations of the majority of the population needs to be furiously denied.

Current education with its neoliberal, basically technicist, principles is really only contributing to and being dragged along by these perversions of globalization. Education, we must admit, has become something less important than the accumulation and greedy enrichment of the few at the expense of limitless suffering for most of the world's population.

We need to emphasize the fact that globalization dictates not only the norms of the commercial and financial markets but also the values, behaviors, and elitist and discriminatory cultural patterns socially consecrated by the dominant interests; affecting the "have," the "want," and the "be" of all the beings on the planet, whether we want it or not, whether we know it or not. There is, and there always has been, a dialectical relationship among education, politics, and power. Thus, I repeat, if we want the transformation of unjust societies, one of the paths is to follow Paulo and Che. Reinvent them—because the world walks with large steps and also because their humanistic and historic comprehension may not jibe with the unalterability of the eternally permanent—and find solutions for present dramas.

The ethical-pedagogical and political-epistemological postures of Paulo and Che were to oppose this state of affairs, to shout that human beings are born to be more. This is one of the principal duties of the progressive educator, if we want to make a better world for everyone. Peter McLaren continues to dedicate himself to this task with competence, fervor, and tenderness, as proved by this theoretical work and his praxis as a committed citizen of the world.

It is necessary, without delay, to ally ourselves with those who, like Peter, are attempting to reinvent the pedagogy of resistance with tactics that will be effective in combating new aspects of the millennial evil of the powerful. And, as romantic and idealistic as it may seem to the astute nonbelievers of the world, the possibility of our intelligently creating a more just, beautiful, and truly fraternal world while resisting all sorts of injustices, degradations, and violences that hold sway on planet Earth is by way of a pedagogy of love.

It is important to nourish hope, that ontologically human thing, which builds faith in a better future and makes us act in the direction of establishing truly democratic societies. We cannot run the risk of everyone dying in the anguish and nostalgia imposed by every kind of neocolonialism and imperialism. We must be certain that hope as a political category is completed by love. Hope is a revolutionary transformer, either through knowledge or through radical ethics, but it loses strength, brilliance, and political clarity without fraternal love. I feel the beneficent presence of Paulo, not only as my husband but also as a man who can still contribute with all his life force through serious and profound reflections as well as through his generous, revolutionary praxis in the field of political education when I see him reinvented, as he so desired to be, by people who possess, above all, the same capacity to love men and women that he and Che had.

I am very happy in the certainty that Peter is continuing to contribute to the transgressive pedagogy of Paulo and Che, recreating them in the current context. My many very special thanks for the opportunity to write this foreword that brings me even closer to Paulo and to you.

> Ana Maria Araújo Freire (Nita Freire)
> São Paulo
> June 6, 1999
> (Translated by Peter Lownds)

A SALUTE TO PETER McLAREN

Luis Vitale

Two men crossed my Latin American University generation:
Ernesto Che Guevara and Paulo Freire.
I still guard as a treasure
my teaching experience
in the good times of Allende,
with my students reclined
on the lawn of the University of Concepción,
in the poor neighborhoods and the coal mines,
seduced by the words and works of Paulo,
lending to us generously and pedagogically
what he had learned from his people,
as did Simón Rodríguez,
teacher of the other Simón: Bolívar
who dreamed of Latin American unity.
A dream which regained vigor with Che
in his liberatory practices and words.

An alternative pedagogy
Appeared in "Our America," in the words of Martí.
It was the method of Paulo
full of content for a better world.

When the "neoliberal" night was darkest,
the dawn broke on the Caribbean coasts,
on "los sin tierra," in the native land of Paulo,
and from behind a tree in Chiapas
the eyes of Marcos, poetically calling
to terminate hopelessness.

New Paulos and new Ches will return
in teachers who apply their wisdom
with a vision of a just society,
in the classrooms and outside of them, all united
giving new meaning to life.

Paulo and Che
they call us and unite us
in this selfish world.

It was, is, and will be UTOPIA,
day after day.

Che and Paulo resuscitated
will return to our paradigms
in new and forceful versions
of revolutionary pedagogies.

And the seed planted by Peter
will bloom into a thousand flowers.
                —28 September 1999
                    (translated by Jill Pinkney-Pastrana and Gustavo Fischman)

Luis Vitale is currently Prof. Titular in the Department of History, Universidad de Chile. He is the author of fifty-six books, including *A General History of Latin America*, *A Marxist Interpretation of the History of Chile*, *Comparative Social History of the People of Latin America*, *Introduction to a Theory of History for Latin America*, *From Marti to Chiapas*, *Che: A Latin American Passion*, and *The Andean Project of Che*.

INTRODUCTION

On a recent voyage to the rain forests of Costa Rica, I rode a bus through the beautiful city of Cartago. From my window I noticed a young man with a long ponytail running beside the bus. As the bus passed him, he glanced up and our eyes momentarily met; I noticed that he was wearing a Che T-shirt with the inscription '¡Che Vive!'. A fleeting sensation of plaintive connectedness overcame me, and I managed to give him a quick 'thumbs-up' gesture of affirmation just in time for him to return a broad smile to the crazy gringo. For a brief moment, I felt that this ponytailed stranger and I were linked by a project larger than both of us. During that instant, I could tangibly sense between us a collective yearning for a world free from the burdens of this one, and I knew that I was not alone. The image of Che that he wore on his breast like a secular Panagia pointed to a realm of revolutionary values held in trust by all those who wish to break the chains of capital and be free. Che has a way of connecting—if only in this whimsical way—people who share a common resolve to fight injustice and to liberate the world from cruelty and exploitation. There was no way of knowing the politics of this young man and how seriously he identified with the life and teachings of El Che. But Che's image brings out the promise of such a connection and the political fecundity of even this momentary reverie.

The great Brazilian educator, Paulo Freire, also shares with Che the ability to bring people together around an animated common trust in the power of love, a belief in the reciprocal power of dialogue, and a commitment to 'conscientization' and political praxis. Few figures among the educational Left are as well known and as universally revered as Paulo Freire. Throughout my travels in Latin America, Southeast Asia, and Europe, I have seen slogans by Freire scribbled on buildings alongside those of Che. Whenever I speak at revolutionary forums or academic conferences about political praxis—whether in Malaysia, Japan, Mexico, Argentina, Brazil, Costa Rica, Finland, Europe, or elsewhere—the names of Che Guevara and Paulo Freire (and more recently, the Zapatistas) inevitably come up. They not only draw attention to the crisis of the times but also provide the singular hope that is necessary to move the struggle forward, *cueste lo que cueste.*

No one has done more to move the struggle forward over the role of education as a vehicle for liberatory praxis than Paulo Freire. From the moment he was jailed by the Brazilian military during the early days of the repression in 1964, to his exile and continuing struggle on behalf of peasants and the working class throughout the world (to whom he was dedicated in helping overcome their centuries-old marginalization from society), Paulo Freire has captured the political imagination of educators around the world. In an introduction to my book *Life in Schools,* the great liberation theologian, Leonardo Boff, affirmed Freire's pedagogical project as one of action in and on the world:

> The pedagogical project is created in order to place . . . lives inside the classroom and to employ knowledge and transformation as weapons to change the world. From the perspective of the social location of the condemned on Earth, it becomes clear that knowledge alone, as intended by the school, does not transform life. Only the conversion of knowledge into action can transform life. This concretely defines the meaning of practice: the dialectic movement between the conversion of transformative action into knowledge and the conversion of knowledge into transformative action. (1997, p. xi)

Although Che is certainly a better known figure than Freire worldwide, one would be hard-pressed to find a more respected and celebrated *'profe'* in the field of education than Paulo Freire anywhere in the world. His most famous work, *Pedagogy of the Oppressed,* has sold over a half million copies and has been translated into more than twenty languages. His theoretical developments have influenced the scholarly domains of sociology, anthropology, literacy, ecology, medicine, psychotherapy, philosophy, pedagogy, critical social theory, museology, history, journalism, and theater, to name just some of the fields indebted to his work. He is even credited with helping to found a new approach to research known as participatory research (Freire and Macedo, 1998). According to Ana Maria Araújo Freire and Donaldo Macedo, Freire was invited to visit approximately 100 cities throughout the world during his lifetime. They write: "His theory, which constitutes a reflection upon his practice, has served as the foundation for academic work and inspired practices in different parts of the world, from the *mocambos* of Recife to the *barakumin* in Brazil and abroad" (1998, p. 27). Even before the death in 1997, numerous schools, student organizations in schools of education, unions, popular libraries, and research scholarships bore his name. A list of his academic awards and honorary degrees would fill several pages.

Though Freire was an advocate of nonviolent insurrection and struggle, he was nevertheless jailed in Brazil as a politically dangerous subversive because of the

counter-hegemonic power of his ideas. Che remained convinced that reclama-
tion of one's land from imperialist settlers by violent means was a form of self-
defense, and that violent insurrection was the only way to defeat fascism and Yankee imperialism and reveal to the masses that the colonial god has feet of clay.
Despite these divergences, Freire and Che remained brothers of the heart,
brothers who never met in prison, in the theater of war, or in the arena of pedagogical struggle, but who shared a fraternal bond that opened up their hearts and
minds to a similar vision of the world—a vision of what the world already was,
where it was headed, and what it could become. As intellectual and political comrades, their lives represented the best of what the human spirit has to offer.

It is a feeling of kinship with Freire and Che that has served as the primary
motivation for this book. In the preface to my book *Critical Pedagogy and Predatory Culture,* Freire writes:

> When such a kinship develops we need to cultivate within ourselves the virtue of
> tolerance, which "teaches" us to live with that which is different; it is imperative
> that we learn from and that we teach our "intellectual relative," so that in the end
> we can unite in our fight against antagonistic forces. Unfortunately, as a group, we
> academics and politicians alike expend much of our energy on unjustifiable "fights"
> among ourselves, provoked by adjectival or, even worse, by purely adverbial dif-
> ferences. While we wear ourselves thin in petty "harangues," in which personal
> vanities are displayed and egos are scratched and bruised, we weaken ourselves for
> the real battle: the struggle against our antagonists. (1995, p. x)

Paulo Freire was a dear friend and loving mentor. His words about kinship
ring true, as do his warnings about the petty jealousies that infect academics,
especially the small-minded ones (and the academy is filled to the brim with
them) whose opportunism is wrapped in charm, whose narcissistic and vainglo-
rious search for attention and personal gain knows no bounds, and who will stoop
to any level to personalize their criticisms and engage in acrimonious intellectual assaults and sell their souls for power or fame. Freire would have none of
that; he was a humble man who always put the project of human freedom ahead
of his own personal gain. One of the first of his many acts of kindness toward me
was helping to arrange an invitation for me to speak at a conference in Cuba in
1987. After that, we would periodically see each other when he came to visit the
United States. Once I had the opportunity to visit with him and his wife, Ana
Maria (or "Nita"), in their home during a visit to São Paulo. Over the past fifteen
years I've written a great deal about Paulo and his work. This is not surprising
for somebody who, for twenty-five years, has been involved in educational transformation both in the domain of grassroots activism and in the politically quar-
antined precincts of the academy. And though the political project that guides
my work has been influenced no less by the teachings and life of Che Guevara,

I have written only several articles about him. Although I never had the opportunity to meet him (I was nineteen when he was executed), his influence on my
understanding of social justice and human courage has been inestimable.

It is saddening to witness how the figure of Paulo Freire has been domesticated by liberals, progressives, and pseudo-Freireans who have tried incessantly
to claim his legacy and teachings—much as they have done to the figure of John
Dewey, whose radical politics have been ominously blunted by his more politically sanguine followers in the academy. Hence, it is necessary to re-possess
Freire from those contemporary revisionists who would reduce him to the *grand
seigneur* of classroom dialogue and would antiseptically excise the corporeal
force of history from his pedagogical practices. It is much more difficult to
appropriate the figure of Che Guevara, given that he was an active *guerrillero*
until the moment he was murdered under the hawkish eye and panoptic gaze of
the CIA. At the same time it is much more difficult to argue for the relevance of
Che for educators today, given that he remained an active opponent of U.S.
imperialism throughout his entire life and called for "Vietnams" to arise on every
continent of the globe. But when you consider that Malcolm X now appears on
a U.S. postage stamp, it might well be the case that one day Che will be included
in the U.S. pantheon of world 'heroes.' After all, the United States has a seduc-
tive way of incorporating anything that it can't defeat and transforming that
'thing' into a weaker version of itself, much like the process of diluting the
strength and efficacy of a virus through the creation of a vaccine. If the United
States could find a Che 'vaccine,' it is more than likely that a stronger version of
the Che 'virus' would rise up somewhere in the world where capital was laying
waste to human dignity and the survival of the poor and dispossessed, in order
to wreak its revenge. As long as Marx and Engels's homage—"The history of all
hitherto existing society is the history of class struggles"(1952, p. 40)—still captures the imagination due to its increasing relevance in the world today, that
much is assured.

This book devotes considerably more space to Che than to Freire in an
attempt to balance the scales, so to speak. Another reason for a disproportionate attention to Che in this book stems from a personal lament that his contribution—both in terms of his teachings and the pristine coherence that marked
the way he lived his life as a *guerrillero*—seldom, if ever, has been discussed at
length in the educational literature on critical pedagogy. In my view, this lack of
attention constitutes an oversight of momentous proportion, both for the educational Left in particular and for teachers and teacher educators in general.

When I first began sketching the ideas for this book, I proposed readmitting
into the debates over educational reform the legacy of Che Guevara as a model
of moral leadership, political vision, and revolutionary praxis. I soon recognized,
without surprise, that Che had never been officially admitted to the court of serious educational debate, most likely for the same reason that provoked Herb
Kohl to write:

> I am still not convinced that . . . [Che] . . . had a pedagogy that is meaningful for our society at this historical conjuncture. We are not at a revolutionary moment and we are the center of capitalist oppression with no strong social movement committed to changing the situation. In fact I cannot think of any school textbooks that treat Guevara with dignity and complexity. (1999, p. 308)

Kohl argues that because Che is not sympathetically portrayed in school textbooks, and because strong social movements against oppression are woefully lacking in the United States, we therefore should not place too much faith in the relevance of Che's message for our current condition. I wish Kohl could have been on the marches in which I have been privileged to participate, from Los Angeles to Porto Alegre, where banners of Che are clutched by proud working hands and held high. Kohl's defeatist comments about Che appear more symptomatic of a growing cynicism among progressive educators than a reasoned and convincing case against Che.

Why Che? Why Freire? Why now? For those who have been following world events, or taking even a cursory look at the conditions in our cities and small towns all across the United States, it is evident that democracy has transmogrified into the negation of its own principles; that there is a counter-tendency growing within it; that a beast is growing in its belly, bloated by capitalist greed; that human beings have made themselves subservient to, and at the very least, accessories of capital accumulation and consumption and the instruments of labor that dominate them through a powerfully cathected social amnesia; and that the international division of labor is widening into a crisis of monopoly capitalism—what Lenin so aptly termed imperialism. Che and Freire have never been needed more than at this current historical moment. It is not necessary to canvas the present political landscape with the discerning gaze of the sociologist or the trained academic eye to see that oppression has not been vanquished by capitalist democracy but continues to emerge unabated in new forms by means of innovative and decentralized production facilities, newly centralized economic power brought about by new media technologies, capitalist warfare against unions and social services, state-sanctioned Latinophobia, and the disproportionate incarceration of Latino/as and African Americans in a rapidly expanding prison industry. Recent events surrounding education professor José Solís Jordán—who taught educational foundations at DePaul University and the University of Puerto Rico, and who was framed by the FBI and found guilty of planting two bombs at military recruitment center—serve as only one of many indications that the U.S. government will stop at nothing short of breaking all peaceful opposition to its imperialist practices in Puerto Rico and elsewhere.[1]

We don't need to chart current corporate strategies with a moral compass crafted by seminarians to know that the globe is fast becoming raw material for corporate greed and quick profit margins, as the gap between rich and poor is growing so large that the 300 largest corporations in the world now account for 70 percent of foreign direct investment and 25 percent of world capital assets (Bagdikian, 1998). Never before have media technologies been so sophisticated that they could effortlessly accelerate assets from the public to the private sector and consolidate so swiftly and smoothly the power of corporations. Not since the end of World War II has the United States been in the position—in military terms, at least—of being the world's only superpower and unchallenged. The neoliberal ideology of the free market—mediated through the triad multilateral institutions of the International Monetary Fund, the World Bank, and the World Trade Organization—is accelerating capital accumulation throughout all parts of the globe. Such an acceleration of capitalist accumulation is occuring in direct proportion to a lack of opposition among world leaders who, at this moment in time, are unbearably burdened by political inertia and ethical quietism. Uneven or unequal development of the world system is devastating the poor and disadvantaged throughout Latin America, Africa, Russia, and elsewhere around the globe, as the world becomes inescapably polarized into peripheral and central economies. Global capitalism is propelling a mass exodus of 'guest workers' to the industrialized West, and fueling in its wake a war against the 'Other.' The legacy of European colonialism is being played out with a vengeance, this time through a deepening of the disparities within the international division of labor brought about by the circuits and flows of finance and monopoly capital. Never before has capital penetrated the spaces of the lifeworld that were previously off limits (previously restricted to wage labor but now commodifying subjectivity itself) and done so throughout the entire planet. Never before has the Malthussian spirit risen up with such violence in the rampant neoliberalism that condemns the worker to remain forever uninivited to capital's mighty feast. As the poor grow in numbers, as the homeless flood the streets of our cities, they are seen more and more as disrupting the 'natural order' of capitalism. And facing this unraveling historical matrix we have, in the Western academy, postmodern theory's avant-garde celebration of cultural hybridity; the incommensurability of discourses; pastiche, indeterminancy, and contingency; the ironic troping of its commodity status; its textual burlesque; and its celebration of cultural detrius such as kitsch, pop iconography, and samizat publications as the apogee of cultural critique. While not all postmodern theory is to be rejected, there is a species of it that remains loyal to capital's promotional culture where parody can be paraded as dissent and cultural parasitism masqueraded as subversion and where one can avoid putting political commitment to the test. The academy is a place where Marxism is dismissed as innocent of complexity and where Marxist educators are increasingly outflanked by fashionable, motely minded apostates in svelte black suede jackets, black chinos, and black '50s eyeglass frames with yellow-tint lenses, for whom the metropole has become a riotous mixture of postmodern mestiza narratives and where hubris shadows those who remain even remotely loyal to causal thinking. For these voguish hellions of the seminar room, postmodernism is the toxic intensity of bohemian nights, where the proscribed, the immiserated, and the wretched of the earth simply get in the way of their fun. Poverty, for them, is at the very least a purgative for an indulgent society and at worst a necessary evil—if you want the material trappings of the American Dream, that is. Where Freire was implacably prosocialist, critical pedagogy— his stepchild—has become (at least in classrooms throughout the United States) little more than liberalism refurbished with some lexical help from Freire (as in words like 'praxis' and 'dialogue') and basically is used to camouflage existing capitalist social relations under a plethora of eirenic proclamations and classroom strategies. Real socialist alternatives are nowhere to be found, and if they are, few have *las tripas* to make them resoundingly heard in the classrooms of the nation.

I don't want to suggest that there are no important debates that postmodernism has ushered in—especially by some post-Marxists who have begun to refigure the topic of labor. Postmodern Marxists view as productivist and laborist the many articulations of orthodox Marxism; revolution becomes the consummation of the logic of the desiring machine where social actors "are reborn as 'bodies without organs' and remade as cyborgs" (Dinerstein and Neary, 1999 p. 1). For orthodox Marxists, postmodern Marxism discards the concrete quality of labor in favor of its more abstract potentialities, where human emancipation becomes an avoidance of reality (Dinerstein and Neary, 1999). This book will not attempt to resolve this debate, but will pull out some elements of this debate for consideration in a discussion of critical agency. Ultimately, one has to approach the relationship between postmodernism and Marxism dialectically. Dialectics is about mediation, not juxtaposition. The issue is not simply *either* Marxism *or* postmodernism. In some instances postmodern theories may be more productive for understanding aspects of social life than current Marxist theories admit. In this book my concern is with arguing against some versions of postmodern theory and their lack of attention to global capitalist social relations and attendant human suffering. However, I am even more concerned with what Marxist theory does best: analyzing and challenging the very viability of capitalism in human society.

We live in unhappy times, in the midst of a global hegemony based on fraud, when our feelings of unhappiness do not appear to be connected to the depredations of capitalist exploitation occurring within the external world. Rather, our feelings are attached to the shimmering surface effects of signs and simulations and the dull radiance that illuminates the spectacles of the everyday. Our external and internal worlds seem to have been split apart. Ana Dinerstein and Mike Neary link this disconnection to the process of *disutopia*, an abstract crisis of theory. Their comments are worth quoting at length:

> *Disutopia* is the most significant project of our time. It is not just the temporary absence of Utopia, but the political celebration of the end of social dreams. *Disutopia* should not be confused with *apathy*, since, although it *appears* in the *form* of indifference, the postmodern condition entails an active process involving

simultaneously the struggle to control contradiction and diversity, *and* the accla-
mation of diversity; the repression of the struggles against *Disutopia* and the celebration of individual self-determination. The result of this is social Schizophrenia.
In so far as diversity, struggle and contradiction cannot be eliminated by political
or philosophical voluntarism, *Disutopia* has to be imposed. Its advocates spend a
huge amount of time in de-construction, repentance, denial, forgetfulness. *Neu-
rotic Realism* in Arts, *the Third Way* in Politics coupled with its academic justifi-
cations, the scientific classification of the horrors of our time, as well as the difficulties for personal relations to become meaningful are some examples that
illustrate how the project of *Disutopia* works. The result of all this together is
Mediocrity. (1999, p. 3; emphasis in original)

To challenge the current project of Disutopia, it is important that we do not
lose sight of the particular in relation to the totality of determinate social relations. Few individuals can show us the expanse of the concrete social forces and
relations that both entrap and enthrall us as powerfully as can Che Guevara and
Paulo Freire. Few can illustrate as effectively through their lives and their teachings how labor and the laboring class must serve as the agent of the transformation of capitalist social relations and why the subjectivity of the working class
must become the starting point for the development of the 'new man/woman' of
revolutionary social struggle. And what better and more effective way can critical agency be developed than through the educational efforts of Che and Freire?
A major task of this book is to begin to tease out ways in which the pedagogy
of these two historical figures can be used as the wellspring for creating the type
of critical agency necessary to contest and transform current global relations of
exploitation and oppression. Of course, many books have already been written
about critical pedagogy, revolutionary pedagogy, feminist pedagogy, and the contributions that Freire has made toward their development. This book is pleased,
naturally, to join such company. However, what sets this book apart is its—albeit
modest—attempt to rescue critical pedagogical work from the kind of bourgeois
humanism that has frequently made it functionally advantageous to existing social
relations, the employer class, and the international division of labor.
This book essays no more than a rudimentary sketch of the lives of Che and
Freire, leaving some biographical details no doubt wanting in nuance. Especially
for those who are aficionados of Che's life, there may be disappointments in the
pages that follow, since I made no claim to offer any new factual information
about the 'historical Che' of official Cheography that is not already available in
the recent plethora of books and articles about Che—many of them impressive
in their fastidious attempt to leave no rock marking Che's history unturned.
What might interest many students of Che perhaps will appear throughout this
book only in ancillary form. Yet although this book may not uncover any new
mysteries surrounding the life and death of Che, I do promise to shape a new

context within which to reappraise his legacy—a 'pedagogical' context for appreciating the way in which he conducted his life—which, after all, is the most profound lesson he has left for us to ponder and to emulate.

Freire managed to outlive Che by over thirty years, and the world has been a greater place because of what he was able to accomplish in his long and arduous journey on the road to liberation. Few individuals have been as successful in moving the human spirit forward as these two men. They have taught us that history cannot erase revolutionary struggle based on the heroic aspirations of the uncommon lives of 'common' people. They have also revealed to us that the wounds of history cannot be healed without revolutionary love and a warrior's spirit tempered to do battle in the streets, in the boardrooms, in the classrooms, and in the factories of the capitalist present—and also in the caverns of the human heart. It is to the memories of these uncommon 'common' people that this book has been written.

Why Che? Why Freire? Why now? Why indeed.

NOTE

1. See Peter McLaren and José Solís Jordán (1999).

REFERENCES

Bagdikian, Ben H. (1998). "Capitalism and the Information Age." *Monthly Review*, vol. 50, no. 7, pp. 55–58.

Boff, Leonardo (1997). "Foreword to The Third Edition." In Peter McLaren, *Life in Schools: An Introduction to Critical Pedagogy in the Foundations of Education*. New York: Longman, pp. xi–xii.

Dinerstein, Ana; and Neary, Michael (1999). "Opening Remarks to the Labor Debate," February 24, 1999. Labor Studies Seminar Series, pp. 1–4. Unpublished manuscript.

Freire, Paulo (1993). *Pedagogy of the Oppressed*. Trans. by Myra Bergman Ramos. New York: Continuum.

Freire, Paulo (1995). "Preface." In Peter McLaren, *Critical Pedagogy and Predatory Culture*. London and New York: Routledge, pp. ix–xi.

Freire, Ana Maria Araújo; and Macedo, Donaldo (1998). *The Paulo Freire Reader*. New York: Continuum.

Kohl, Herbert (1999). "Social Justice and Leadership in Education: Commentary." *International Journal of Leadership in Education*, vol. 2, no. 3, pp. 307–11.

Marx, Karl; and Engels, Friederich (1952). *The Communist Manifesto*. Moscow: Progress Publishers, p. 40.

McLaren, Peter; and Jordán, José Solís (1999). "The Struggle for Liberation: La Lucha Continua! José Solís Jordán's Fight for Justice." *International Journal of Educational Reform*, vol. 8 no. 2, pp. 168–74

ACKNOWLEDGMENTS

The chapter on Che evolved from a paper that was originally presented at the conference Thirty Years Later: A Retrospective on Che Guevara, Twentieth-Century Utopias, and Dystopias, held at the University of California, Los Angeles, October 24–25, 1997. It was revised as the keynote address at the annual convention for the National Association for Multicultural Education, Albuquerque, New Mexico, October 31, 1997. An early version of this chapter was published as "The Pedagogy of Che Guevara" in *Cultural Circles*, vol. 3, summer 1998, pp. 28–104; and a highly condensed version of this article—"Revolutionary Leadership and Pedagogical Praxis: Revisiting the Legacy of Che Guevara"—has been published in *The International Journal of Leadership in Education*, 1999, vol. 2, no. 3, pp. 269–292. The chapter on Freire has been expanded from a short essay—"Paulo Freire's Legacy of Hope and Struggle"—that appeared in *Theory, Culture & Society*, vol. 14, no. 4, November 1997, pp. 147–153; and from another short essay: "A Legacy of Hope and Struggle," in *Reclaiming Our Voices: Emancipatory Narratives on Critical Literacy, Praxis, and Pedagogy*, in a special issue that was guest edited by Antonia Darder, *Teaching as an Act of Love: Reflections on Paulo Freire and His Contributions to Our Lives and Our Work*, Los Angeles, California Association of Bilingual Education, 1998, pp. 19–23. Two essays also contain some condensed sections of the chapter on Freire: "A Pedagogy of Possibility: Reflecting upon Paulo Freire's Politics of Education," in *Educational Researcher*, vol. 28, no. 2, March 1999, pp. 49–56; and "Paulo Freire's Pedagogy of Possibility" in *Freirean Pedagogy, Praxis and Possibilities: Projects of the New Millennium*, edited by Stanley S. Steiner, H. Mark Krank, Peter McLaren, and Robert E. Bahruth.

The brilliant exhibition at UCLA's Fowler Museum of Cultural History, "Che Guevara: Icon, Myth, and Message," curated by David Kunzle, and the subsequent invitation to present at the international symposium on Che, also held at UCLA during the time of the exhibition, helped to inspire me to write the original essay on Che. Kunzle's own writings have been illuminating, as have been my discussions with Maurice Zeitlin, Richard Harris, Doug Kellner, and James Petras.

I want to thank Dean Birkenkamp and Jill Rothenberg for their unflagging support of this project and excellent editorial assistance. Christine Gatliffe deserves a special thanks for her dedication to and hard work on this project, as does Kathleen Silloway for her excellent copyediting. Thanks to Ramin Farahmandpur for his important research and editorial efforts on my behalf, to Jayne Spencer for her perceptive insights into Che's history, to Jennifer McLaren for her conversations about revolutionary ideals, to Robert Bahruth for his excellent editorial suggestions, to Roberto Flores González for his interpretations of the Chiapas conflict, to Marcos Aguilar for his perceptive editorial advice, and to students and colleagues who have helped in the preparation of this manuscript.

Special thanks to Joe Kincheloe, Ana Maria Araújo Freire, Shirley Steinberg, Donaldo Macedo, Pepi Leistyna, Henry Giroux, Gustavo Fischman, Ira Shor, Antonia Darder, Rudy Torres, Lou Mirón, Moacir Gadotti, and Colin Lankshear. I would also like to thank the students in my Pedagogy of Revolution class at UCLA: Jaime Soto, Josefina Santiago, Martha Guerrero, Yvette LaPayese, Christer Berntzen, Michael Richter, Chitra Golestani, Rachel Estrella, Anita T. Revilla, Gilbert Contreras, Hua-Lun Lee, and Erica Friedman. Peter Lownds deserves a special thanks for the poetry of his ideas and his expertise in the Portuguese language. I want to acknowledge, with gratitude, the support of Luis Ernesto Morejón, Itamys Garcia Villar, the editors of Pathfinder Press, Fidel Rodriguez, Edgar Gonzalez, Alicia de Alba, Bertha Orozco Fuentes, Nize Maria Campos Pellanda, Marcia Moraes, Silvia Serra, Estanislao Antelo, Tomaz Tadeu Da Silva, Bebel O. Schaefer, Timothy Speed Levitch, Gayle Shangold, Veronica Poses, Dave Hill, Mike Cole, Rodolfo Chavez Chavez, Herman García, Glenn Rikowski, Peter Mayo, and Bill Tierney. I am also grateful for the support of the rest of my family, Laura McLaren-Layera, Marcelo Layera, Jon Fleming-McLaren, and Julie Fleming-McLaren. I take full responsibility for any errors that may appear in this text.

PART ONE

THE MAN IN THE BLACK BERET

No porque hayas caído tu luz es menos alta. (Not because you have fallen is your light less high)

—Nicolás Guillén, *Che Comandante (October 15, 1967) (in Löwy, 1973)*

Che considered himself a soldier of this revolution, with absolutely no concern about surviving it. Those who imagine that Che's ideas failed because of the outcome of the struggle in Bolivia might as well use this simplistic argument to say that many of the great revolutionary precursors and thinkers, including the founders of Marxism, were also failures because they were unable to see the culmination of their life's work and died before their noble efforts were crowned with success.

—Fidel Castro, *Che: A Memoir*

The peasants of Cochabamba have evolved a litany, a strange kind of prayer: "Little soul of Che, by your leave please work the miracle that will make my cow well again. Grant me that wish, little soul of Che."

—Paco Ignacio Taibo II, *Guevara: Also Known as Che*

Che Guevara making a point with his cigar, which he often did, circa 1964, Havana (Roberto & Osvaldo Salas/Liaison Agency)

Che Guevara speaking before the Central Organization of Cuban Trade Unions (CTC), circa 1962/3, Havana (Roberto & Osvaldo Salas/Liaison Agency)

ENCOUNTERING CHE IN OCCUPIED SPACES

In the midmorning on October 9, 1967, at the request of Colonel Zenteno, Warrant Officer Mario Terán of the Bolivian Rangers fires a six-round volley from an M2 rifle into the emaciated body of Che Guevara de la Serna. The shots ring out seconds after the famous revolutionary figure, laying wounded and exhausted on the dirt floor of a schoolhouse in La Higuera, near the Vallegrande military base, utters the now famous words: "Shoot, coward you are only going to kill a man."[1] That day, "El Che"—the man whom Jean-Paul Sartre had declared to be "the most complete human being of our age," and whom Frantz Fanon had described as "the world symbol of the possibilities of one man" (cited in Kunzle, 1997)—joined the ranks of fallen revolutionary martyrs such as José Martí, Emiliano Zapata, Augusto Sandino, Farabundo Martí, Camilo Torres, León Trotsky, María Lorena Barros, and Rosa Luxemburg. He was slain by a half-drunk executioner who was celebrating his birthday and who had argued for the right to kill Che because three friends from B company with the name "Mario" had been killed by the guerrillas.[2] As Terán is blasting away at Che, Sergeant Bernardino Huanca, who had volunteered to kill Che's comrades (and whose burst of machine-gun fire had caused the bullet hole in Che's beret just prior to his capture), enters the room next door and riddles the Peruvian, Juan Pablo Chang-Navarro (El Chino) and the Bolivian Simón Cuba (Willy) with bullets.[3] A short time later, Sergeant Major Carlos Pérez Panoso and Private Cabrero enter the schoolhouse and fire two postmortem shots into Che's body.[4]

The executioners and the guards stationed around the schoolhouse have already divided among themselves the money and personal objects removed from Che when he was captured—two berets (including the one bearing a bullet hole), a Parker fountain pen, a belt, one German 45-gauge pistol, a stainless-steel Solingen dagger, two pipes (one of which Che had used in his final hours to smoke the tobacco from two Astoria cigarettes offered to him after his capture by Captain Gary Prado Salmón), a notebook containing "Canto General" by Pablo Neruda and "Aconcagua" and "Piedra de Hornos" by Nicolás Guillén copied in his handwriting, one altimeter, and a cigarette holder (Harris, 1970). Two identical stainless-steel Rolex Oyster Perpetuals (one belonged to Che fallen comrade, Carlos Coella—Tuma—who, before dying, asked Che to give to his son) had been given by Che to Captain Gary Prado Salmón for safekeeping [with an "x" scratched onto the side of his own watch with a pebble that found on the dirt floor of the schoolhouse, the day before his execution (Ha 1970)]. Che's damaged Garand rifle was kept as a personal 'trophy' by Col Zenteno Anaya.

Orders for the executions had come in coded instructions from the M res general headquarters in La Paz but had originated from the office of P President, General Rene Barrientos (who was also Commander-in-Chie

armed forces), in accord with General Alfredo Ovando Candia, and Chief of Staff Juan José Tórrez. The military wanted the public to believe that Che had been killed in combat, and for that reason Che was not shot 'coup de grace'–style, in the head. The High Command of the Armed Forces issued Communiqué 45/67 early on October 9, stating that Che had been killed in an encounter marked by "fierce fighting" between "a red detachment" and Assault Regiment 2 (Rangers) in the Quebrada de Yuro region.

Slumped in a canvas stretcher lashed to one of the landing skids of a helicopter, the body of Che is transported from La Higuera to Vallegrande, 8th Division Headquarters of the Bolivian military. Riding in the helicopter is Colonel Joaquín Zenteno Anaya, and beside him in a Bolivian army captain's uniform sits "Captain Ramos," a tall and grim-faced CIA operative and Cuban émigre, Félix Ismael Rodríguez Mendigutia [who had, as the radioman at La Higuera, confirmed Che's execution (he had been a member of the CIA-trained anti-Castro 2506 Brigade, and later went on to train the infamous Nicaraguan Contras and to become part of Ronald Reagan's Iran-Contra scandal as Oliver North's "point man")]. The helicopter arrives at exactly five o'clock in the afternoon and is met by a huge entourage of soldiers. The weather is bright and clear. Waiting at the landing strip are groups of reporters from Brazil's TV Globo, Swedish and British newspapers, and Bolivia's daily, *Presencia*. The soldiers quickly cut the stretcher loose from the landing skid, load it into the back of a white Chevrolet panel truck, and dispatch it expeditiously through the narrow streets of Vallegrande. With a jeep occupied by British journalists in hot pursuit, the truck takes a route that brings them near the dried-up fountain of the main square, the town hall with the clock permanently stopped at ten past five, Julio Durán's drugstore, the Montesclaros grocery, Doña Eva's store that doubles as a boardinghouse, and the church whose parishioners yearn to win for it the title of 'basilica.' Moments after they roar through the great iron gates of the Nuestro Señor de Malta Hospital, the stretcher is hastily removed to an adobe shack apart from the main hospital building (Bermejo, cited in Taibo, 1997, p. 564). Che's corpse is placed on the floor of the hospital's laundry. British journalists who quickly descend upon the scene initially are prevented from taking photographs by a terse and unsmiling Dr. Eduardo González (the *nom de guerre* of Gustavo Villoldo Sampera, the senior Cuban CIA operative present at the autopsy and disposal of Che's body, and chief CIA field officer in Bolivia). When the reporters ask in English where Dr. González is from, he retorts sarcastically: "From nowhere!" Villoldo kicks Che's corpse (Cupull and González, 1997) while Captain Ramos (Félix Rodríguez) hovers somewhere at the edge of the gruesome spectacle, making notes for his superior, Dr. González, and for his CIA bosses back in Washington. Che's corpse is placed on a sink and Villoldo immediately its its face. Colonel Roberto Toto Quintanilla, chief of the Intelligence Depart ent of the Bolivian Ministry of Interior, takes Che's fingerprints. With the he

of the hospital's laundress, Graciela Rodríguez, Nurse Susana Osinaga undresses Che's body, hurriedly mops the blood from Che's cold flesh, and unties the handkerchief that Captain Gary Prado Salmón had, in Higuera, placed around Che's lower jaw and tied at the top of his head to "prevent further distortion of the guerrilla chief's face" (because he felt that the faces of guerrillas in death "showed an angry expression, with their mouths open and their glance wandering," whereas dead Bolivian soldiers "always seemed to be sleeping with peaceful faces": Salmón, 1990, p. 254). British journalist Richard Gott, on assignment in Bolivia for the *Manchester Guardian,* is known to have met Che in the past and therefore is asked to identify his corpse and to confirm for the rest of the media present that this is indeed 'El Che.' (Gott's filed reports broke the news that the CIA was involved, something the U.S. newspapers chose not to report for months.) Photographs of Che's corpse are taken, including separate pictures of Che's calves and feet wrapped in three pairs of socks and handmade shoes. Hospital Director Moises Abraham Baptista and an intern, Jose Marinez Caso, slit Che's throat and inject his body with formaldehyde to prevent decomposition. Intelligence experts run numerous identification checks on the body. Once the officials have done their work, the soldiers allow waiting newsmen to enter the shack and take photographs of Che's corpse. The nervous newsmen are also permitted to take fingerprints if they wish. Earlier that day, Roger Schiller, the Swiss Jesuit parish priest from Pucara, had closed the eyes of Che after his body had been attached to one of the skids of the helicopter; now Che's eyes are reopened to heighten the dramatic exhibition of his corpse. Che lies on a stretcher suspended across the length of the concrete laundry sink, seemingly appareled in a mystical light, his green eyes almost transparent, his purpling lips tracing an enigmatic smile, and his body lying peacefully, seemingly in a state of grace—a position that dovetails quite nicely with Christian iconography. His gaze is refulgent, even in death, as if God had embalmed the corpse with moonlight. To many of the Vallegrande women, the hospital nuns, and to nurse Osinaga, Che bears an extraordinary resemblance to Jesus Christ; so taken are they by Che's mystical visage that some of the women surreptitiously snip off clumps of his hair to be used in good-luck talismans (which they have kept to this day to pray for Che's soul on the Day of the Dead; Anderson, 1997, p. 742). Early in the morning on October 10, Vallegrande *campesinos,* soldiers, and townspeople are allowed to slowly file past the corpse. When the soldiers try to control access, "an avalanche of people [break] through the cordon of soldiers" (Taibo, 1997, p 565).

Later that evening, after the spectacle of viewing the corpse is completed, Drs. Baptisa and Casso perform an autopsy in the presence of Toto Quintanilla and CIA operative, Eduardo González. More fingerprints and photographs are taken. Lieutenant Colonel Andrés Selich and Major Mario Vargas Salinas pose for photographs beside Che's corpse. What the photos capture is no less macabre than the spectacles reported to have taken place at the Theatrium Anatomicum in Leiden in the 1590s. General Alfredo Ovando Candía wants to decapitate Che and to keep his head in storage for identification purposes. Félix Rodríguez opposes the severing of Che's head (Anderson, 1997, p. 742), claiming that the Bolivian government would look barbaric to the rest of the world (Taibo, 1997, p. 566). He suggests instead that a single finger be severed (Anderson, 1997, p. 742). A compromise is reached. With long, brisk strokes, Dr. Abraham Baptista saws off Che's hands at the wrist and plops them into a flask of formaldehyde (Taibo, 1997, p. 566).[5] Two attempts are made to make a wax mask of Che's face. The attempts fail miserably and the face is destroyed. The butchering of the corpse is so troubling to Martínez Caso, the intern, that he returns home and gets drunk. Two Argentine police forensic experts arrive to match Che's fingerprints with those on file in Buenos Aires. The following day, the military is ready to incinerate Che's corpse with four tanks of gasoline. But because it is almost dawn and the townspeople of Vallegrande are highly sensitized to ongoing events, and because foreign journalists are lurking about in the area, the decision is made to bury him in a ditch (Cupull and González, 1997). A bulldozer parked on the construction site at Vallegrande's new airport project is drafted into service, and a pit is dug at the end of the runway site into which the bodies of Che and six of his combatants—from Bolivia, Simón Cuba (Willy) and Aniceta Reinaga; from Peru, Juan Pablo Chang-Navarro (El Chino); from Cuba, Alberto Fernández Montes de Oca (Pachu or Pachungo), René Martínez Tamayo (Arturo), and Orlando Pantoja (Antonio or Olo)—are summarily dumped. That night, candles for Che are lit among the small holdings around Vallegrande.[6]

Twelve days after his death, approximately 55,000 Americans stood silently, their heads bowed, before the Lincoln Memorial in Washington, D.C., marking the death of Che Guevara. Henry Butterfield Ryan remarks: "Almost all of them young people, sharing varying degrees of rage against the policies of the U.S. government, they easily agreed with the implicit suggestion by one of the demonstration's leaders that Guevara was a kindred spirit, and they stood silently in his homage" (1998, p. 162). In contrast, and with no small historical irony, the only public demonstration of homage to Che held in Moscow was a rally by a handful of Latin American students from the city's Patrice Lumumba University in front of the U.S. embassy (Ryan, 1998).

The death of Che Guevara marked a singular historical moment, when the execution of an heroic guerrilla commander transformed itself into a sign announcing history's silence, when the impossibility of capitalism was visibly registered in the blood of a martyr and its logic fully impugned. A reminder of history's deafening silence took place on June 28, 1997, when the body of Che Guevara was discovered near the airstrip where it had been discarded thirty years earlier. A sense of wonder at the discovery of Che's remains afforded a steady undertow to the anticommunist moralizing that had reached its crescendo in the gleeful celebration of the fall of the Soviet Union. No matter how mightily the guardians of the new world order strove to wrest this symbolic victory from the Left, they were haunted by the pulsating afterglow of Che's luminescence.

Che's posthumous rebirth brought about by the recent discovery of his physical remains has given him a postcontemporary presence; he is now a man among us once again. The discovery of Che's remains metonymically activated a series of interlinked associations—rebel, martyr, rogue character from a picaresque adventure, savior, renegade, extremist—in which there was no fixed divide among them. The escalating cycle of fear and condemnation sustained by the Cold War had positioned the North American reception of Che before an unbreachable moral chasm, causing Che-gazers to react differently to his legacy—sometimes even violently—depending upon which side you saw him standing within the irreduceable Manichean struggle between good (democracy) and evil (communism). In today's North American society with the softening of crusted-over Cold War antagonisms, Che's storied life has become part of a regime of the unpresentable, the incomprehensibility and threatening import of his ideas and actions no longer reduced to a reassuring friend-or-foe narrative. The contextual overlay of conflicting representations of Che evokes meanings that are ultimately open-ended.

The current court of opinion places Che on a continuum that teeters between viewing him as a misguided rebel, a coruscatingly brilliant guerrilla philosopher, a poet-warrior jousting at windmills, a brazen warrior who threw down the gauntlet to the bourgeoisie, the object of fervent paeans to his sainthood, or a mass murderer clothed in the guise of an avenging angel whose every action is imbricated in violence—the archetypal Fanatical Terrorist. For the Radical Left, Che has become the *über-guerrillero*, the all-purpose Saint; and for the persecutory, diabolical, and annihilative forces of the New Right, he is the all-purpose sinner. Even though there appears to be more of a willingness by rank-and-file North American commentators to de-reify Che as either saint or sinner and to place him somewhere in-between, we must remember that every encounter with that irrepressible force known as Che occurs in an occupied space. It is a space of reception dense with public signs and personal memories, a space delimited by the discourses and 'ways of telling' that are most available to society, most overdetermined within society, and carrying the most currency within today's economy of ideas—especially in the public media. The explanatory range of Che's image is not limitless but rather overdetermined by bourgeois reading formations. Such formations themselves are not homogeneous—in fact, they are often contradictory—and are dependent upon, among other things, the extent to which the colonizer accepts or derives a reciprocal relationship with the colonized.

Individuals within state-free formations are more likely to recognize themselves in others than are individuals in class-stratified societies with strong state formations. With the collapse of the Soviet Union and the subsequent fervent proclamations about the "end of history," U.S. citizens are still motivated to align themselves, for the most part, with the inconceivable ideological discrepancy of capitalist democracy as good and socialism as evil. Capitalism, we are told, is that naturally pure social relation that constitutes the substratum of democracy. Although the image of Che exists simultaneously in two different registers, the public is still encouraged to disclaim him as a glamorous anachronism of political struggle, a shot-to-fame eccentric who turned the battlefield into an arching chasm of moral idealism, reaching its peak in the creation of the new socialist agent, an heirloom of a defeated Left, or as a rhetorician with a gift for transforming the ineffable into fiery trope and oratory. To invoke the old gallery of revolutionaries—Che, Sandino, Martí—is supposedly to be diswitted in the search for the so-called evolution of democracy and its attendant social and cultural 'progress.' Richard Alcarón, president of Cuba's National Assembly, writes:

> There are attempts to present Ernesto Guevara as a symbol of a bygone era, as something from the past. In the euphoria following the crumbling of the Soviet Union, the imperialist academic establishment—which has joined with others, since cloning existed in the ideological sphere well before it was discovered in the laboratories—has tried to make people believe that the defeat of that model meant the death of the socialist ideal and that this would forever put an end to the movement by workers to achieve that goal. (1998, p. 33)

Yet because the image of Che is informed by such mimetic excess and fecund indeterminacy, he rides a nervous trajectory of meaning that can navigate between those minefields of forces that would otherwise condemn him to the dustbin of history. This is because the image of Che ultimately embeds the mythic in the ordinary and is able to gather the past and the future into a single moment: the promise of redemption and the anticipation of a new order of being and becoming. Today, his story can be retold and remembered in spaces less resistant to counternarratives that challenge political orthodoxy and less cluttered by negations and official prohibitions. To retrieve the memory of Che is to break the trance of inevitability by mocking the blatant exploitation that marks the present capitalist moment. It is to dislodge what appears to be the intractable hegemony of commonsense, quotidian reality, and to describe and ultimately change it. This, of course, is one of the purposes of this book.

Because one of the occupied spaces in which Che is read is virulently overpopulated by libidinal discourses—the heterophilic culture of entertainment—and because North America loves sexy heroes, Che continues to be revered for the market value of his masculinity. Once attracting mainly the off-ramp, below-the-radar interest of fringe culture intelligentsia who saw Che as a mixture of Anton LaVey (the founder of the San Francisco–based Church of Satan) and

Robin Hood and who would hang their Che-a-Go-Go posters in their offices and discuss the merits of revolutionary art at coffee-klatch meetings, Che has gone mainstream pop culture. The long hair and beard of Che, Camilo Cienfuegos, and the *guerrilleros* that had been in the mountains with Fidel—*los barbudos*— made a strong impression on members of the U.S. counterculture when the *guerrilleros* visited Washington in 1959. Before the British invasion of the 1960s, with the Beatles and the Rolling Stones as the vanguard, the image of Che wearing long hair and military fatigues, coupled with his revolutionary ardor, captured the imagination of a generation of young people poised for cultural rebellion. Before Zippergate and Monica Lewinsky's boutique beret, there was the black military beret adorning a noble head with captivatingly handsome features. (Prior to the beret, Che had worn a military cap that had belonged to Ciro Redondo, which he had worn ever since Ciro's death. He lost the cap crossing Camaguey during the Cuban campaign.) Recently, June Casagrande of the *Los Angeles Times* described Che's presence in the structural unconscious of the United States: "Guevara has always been the Jim Morrison of machine-gun Marxism: a sexy, dirty . . . idealist who danced with death as a way of life. But in 30 years, Americans have reinvented Guevara in the image of his creator, remembering his convictions and his message, while brushing over the parts of Guevara that once seemed too threatening: the armed rebel and the Marxist" (1997, p. 9). Though Casagrande's sentiments are clearly overstated, there is some truth to her remarks. However, Casagrande would have us think that the relationship between Che and the public is one of unbridled love. If such a relationship does exist, then some of it is only market deep.

By disguising itself as human nature, capitalism's brutal and unremitting logic has prevented most citizens in advanced capitalist countries such as the United States from locating the importance of Che's martyrdom beyond the market logic of bargain-basement capitalism. The colonial gestures and tropes used to "construct" Che through the operation of difference persistently forecloses the emancipatory character of his ideas and his life. The has been unable to escape the imperial categories and colonial epistemologies that have both created and 'trapped' his legend in the discourse of the Western metropolitan subject. Che's message is a political constant residing in the margins of the social as an exercise of dangerous memory—a recovery of subjugated knowledge—that can never be fully contained by the silence of official history. When Che's blood was shed, a hemorrhage of signifiers occurred at the threshold of the imperial imagination, staining its pristine marble battlements with a message that cannot be wiped clean of its implications for the human condition. While we remain haunted by the photo of the corpse of Che placed across a cold tub—an image described by Paco Ignacio Taibo as "a hyperrealist version of Rembrandt's painting of Dr. Tulip's Anatomy Lesson" (1997, p. 565)—we need to remember that the birth of this secular saint was possible only because of the sacrifices made by Che on behalf of suffering humanity. This sentiment was not lost on those who were despoiled the most by the putrid power of capitalism:

> The campesinos paraded in front of the body, in single file, amid an awesome silence. When the army tried to control access, an avalanche of people broke through the cordon of soldiers. That night, candles for Che were lit for the first time in the small holdings around the little town. A saint was being born, a secular saint of the poor. (Taibo, 1997, p. 565)

The image of the corpse of Che stretched out on a washtub in Vallegrande, so mystically rendered by photographer Freddy Alborta, appears bathed in a transcendental aura, giving Che a luminescent presence among the sallow visages of the soldiers, journalists, photographers, and officers present. The portrait-in-death of this *guerrillero* Christ, whom José Arce Paravicini denominated the "gunshot Christ" (*Cristo de metralla*), inspires a mythological reverence not only because Che's emaciated corpse bears a striking similarity to famous artistic depictions of the corpse of Christ (such as those by Mantegna and Holbein), but also because Che's life and teachings reflected a wisdom, compassion, and sacrifice for humanity that has been compared to that of Christ. Thirty years after his execution by the Bolivian military aided by the CIA, North American teachers and teacher educators recognize Che more as a Third World symbol and romantic icon of an idealized and distant past than as a man whose life and message have serious implications for understanding—and perhaps even shaping—today's world-historical events. After all, the future as prophesied by Che has not arrived, and the situation of the oppressed in Asia, Africa, and Latin America—the three continents dominated by imperialism to which Che's project of internationalism was directed—are more securely in the grasp of capitalist powers than ever before.

Yet it would be wrong to assign to Che—as the dominant U.S. media are compelled to do—a legacy of mainly commercial, "posterized" Guevarism in the form of T-shirts, pins, sloganizing posters, and keychains festooned with romantic portraits of Che and sold throughout the world. Che, who discerned an encroaching totalitarianism throughout the Americas that was fueled by U.S. imperialism, and who put capitalism on trial before the court of history, has become reduced to a type of freelance revolutionary—as his image becomes an accoutrement of the respectable middle class, as his beret appears on the head of a talking Chihuahua in a Taco Bell commercial, and as his military-style shirts now constitute the inventory of upscale chain stores. All of this is occurring within a major epidemic of deniability on the part of the rank-and-file citizen, characterized by an almost complete disavowal of intention on the part of the capitalist class in relation to the disastrous consequences that capitalism has had for the poor and the powerless. This is a far cry from the reverence accorded Che throughout Latin America; from photos enshrined in the vestibules of private homes; to his five-story high portrait that graces a government building in Cuba's Plaza de la Revolucíon; to the cries of Cuban students, "seremos como Che"; to his image carried aloft by protesters from Mexico City to Porto Alegre, Brazil; to his secular canonization by the campesinos in La Higuera. The commercialized Che, however, is where the numinous and numismatic meet. Just as the message of Malcolm X has been buried by his visual iconography, Che's message has been overcoded by radical-chic consumer culture and must be pried away from the Christlike image of the man in the beret that adorns the walls of alternative bookstores, which was once "sold as a *de riguer* [*sic*] decoration for the campus dorms" (Sandison, 1997, p. 148). The 'Chesucristo' or Christification of Che speaks to Che's love of humanity and determined willingness to sacrifice himself for the common good, yet tends to obscure the substance of his political mission (see Kunzle, 1997; see also González, 1997). His thoughts on revolutionary class struggle and his vision for world socialism represent more than the romantic musings of a naive and misguided guerrilla. And his death should contribute more than an opportunity for hucksters to transform his image into kitsch *objets d'art* or to purchase his legend in quick-buck, souvenir-shop franchises. A week prior to the memorial services for Che held in Cuba in October 1997, Che's daughter, Aleida Guevara, decried the commercialization of her father's memory, which she said represented the antithesis of Che's politics. She remarked: "I hate to see my father's face in ashtrays and on somebody's bottom of their jeans. This is mercantilism. It's opportunism. These people are just trying to make money. But I also have the hope that there are some young people who follow not the fashionable image but who search for the man in a global society that is losing all its values" (Fineman, 1997, p. A12).

Even the church has gathered the symbol of Che into its mighty embrace. Exploiting the image of Che the revolutionary, the Churches Advertising Network in England recently sparked a bizarre controversy in their national poster campaign by putting a decidedly kitschy image of Che—wearing a crown of thorns, sporting a rugged visage and exuding the macho-cum-sensitive allure of Sunday afternoon jocksniffery—on five-foot posters and asking 50,000 churches to buy them as a way of motivating people to come to church on Easter. With the desire that the image "would be pinned to the walls of teenage girls' rooms" and wishing to get away from "the wimpy Nordic figures in a white nightie," Rev. Peter Owen-Jones steadfastly supported the campaign (Combe, 1999). This strategy of 'revolutionizing' the image of Jesus allowed Tory member of Parliament and sponsor of the Conservative Christian Fellowship, Harry Greenaway, to harrumph that "Jesus was perfect" and that it "is grossly sacreligious to liken him to Che Guevara" (Miller, 1999a). He also added that "those who are in any way responsible should be excommunicated" (Miller, 1999b, p. A7). Judie Beishon, of the executive committee of the Socialist Party, remarked sardonically that the comparison itself "is probably a bit unfair to Che Guevara" (Combe, 1999).

The Christlike Che, circa 1963, Havana (Roberto & Osvaldo
Salas/Liaison Agency)

Alexander Cockburn writes that "the famous image of Che, snapped by
Alberto Korda in 1960 the day Cuba's leaders were publicly mourning those
killed in the explosion of a munitions ship, survives its immersion in kitsch
because Che himself cannot be diminished to kitsch. He lives in history, just as
his image has been brandished at 10,000 rallies, marches and processions,
among them Bolivian peasants marching on La Paz in the early 1990s" (1997, p.
4). His black beret with the 'identity star' (pinned to it by Celia Sanchez in the
Sierra Maestra in May 1957 to mark his promotion to Commander) has become
a symbol of heroic leadership. He was a romantic figure in a youthful rebel
Cuban government, whose average age was thirty-three and his image looms
even larger today.

In retrospect, Che was correct in his perspicacious assessment of Vietnam's
potential to defeat the U.S. military and to inspire other revolutionary movements. According to Löwy, "Subsequent to Che's assassination, events vindi-
cated Che's global analysis as well as his comprehension of the maturing subjective conditions. Vietnam did temporarily undermine Washington's capacity
for massive military intervention, thus facilitating the overthrow of U.S. clients
in Iran, Ethiopia, Nicaragua, and Grenada" (1997, p. 9). More than an intrepid

Controversial advertisement by the Anglican Church of England
(courtesey of David Kunzle)

polymath, Che had a singular, analytical grasp of the potentialities and possibilities of anti-imperialist struggle, and there is no question that, as James Petras puts it; "the figure and ideas of Che Guevara have been influential and prescient in shaping the revolutionary debates and understanding their potentialities" (1997a, p. 8). Bivouacked in the dense thickets of the Bolivian countryside, Che put the *ancien régimes* of Latin America and the North American continent on notice in his firm unshakeable commitment to socialist revolution through armed struggle directed by a revolutionary vanguard. In his attempt to deal a sledgehammer blow to a renascent U.S. imperialism and to inspire 'new Cubas' throughout Latin America, Che called upon the poor and dispossessed—*los pobres de la tierra*—to rise up against their oppressors.

Che's spirit lives and beckons us to still the swirl of confusion that envelopes us and to steady our gaze toward the future. The eyes that stare out at us from posters and T-shirts have become not only apertures to the past but also windows of historical possibility. As Ariel Dorfman writes:

Even though I have come to be wary of dead heroes and the overwhelming burden their martyrdom imposes on the living, I will allow myself a prophecy. Or maybe it is a warning. More than 3 billion human beings on this planet right now live on less than $2 a day. And every day that breaks, 40,000 children—more than one every second!—succumb to diseases linked to chronic hunger. They are there, always there, the terrifying conditions of injustice and inequality that led Che many decades ago to start his journey toward that bullet and that photo awaiting him in Bolivia.

The powerful of the earth should take heed: deep inside that T shirt where we have tried to trap him, the eyes of Che Guevara are still burning with impatience. (1999, p. 212)

In the end, Che was not defeated by a better equipped Bolivian fighting force of superior numbers, but by an ideological campaign that included a well-renumerated, anti-communist campaign spearheaded by the CIA, by the colonist revanchism of U.S. politicians who were attempting to rehabilitate Euro-American values as the pinnacle of civilization, by the rodomontade of Latino-phobic U.S. politicians, by the imperializing heritage of U.S. foreign policy, and by the powerful U.S. military-industrial complex. Yet in his military defeat he won the battle of the human spirit and became "the most important martyr of revolutionary struggle in Latin America in the twentieth century" (Loveman and Davies, 1985, p. x) and "one of the twentieth century's most glorified fighters— a symbol of the power of human volition and determination" (Loveman and Davies, 1985, p. ix).

But Che's death was more than a loss to the Marxist Left.[7] As Graham Greene opined:

The death of Che Guevara brought a sense of grief and disappointment to people who had no Marxist sympathies. He represented the idea of gallantry, chivalry, and adventure in a world more and more given up to business arrangements between the great world powers: he expressed for us the hope that victory did not always go to the big battalions. . . . They were afraid to bring [Che] to trial: afraid of the echoes his voice would have aroused in the courtroom: afraid to prove that the man they hated as loved by the world outside. This fear will help to perpetuate his legend, and legend is impervious to bullets. (cited in Kunzle, 1997, p. 19)

Just as an earlier generation had viewed the Spanish Civil War as a pivotal moment in world struggle against fascism and imperialism, so the war in Vietnam for my own generation became the signal moment that identified a new struggle against imperialist aggression on a world scale. Sounding the challenge of "One, two, three Vietnams," Che was the most shining example of this revolutionary struggle—what Ernesto Sábato called "the struggle of Spirit against Matter" (Kunzle, 1997, p. 19). James Petras remarks that Che's most significant contribution to revolutionary thought was "his recognition that imperialism was everywhere organizing the exploitation of every crevice on the earth's soil, intervening militarily in the most remote villages, undermining the most cherished cultural practices" (1997a, p. 20). Frei Betto noted recently: "The image of the Sierra Maestra guerrillas, with their beards, boots and olive-green uniforms, greatly contributed to the political ideals of Brazil's student movement in the 1960s. In the Calabouço restaurant in Rio de Janeiro, or the bars along Maria Antonia Street in São Paulo, we thought history was offering us a chance to defeat U.S. imperialism" (1997, p. 5).

Here was a medical doctor (Che was awarded his M.D. in Buenos Aires in 1953, with a thesis on allergies) who in some ways represented the appeal of top-drawer Argentine society—yet who became a revolutionary, an organic intellectual in the Gramscian sense, a critic of capitalism who possessed an unvarnished clarity of thought, and a guerrilla leader instrumental in bringing the corrupt Batista regime—which outnumbered his rebel force militarily by more than a hundred to one—to its knees (Markee, 1997) and who finally stayed the hand of Washington during the Bay of Pigs invasion (what Cubans call the invasion of "Playa Girón, Bahia Cochinos," after the beach on the Bay of Pigs where the mercenaries landed). Here was a man who possessed the brazen courage to set forth a sophisticated internationalist indictment of the capitalist world powers on behalf of the entire Third World (Markee, 1997). Not only did he advance his ideas at a 1961 Montevideo conference where the Kennedy administration's Alliance for Progress was unveiled, but in later years Che boldly extended his critique to the Soviet Union (whom he had vigorously supported in the early years of the postrevolutionary Cuban government), which he felt was doing little to assist the development of socialism in the developing world (Markee, 1997). Here was a statesman, but also a tragic figure who, weighing less than 110 pounds due to severe bouts with asthma and dysentery, had barely escaped a 1965–66 guerrilla campaign in the Congo; and who, having been abandoned by the Bolivian Communist Party and captured by the Bolivian military and CIA, remained true to his principles even unto death.

Che had been fearless enough to stage his 'last gamble' in Bolivia, from where he planned to begin an insurrection in his native Argentina. With a government *recompensa* of *la suma de 50,000 pesos bolivianos a quién entregue vivo o muerto* (about U.S. $4,200 reward for information leading to his capture, dead or alive) hanging over his mission (Barrientos personally announced the reward in Vallegrande during an inspection tour of the combat zone when the body of the *guerrillera*, Haidee Tamara Bunke or 'Tania,' a German-Argentine woman, was brought in for burial), Che pressed forward, ignoring the odds against his survival. Chilean radio had broken Bolivian censorship to inform Che that there were 1,800 Bolivian troops involved in the hunt. His intended destination of a cave hideout was taken over by a force of 150 soldiers, and two safe-house destinations were also overrun by soldiers. Supplies were unavailable (including medical supplies for Che's asthma), and Che's weary twenty-two-man group was forced to eat some of their packhorses and drink their own urine as overflights by spotter planes and helicopters became more frequent (Sandison, 1997). Learning of the death of Tania and the imprisonment of his ex-Young Communist Party *compañera*, Loyola Guzmán (the army had arrested in La Paz a total of sixteen youths who had worked as liaisons for the guerrillas), Che prepared himself and his men to fight to the death. This was a man who commanded respect and admiration in an era in which politics and a culture of optimism were inseparably—and one could even add 'valiantly'—wedded. Che had progressed from being a middle-class intellectual and political activist to a full-blown revolutionary. Andrew Sinclair writes:

> Previously he had merely been a young, asthmatic and quixotic urban intellectual, who considered himself a revolutionary because of travel among the Latin American poor and a study of Marx and Lenin. He had been in no way different from thousands of other progressive middle-class Latin Americans in the liberal professions. Yet by the time Fidel Castro's provisional government took over from Batista in January 1959, Che was a proven guerrilla fighter of great courage, power and ability. (1998, p. 35)

As progressive educators throughout the United States, pulled into the ferocious orbit of the current transnational phase of capitalism, remain bound up in the confusion among territoriality, class struggle, and the nation-state, the spirit of Che Guevara continues to haunt the moral conscience of all those who refuse to dedicate themselves to the pursuit of freedom and justice. The narrativized world of Che imbues his image with memory and a haunting presence. Born under the Chinese sign of the Dragon (according to the ancient Chinese horoscope), and destined to be born a thousand times in one lifetime (Sinay, 1997), Che

> has become one of the greatest legendary figures of our times. He is regarded as a popular hero among the youth in every part of the world. His name, his ideas, and his romantic image have become part of the symbolism of those who believe that the injustices of this world can be erased only by revolutionary means. Rarely in history has a single figure been so passionately and universally accepted as the personification of revolutionary idealism and practice. Moreover, even those who feel no sympathy for the ideals he upheld seem to be affected by the charisma of his almost mystical image. (Harris, 1970, pp. 11–12)

Che lives today in allegorical space, where references to his life do not so much symbolize particular meanings as they open up an entire field of referentiality and illuminate it. But in the illumination of meaning we have simultaneously the act of forgetting, a motivated amnesia or structured silence elevated to the status of common sense. The challenge is to unconceal Che's relevance for today, in a process of historical unforgetting. Frei Betto remarks that "today, 30 years after his death, Guevara's memory continues to challenge all people who do not dedicate their lives to an altruistic cause" (1997, p. 5).

FEARING SYMMETRY: CAPITALISM AGAINST DEMOCRACY

New questions now face leftist groups throughout the globe: Given that the leading industry in the United States is financial services, and that the imperial ambition of the United States—the undisputed world-governing hegemon and rogue superpower *par excellence*—is the domination of world markets through the U.S. Treasury/International Monetary Fund complex, what are the implications for those countries who refuse to submit to a new global *pax Americana*? Or have international financial institutions and multinational corporations hollowed out the nation-state to become the major players in the theater of global power? What does it mean for undeveloped countries that the United States now perceives the concept of national security as any instability throughout the globe that might threaten the interests of the United States? Although it is true that the imperial power of the United States has no contemporary parallel nor historical precedent, is the United States an ascending hegemon or a hegemon in decline? Can the present period be characterized as the last great gasp of U.S. hegemony? Is the United States living on borrowed economic time? Given that the United States has been on the wrong side of history in its aggression toward countries shaking off their colonialist shackles—in Latin America and Southeast Asia, for instance—will there be any significant force that can dethrone U.S. hegemony? Will things get worse, or has neoliberalism reached its high-water mark? Will the interstitial emergence of new agonistic forces of opposition and contestation—from nongovernmental organizations to revolutionary social movements—really amount to a serious challenge for the world's ruling elites?

New questions currently face the educational Left: What is the best way to map the changes that we are witnessing in the relationships among the nation-states, state power, and class power? How does transnational capital's need for services from the neoliberal nation-state affect educational restructuring, such as the move toward privatization and corporate models of citizenship? How can the North American educational Left develop strategies of resistance to the monopolistic, transnational capital of the 'free world'—what Roberto Fernández Retamar calls "the hilarious name that capitalist countries today apply to themselves and bestow in passing on their oppressed colonies and neo-colonies" (1989, p. 36)—and its exploitation of global labor while effectively fighting its principal agent, the global corporation and its implicit model of citizen/consumer? Can revolutionary groups such as the Zapatistas in Chiapas, Mexico, and their indigenous and *campesino* counterparts throughout Latin America push the levers of history far enough to enable them to resurrect and galvanize an internationalization of proletariat struggle and achieve the conditions that Che set for epochal change? Which will be more effective in the long run, fax machines or AK-47s? Does the scholarly exegesis of academic new leftists influenced by the insights of French postmodernists add to our detract from the struggle for liberation?

This book puts forth the theme that in the wake of the demise of the Soviet Union, in the face of the global restructuring of accumulation and the transnationalization of factions of the economic elite, and in the midst of the current entrenchment of the culture/ideology of consumerism and individualism, the ideas and example of Che Guevara (and Paulo Freire) can play a signal role in helping educators transform schools into sites for social justice and revolutionary socialist praxis, particularly those educators who work in teacher education institutions. The potential for rethinking global capitalism—in all of its "tycoon," "casino-style," "quick-fix," and "bargain basement" incarnations—and for re-examining the social disenfranchisement of labor that is afforded by revisiting Che's legacy are two of the many reasons why Cuba declared 1997 to be *Año del 30 aniversario de la caída en combate del guerrillero heroico y sus compañeros* [The year of the thirtieth anniversary of the death in combat of the heroic guerrilla and his comrades (*Los Angeles Times,* Nov 9, 1997).]

Zygmunt Bauman elaborates on the relationship between capital and spatial compression, forcefully arguing that the new capitalism respects no spatial borders or constraints whatsoever:

'The economy'—capital, which means money and other resources needed to get things done, to make more money and more things yet—moves fast; enough to keep permanently a step ahead of any (territorial, as ever) polity which may try to contain and redirect its travels. In this case, at least, the reduction of travel time to zero leads to a new quality: to a total annihilation of spatial constraints, or rather to the total 'overcoming of gravity.' Whatever moves with the speed approaching the velocity of the electronic signal, is practically free from constraints related to the territory inside which it originated, towards which it is aimed or through which it passes on the way. (1998, p. 55)

In a recent introduction to the journal, *Race & Class,* John Berger likens the impact of global capitalism to a world set in flames and with no horizon—in a word, to hell. In fact, he compares it to the right-hand panel of the *Millennium Triptych* painted by Hieronymus Bosch. He writes that "this lack of sense, this absurdity, is endemic to the new order" (1998/1999, p. 3):

There is no horizon there. There is no continuity between actions, there are no pauses, no paths, no pattern, no past and no future. There is only the clamour of the disparate, fragmentary present. Everywhere there are surprises and sensations, yet nowhere is there any outcome. Nothing flows through: everything interrupts. There is a kind of spatial delirium. Compare this space to what one sees in the average publicity slot, or in a typical CNN news bulletin, or any mass media commentary. There is a comparable incoherence, a comparable wilderness of separate excitements, a similar frenzy. (pp. 1–2)

For Berger, the world of global capitalism is compressed into a prison house where all knowledge is forced into the bed of Procrustes and put into the service of a "wicked greed." He is worth quoting further:

As Bosch foresaw in his vision of hell, there is no horizon. The world is burning. Every figure is trying to survive by concentrating on his own immediate need and survival. Claustrophobia, at its most extreme, is not caused by overcrowding, but by the lack of any continuity existing between one action and the next which is close enough to be touching it. It is this which is hell. The culture in which we live is perhaps the most claustrophobic that has ever existed; in this culture of globalisation, as in Bosch's hell, there is no glimpse of an elsewhere or an otherwise. The given is a prison. And faced with such reductionism, human intelligence is reduced to greed. (1998/1999, p. 3)

It should be remarked here that Berger's "hell" brought about by global capitalism is precisely the system of equivalences that many conservatives believe constitutes a true reflection of both heaven and democracy: sheer contingency, virtual reality, lack of a systematic opposition, individuals fending for themselves. From the days in 1855 when Sir John Bowrigg, the Victorian bureaucrat, proclaimed, "Free Trade is Jesus Christ and Jesus Christ is Free Trade" (Perera, 1998/1999, p. 199) to the current era where Christian fundamentalists such as the Reverend Jerry Falwell proclaim capitalism, democracy, and Jesus to be as seamlessly connected as the Shroud of Turin and equally as mystical, there has been a willful ignorance surrounding the paralyzing effects that the victorious embrace of capitalism has had on the powerless and destitute of the world. For it cannot be denied that the globalization of labor and capital have brought about material shifts in cultural practices and the proliferation of new contradictions between capitalism and labor that progressive educators who work in schools of education have been hard-pressed to respond to, as opposed to react to, successfully. As Stuart Hall remarks, "Economic Man or as s/he came to be called, The Enterprising Subject and the Sovereign Consumer, have supplanted the idea of the citizen and the public sphere" (1998, p. 11). The current phenomenon of globalization has been referred to as "the revenge of the economy over the social and the political" (Adda, 1996, p. 62). It has been mightily announced as the "grand finale of the explosion of Western modernity" (Engelhard, 1993, p. 543).

In the United States, the logic of capitalism has been scalded into the historical imagination of its subjects. In fact, the goal of the U.S. political elite is to make the world safe for the global domination of capital and the U.S. way of life.

A truly world-class dream of capitalist domination on a global scale could be glimpsed by discerning guests at a special convention held at the Fairmount Hotel in San Francisco in 1995. From the office of his foundation on an abandoned military area south of the Golden Gate, Mikhail Gorbachev had invited what he called his 'global brains trust'—500 leading politicians, businessmen, and scientists from around the world—to a big gala congress at the Fairmount. Ted Turner, Margaret Thatcher, David Packard, John Gage, George Bush, George Schultz, and countless other millionaires and billionaires jostled hugger-mugger amid the plush carpets of the convention ballrooms in an orgy of carving up the planet into the haves and the have-nots. Among such a succulent group of wheeler-dealers, a quick consensus was reached: During the next century, there would be no new regularly paid jobs in any segment of the economy in the growth markets of affluent countries. Only 20 percent of the population would be needed to keep the economy going in the next century. In fact, 80 percent of the population would be dispatched into the vast armies of the unemployed (Martin and Schumann, 1997). These new armies of the night would have to be pacified through entertainment—what Zbigniew Brzezinski archly called "tittytainment" (Martin and Schumann, 1997). People in the industrialized countries of this 'two-thirds society' who will be searching for something to make their lives remotely meaningful will not be able to look to business (it's too unreasonable to expect a social commitment from the business community) but rather to the benevolent domain of volunteer work. People will be sweeping the streets for next to no pay (Martin and Schumann, 1997), or else they will be sitting in front of their television screens, their spirits (and presumably certain body parts) raised by the captains of tittytainment.

Capitalism has entered a global crisis of accumulation and profitability. Neo-liberalism has become the lodestar for the new world order's conquest of the next millennium. Wages have been compressed worldwide, income is steadily being transferred from labor to capital, corporations are struggling for a comparative advantage in cheap labor and in acquiring state-subsidized access to national resources while abandoning public obligations to the poor. The result is class polarization, downward mobility, and class secession. Self-destructing as a result of its own production overcapacity, the new era of flexible accumulation requires a number of ominous conditions: the total dismantling of the Fordist-Keynesian relationship between capital and labor; a shift toward the extraction of absolute surplus value; the suppression of labor incomes; longer working hours; more temporary jobs; the informalization of labor; and the creation of a permanent underclass—to name just a handful of developments. William Greider has noted in a recent issue of *The Nation* that "in different ways, labor incomes are suppressed on both ends of the global system—usually by labor-market forces (including mass unemployment or temp jobs) in the advanced economies, often by government edict and brutal force in developing ones. Meanwhile, companies must keep building more production or locating factories to keep up in the cost-price chase" (1997, p. 12). Managers ponder Joe Kincheloe's (1999) question: How do we tell the workers?

A. Sivanandan further captures the ominous condition of the 'free' market when he warns:

> For the free market destroys workers' rights, suppresses civil liberties and neuters democracy till all that is left is the vote. It dismantles the public sector, privatizes the infrastructure and determines social need. It free-floats the currency and turns money itself into a commodity subject to speculation, so influencing fiscal policy. It controls inflation at the cost of untold poverty. It violates the earth, contaminates the air and turns even water to profit. And it throws up a political culture based on greed and self-aggrandizement and sycophancy, reducing personal relationships to a cash nexus (conducted in the language of the bazaar) even as it elevates consumerism to the height of Cartesian philosophy: 'I shop, therefore I am.' A free market presages an unfree people. (1998/1999, pp. 14–15)

William Robinson (1998) holds to the idea that there has occurred a "postmodernist" expansion of capitalism into its current global stage. Globalization has, in other words, moved from a linkage of national societies (world economy) to an emergent transnational or global society (global economy) that has superseded the nation-state stage of capitalism. This is because, as Robinson notes, new patterns of accumulation based on informatics, computerization, communications, and other forms of "third-wave" technology requires a more generalized commodification.

According to Greider, we are returning to a form of prewelfare, competitive capitalism that is driven by the motor of conservative political ideology—an ideology that is capable of deceitfully suturing together the discourses of freedom, family values, civic authority, nationalism, and patriotism. Of course, the term 'freedom' is used in a decidedly manipulative fashion, since only the market remains 'free,' and people must submit to the dictates of the market. This is most painfully evident in cases where the International Monetary Fund and the U.S. Treasury regularly impose forced-austerity terms on poor countries such as cutting wages and public spending and raising interest rates so that endangered banks can fix their balance sheets (Greider, 1997). Thus, Jorge Larrain is compelled to write that

> unemployment is treated as laziness and pricing yourself out of a good job, workers' strikes are transformed into a problem of public order. Criminality and new forms of violence are treated as the result of lack of authority in the family, not enough law and order, lack of Victorian values, and so on. Terrorism is successful because of the free press and the excessive leniency of the law. Divisions and forms of discrimination are partly blamed on immigration and partly conjured away by patriotism and jingoism. (1996, p. 68)

THE ECONOMIST FROM HELL

Friedrich von Hayek began his reputation as a formidable defender of the free market in the bourgeois salons of the 'Red Vienna' of the early 1900s. Here, evenings were marked by a combination of Virginier cigars, Moyet cognac, Pantagruelian chatter, and resilient thinking dipped in anticommunist invective. Von Hayek was soon to become the prime *animateur* of neoliberal economics. The goal of this Austrian economist and, later, a University of Chicago professor, was simple: to crush socialism in his lifetime and to gloat during its obsequies. Hayek rejected unfettered, laissez-faire capitalism and instead urged active government involvement to protect the smooth functioning of a free market. He advanced what he called "the catallaxy" or the spontaneous relations of free economic exchange between individuals. Under the influence of Ludwig Von Mises, Secretary of the Vienna Chamber of Commerce, and Carl Menger, founder of the Austrian School of Economics—not to mention the theories of knowledge developed by Ernst Mach and Michael Polyani—Hayek developed his epistemology of citizenship in relation to the figure of the global entrepreneur. Hayek's concept of the catallaxy rests on the notion that there exists no connection between human intention and social outcome and that the outcome of all human activity is essentially haphazard (see Wainwright, 1994). Hayek was against government regulation in general, except when it came to protecting the free, unfettered functioning of the market.

Hayek conceived of a monetarist economics of free-market constitutional liberalism in order to fuel the engine of his ideological and moral crusade against socialism. Hayek expressed faith—almost to the point of religious zealotry—in the unregulated price mechanism as the means of economic coordination and argued that the role of the state must be to blunt human agency and protect the spontaneous social order form the persistently messy efforts of human design. As a philosophical naturalist, Hayek reveled in whatever transpired outside of the conscious attempt at social control; he abhorred what he believed to be the human engineering aspects of market intervention (Wainwright, 1994). Market ruthlessness was seen as the aggregate effort of consumer choices, and in Hayek's view it was more important to protect the spontaneity of the market—despite its often deleterious consequences for the poor—than to protect individuals or groups from the shameful effects of market 'justice.'

Criticizing neoclassical equilibrium theory as too abstract, Hayek believed that business monopolies were always more benign than the monopolies of labor and the state. Competition is what ensures the spontaneity of the market, and this, in turn, is what creates necessary entrepreneurial opportunities that comprise the evolution of the market system—a natural evolution that must be safeguarded at all costs (and for Hayek, this meant that a *cognoscenti* of males over forty years of age would oversee the market and would be up for election every fifteen years). Under Hayek's scheme of free-market orthodoxy, the everyday citizen has no right to choose what is better for him or her. Only existing, objective, economic conditions can work as the motivating force for choice, guided by a cadre of experts enforcing a "hands off" policy of market protection (Wainwright, 1994). Polycephalous capitalism is permitted—even encouraged—to devour the world's resources with its thousand sets of razor sharp teeth and its insatiable, tongue-smacking appetite for profits. It is to be religiously protected from interference and—when necessary—provided with a military escort.

· The educational epistemology that follows from these neoliberal perspectives flows directly from the idea that knowledge is irredeemably individual. Ignoring the sociohistorical context of economic systems, Hayekian economic science depends upon statistical calculation, macroeconomic ecometrics, and methodological individualism. Econometrics is a pseudo-science designed to promote profit at all costs. As Joel Spring notes, Hayek advanced a new form of totalitarianism wherein the individual is controlled in order to ensure favorable market conditions (Spring, 1998). In both the United States and the United Kingdom, Hayek's ideas—namely, that markets are self-regulating—provided the underpinnings for discussions of school choice, national standards and curricula, eliminating the welfare state, and lifelong learning.

Hayek's pecuniary and political ideals were adopted by his fellow demon at the University of Chicago, Nobel Laureate Milton Friedman, who put them to use in his support of government-financed vouchers for school choice. Hayekian economics underwrote the conservative countertides of both Thatcherism and the so-called Reagan revolution, and eventually influenced global economic planning. Classical liberals reject state intervention in economics and education, but neoliberals in both economic and educational arenas advocate it in order to ensure the operation of a free market and the unrestricted advance of capital. Neoliberal education policy is thus a conservative force, often blending Christianity, nationalism, authoritarian populism, and free-market economics, and calling for such creations as a national history curriculum that celebrates the virtues of Christian values, minimal government regulation (except to ensure a 'free market'), and individual freedom (Wainwright, 1994). This position opposes that of Guevarian-inspired criticalists who emphasize the sociohistorical context of economic systems and who stress the socially constituted ways in which knowledge about social life might lead to revolutionary action on behalf of the oppressed. Educational criticalists who underscore the social character of knowledge stipulate that people can, through cooperation, increase their understanding of the social consequences of their actions, even though they will never fully know their consequences. Highlighting the socially constituted way in which knowledge is produced (a fundamental axiom among Freireans, for instance) provides a basis for questioning the values and mechanisms for regulating the social order. This, of course, contravenes Hayek's pitchforked prohibition against human design and his valorization of the political neutrality of 'accidental' market transactions.

Eric Hobsbawm describes the current neoliberal conjuncture as underwritten by a now defunct consensus of neoclassical academic economists

> who dream of a nirvana of an optimally efficient and frictionless economy of a self-adjusting global market, that is to say an economy with minimal interference by states or other institutions. . . . Some of them, starting with Friedrich von Hayek and Milton Friedman, did so for ideological reasons, but mostly they did so, I guess, out of a taste for abstract technical elegance, combined with a total lack of sense for the real-life context of their propositions. Theirs is economics without political, social or any other non-mathematical dimension. In practice, of course, it is an economics which fitted the economy of transnational corporations and other operators in a period of boom. This consensus is now at an end. (1998, p. 5)

Robert Brenner (1998a; 1998b) reports that, outside of the United States and Europe, the international economy is experiencing an economic downturn that is more severe than any that has occurred since the 1930s. The Left consensus that the growing economic turmoil that is also engulfing Europe and North America is mainly a crisis linked to the irresponsibility of short-term investment is woefully short-sighted. Brenner argues that the rise of finance capital and of neoliberalism is not really the cause of the current international economic crisis as much as a result of it. Brenner links the cause to the rise of overcapacity and overproduction, leading to the falling profitability in manufacturing that began in the late 1960s. Neoliberalism and monetarism resulted from the failure of Keynesian deficit spending to restore profitability and reignite capital accumulation. It is becoming evident, even to many conservatives, that the principle of free market allocation per se will always bring about the best possible conditions. According to Brenner, what is needed is a society built upon the principles of socialism and democratic social control over the economy from the bottom up by the working classes.

HOW HELL BECAME HEAVEN

U.S. world supremacy was maintained through the late seventies and eighties by economic force. From 1984 to the 1990s, global Reagonomics and the instability of the formal markets, the fall of the dollar, and all the consequences therein, posed overwhelming problems for U.S. hegemony over the Western bloc. The global restructuring of industries and work organization has had devastating consequences for developing countries. In the 1960s, failed attempts at import substitutions were replaced (under pressure by international monitors of development such as the United Nations) by a renewed emphasis on export functions. Raw materials and crops were exported, along with goods manufactured in 'Free Trade Zones' (FTZs). To assist export industrialization and to attract foreign capital, tax-free privileges in trade were granted, and incentives such as new buildings and utilities were offered by local governments (Giri, 1995). At the dawn of the new 'green revolution' sponsored by the World Bank and the International Monetary Fund in the 1970s, global assembly lines began to form in Southeast Asia and at the U.S.–Mexican border. In Southeast Asia and Mexico, export manufacturing often occurred outside of the FTZs, as subcontracting arrangements were dispersed to the peasant population, who work part-time. Japanese and Western countries set up offshore production companies in Southeast Asia, the Caribbean, and Latin America in order to bypass high production costs, labor initiatives, and environmental controls at home. And now the International Monetary Fund wants poor countries to improve their balance-of-payments position by liberalizing their economies, devaluing currencies, and increasing imports in proportion to exports. This has brought nothing but havoc for the poor. And international trade conventions such as the General Agreement on Tariffs and Trade (GATT) have made the pursuit of ecologically sustainable food security increasingly more difficult (Giri, 1995; see also Gabbard, 1995). According to A. Sivanandan:

> Education, the staple diet of Third World countries' economic and social mobility, has been priced out of the reach of the poor to produce an elite which owes allegiance not to its own people but to 'opportunities in the West.' The farmers have no land, the workers have no work, the young have no future, the people have no food. The state belongs to the rich, the rich belong to international capital, the intelligentsia aspire to both. Only religion offers hope; only rebellion, release. Hence the insurrection when it comes is not class but mass, sometimes religious, sometimes secular, often both, but always against the state and its imperial masters. (1998/1999, p. 14)

The regional and liberalization pacts that have emerged in the past decade—the World Trade Organization (WTO), the North American Free Trade Agreement (NAFTA), the European Union (EU), Latin America's Mercosur, and the recent negotiations of the Organization for Economic Cooperation and Development surrounding the Multilateral Agreement on Investment—are shaping the New World Order in accordance with the most ideal investment conditions for transnational corporations. The slithering tendrils of capitalism continue to creep, even if they do not find their mark. Anything hindering foreign investment—rules and regulations that protect workers and jobs, public welfare, the environment, culture, domestic businesses, and the like—are being suctioned into the feral beak of oblivion.

The World Trade Organization (which was created on January 1, 1995, following the signing of the GATT global free trade agreement in 1994) and the International Monetary Fund (IMF) both work to obtain trade concessions from those countries whose economies are in distress and to gain access to unprotected sectors of Third World economies. (It is worth noting that the World Trade Organization's Second Ministerial in Geneva in May 1998, where delegates toasted the fiftieth anniversary of the GATT/WTO, was picketed by 10,000 angry protestors.) The WTO, the IMF, the OECD, the International Chamber of Commerce, the European Round Table of Industrialists, the Union of Industrial and Employers Confederation of Europe, the United States Council for International Business, the International Organization of Employers, the Business Council on National Issues, the World Business Council for Sustainable Development, and the Business and Industry Advisory Committee all betray a sympathy for the Devil and work to ensure market control and assist transnational corporations in becoming some of the largest economies in the world. In the United States, research centers in Silicon Valley, on route 128 in Boston, in the Research Triangle in North Carolina (Raleigh/Durham), in Fairfax County, Virginia, and at other locations throughout the country are not only facilitating possibilities for warp speed electronic commerce but are also creating technological contexts for corporate mergers and take-overs.

The "free market revolution" driven by capitalism *à discrétion* and continuous capitalist accumulation has not redounded to the benefit of all. In fact, the "revolution" has left the social infrastructure of the United States (not to mention other parts of the globe), in tatters and has, through its policies of increasing its military-industrial-financial interests, continued to suck the lifeblood from the open veins of South America and other regions of the globe.

For instance, one of the many glorious companies supported by investments from universities is Shell, which has confessed to paying the Nigerian government for military assaults against opponents of multinational oil companies, resulting in the 1995 executions of nine Ogoni activists who opposed Shell, including Nobel Peace Prize nominee Ken Saro Wiwa.

The sudden collapse of the Soviet Union in the 1990s and the shift to capitalism in Eastern Europe has brought nearly five billion people into the world market under the auspices of "shock therapy" capitalism. Aleksandr Buzgalin (1998) has described this form of capitalism as a neoliberal "straightjacket" (the 'shock' without the 'therapy') that is basically a continuation of the "speculative nomenklatura capitalism of the Brezhnev regime" (1998, p. 79). The globalization of capitalism and its political bedfellow, neoliberalism, work together to democratize suffering, obliterate hope, and assassinate justice. The logic of privatization and free trade—where social labor is the means and measure of value, and surplus social labor lies at the heart of profit—now odiously shapes archetypes of citizenship, manages *in tenebris* our perceptions of what should constitute the 'good society,' and creates ideological formations that produce necessary (and necessarily deleterious) functions for capital in relation to labor. As schools are financed more by corporations that serve as service industries for transnational capitalism, and as

Mural on a wall in Chile: You may have to be tough, but not lose your tenderness/You may cut the flowers, but it will not stop the Spring
(courtesy of Jill Pinkney-Pastrana)

bourgeois, think-tank profiteerism continues to guide educational policy and practice, the U.S. population faces a challenging educational reality. At the same time that liberals call for the need for capital controls, controls in foreign exchange, the stimulation of growth and wages, labor-rights enforcement for nations borrowing from the United States, and the removal of financial aid from banking and capital until they concede to the centrality of the wage problem and unless they insist on labor rights (Greider, 1997), very few are calling for the abolition of capital itself.

Let's take the example of Chile, a country frequently used as the poster child for neoliberal economics. For all the talk about Chile's privatized pension system and its new status as an 'economic jaguar,' and for all the praise heaped upon it by the U.S. media such as the *New York Times* (which recently credited Pinochet with a coup that began Chile's transition from a backward economy to one of the strongest economies of Latin America), Chile currently "boasts one of the most unequal economies in the world" (Cooper, 1998, p. 66) in which only 10 percent of the Chilean population earns almost half the wealth and in which the 100 richest people in Chile earn more than the state spends on social services. Real salaries have declined 10 percent since 1986 and are still 18 percent lower than they were when Allende was in power. Cooper reports that a high percentage of people ticketed for using cell phones while driving around the posh Vitacura neighborhood in Santiago were found to be using toy phones or wooden replicas. He writes:

Workers at the ritzy Jumbo supermarket complain that on Saturday mornings the dressed-to-kill clientele fill their shopping carts high with delicacies, parade them in front of the Joneses, and then discreetly abandon them before having to pay. In the rickety shantytowns around Santiago, readily available Diners Club cards are used to charge potatoes and cabbage, while Air Jordans and Wonderbras are brought on a 12-month installment plan. (1998, p. 67)

These are the fruits of the legacy of Friederich von Hayek, Milton Friedman, and their University of Chicago hacks, who were invited to restructure Chile's economy during the days of the dictatorship. Of course, the United States provided more than 'guest' economists. It helped to create the necessary political conditions for its structural-adjustment policy and continued influence in Latin America. The corporate powers within the United States were instrumental in the overthrow of Salvador Allende's elected socialist government.

I have been sickened by comments made by former Secretary of State Henry Kissinger that were released recently in a declassified secret memorandum of his private conversation with General Augusto Pinochet in July 1976. At the height of Chile's policy of genocide directed against professors, intellectuals, student leaders, human rights workers, and others, Kissinger told Pinochet: "In the United States as you know, we are sympathetic with what you are trying to do here" (Kornbluh, 1999, p. 5). He also remarked: "*My evaluation is that you are a victim of all left-wing groups around the world and that your greatest sin was that you overthrew a government that was going Communist*" (p. 5 italics in original). Kissinger concluded: "We want to help, not undermine you. You did a great service to the West in overthrowing Allende. Otherwise Chile would have followed Cuba. Then there would have been no human rights" (p. 5). These comments directly contradict Kissinger's third installment of his memoirs, *Years of Renewal,* in which his account of his meeting with Pinochet added insult to injury by portraying himself as an advocate for human rights. Kissinger failed to mention Pinochet's regime of torture, disappearances, and international terrorism, and his strategic silence may have paved the way for the car-bomb assassination of the former Chilean Ambassador to the United States, Orlando Letelier, and his associate Ronni Moffit. Kissinger said nothing when Pinochet twice accused Letelier of giving false information to the U.S. Congress.

The educational Left in the United States is finding itself without revolutionary *firmeza* or a revolutionary agenda for challenging the scoundrels who run the country whose hands are coated in innocent blood, and their strategies for challenging the capitalist curriculum in the classrooms of the nation remain detumescent. We occupy a time that is witnessing the progressive merging of pedagogy to the productive processes within advanced capitalism. Education has been reduced to a subsector of the economy, designed to create cyber citizens within a teledemocracy of fast-moving images, representations, and life-style choices. Capitalism has been naturalized as commonsense reality—even as a part of nature itself—and the term 'social class' has been replaced by the less antagonistic and more domesticated term 'socioeconomic status.' It is impossible to examine educational reform in the United States without taking into account continuing forces of globalization and the progressive diversion of capital into friction-free financial and speculative channels—also known as 'fast capitalism,' 'turbo capitalism,' 'crony capitalism,' 'tycoon capitalism,' 'nihilo capitalism,' 'fat cat capitalism,' 'Klondike Capitalism,' or 'casino capitalism on a world scale.'

Perhaps more than any other political revolutionary, Che recognized the dangers of capital and the exponentiality of its expansion into all spheres of the lifeworld. Today capital is in command of the world order as never before, as new commodity circuits and the increased speed of capital circulation work to extend and globally secure capital's reign of terror.

It is important to recognize that unless we do away with the controlling presence of capital—the social economic foundation of society—we will be severely limited in our ability to confront and overcome racism, sexism, and homophobia. Following the advice given by Marx in the *Grundrisse*, Joel Kovel (1997) underscores the importance of "finding the proper level of abstraction in order to grasp the concrete nature of things" (p. 7). The site where the concrete determinations of industrialization, corporations, markets, greed, patriarchy, technology, all come together—the center where exploitation and domination are fundamentally articulated—"is occupied by that elusive entity known as *capital*" (p. 7). Kovel notes that "capital is elusive because it cannot be singled out in isolation from anything else. It is a social relation grounded in the commodification of labor-power, in which labor is subject to the law of value—a relation expressed through wage labor, surplus value extraction, and the transformation of all means of production into capital" (p. 7). The insinuation of the coherence and logic of capital into everyday life is something that has occurred without serious opposition, and the economic restructuring that we are witnessing today offers both new fears concerning capital's inevitability and some new possibilities for organizing against it. Teacher education is, or course, one necessary (but not sufficient) possibility.

ADVANCED CAPITALISM AS PARANOIA

I register the homomorphic claim that capital is paranoiac on the grounds that it possesses at this historical juncture an identity distinct from the rest of humanity, moving well beyond human subjectivity. Thomas T. Sekine (1998) has captured this relationship in his assertion that logic coincides with economics, and that economic characteristics that represent characteristics of capital reflect humankind's economic motives "made infinite" (1998, p. 437). Capital's logic, in other words, is an extension of our own. Put another way, "we are privy to the subjectivity of capital. Our finite subjectivity and capital's infinite subjectivity are different, and yet they are connected by what Marx called the 'force of abstraction.' . . . By being subsumed under capital and becoming its agent, we can think like capital" (1998, p. 437).

Advanced capitalism—that brakeless train wreaking destruction on all those caught in its path—bears a chilling resemblance to the clinical forms of psychosis known as paranoia and megalomania. The habits and flows of transnational capitalism inscribe a fantastic logic, one that is fiercely unstable if not impossible. In this context, commodity fetishism as discussed by Marx becomes the effective counterpart to paranoid perceptual mechanisms in which the citizen is perceived in relation to his or her value as a consumer.

The binary opposition between capitalism and socialism creates a logic for capitalist intervention on a global scale because it constructs a view of capitalism as an antidote to socialism. Capitalism becomes a signifier for a range of attributes, including human rights, freedom, democracy, justice, and equality. Socialism becomes the "other" by which the United States marks its superior traits of civilization. The power of capitalism to define the meaning of socialism is masked by a discourse of rationality that is carried throughout the industrialized and post-industrialized world by means of far-reaching media networks. These networks enable capitalism to create the conditions for relearning and reproposing the representational heritage of the imperial state.

According to a summary of the literature on paranoia by Paul Smith (1988), paranoia represents a psychosis, not a neurosis. Neurosis can be cured, because it has internal resistances that can be broken down by an analyst. However, paranoiacs have already exhibited those symptoms that have to be "discovered" in a neurosis in order to be cured. That is to say, in the case of paranoia, those symptoms no longer need to be discovered because they have already been naturalized as part of the everyday reality of the paranoiac. Since the paranoiac has no internal resistances to overcome, he or she rejects the logic of the analysts' interpretive strategies. One cannot reason with a paranoiac because, as Lacan notes, paranoia already exists as an interpretation (Smith, 1988).

The paranoiac's internal economy—the imaginary identifications that are forged out of the subject's primary narcissism—structures a libidinal disturbance between the subject and the reality that he/she perceives. The libido is turned upon the ego so that whatever provokes disgust in his/her own ego is projected upon external objects. The external world is endowed with the subject's own worst qualities and characteristics. This process sustains the illusion or fiction of the subject's internal economy or the 'I.' Whereas the 'I' is perceived as good, everything outside the 'I'—perceived as external to this 'I'—is regarded as the repository of destruction, and it is where the subject expels its own impropriety and vomits up its turmoils. This can be seen within predatory capitalism in the reduction of the citizen to his or her labor power, and in the recent government attacks on immigrants, welfare recipients, and undocumented workers who are accused of stealing money from taxpayers. Controversial California propositions 187, 209, and 227 are written in zero degree, white heat, hate-filled paranoia, and a type of mass paranoia activates votes in favor of them. In addition, regulatory boards within the government who oversee trade and commerce are seen as the enemy. Anything that blocks mergers, profits, and accumulation becomes a barrier to 'freedom and democracy.' The ego of the paranoiac must be aggrandized, while the outside world must be continually demonized. Such a separation of the inside and outside demands interpretive delusions or a form of willful ignorance that prevents the development of moral agency. This is because the ego is cut off from the historical memory of the larger social order as well as from its capacity for imaginative production, since it cannot admit to or acknowledge the illusory nature of the world that it has created. The paranoiac cannot recognize the outside world as his or her own creation. The outside world can only be reacted against, not responded to. It is interesting that the last entry in the index in Che's diary on Marxism was attributed to Freud, citing Dscheladin Rumi in "Clinical Histories," and reads: "There, where love awakens, dies the I, dark despot" (Anderson, 1997, p. 189).

The outside world is important to the paranoiac only in terms of how it bolsters the ego's feelings of autonomy. The ego of the paranoiac personality is incapable of self-reproach. In other words, the paranoiac is unable to recognize the conditions of its own interpretative fictions. Paranoiacs reconcile their own defensiveness with what is considered to be an objective formation. The paranoiac stands behind these fictions as their guarantor, claiming them to be interpretations of an already existing world, to be conditions of an objective reality. Paranoiacs seek to conceal their megalomaniacal obsession by revindicating their authority at each moment of conflict with the outside world. Similarly, capitalism works from a discourse of metaparanoia, in which the outside world is constructed in the service of its own agenda of accumulation, of profit-making, of reproducing its own advantage and control over the marketplace. The masses become both the object of its desire and its repulsion as they are libidinalized, hellified, and produced only in relation to their surplus value.

Take the case of 'corporate welfare,' in which corporate tax breaks are disguised as 'economic development' or 'public-private partnerships.' When governments give a corporation or an entire industry a benefit not offered to others—such as an outright subsidy, a grant, real estate, a low-interest loan, a government service, or even a tax break in the form of credit, exemption, deferral, or deduction, or a lower tax rate than what others pay—it is quite often at the expense of another state or town or other corporate taxpayers. And yet traditional welfare programs, such as Aid to Families with Dependent Children and food stamps, come under furious fire by those same politicians and business leaders who benefit either directly or indirectly from corporate welfare. The Lords of Capital, in their chrome-and-glass high-tech offices, refuse to acknowledge the hypocrisy of capital accumulation or the limits to environmental sustainability. When confronted by its contradictions, capital becomes even more voracious, as if it has now replaced the natural environment itself. It announces itself through its business leaders and politicians as coterminous with freedom, and indispensable to democracy such that any attack on capitalism as exploitative or hypocritical becomes an attack on world freedom and democracy itself. Every critic of democracy is thus demonized and mutated into a latent or covert socialist or communist working against freedom. And El Che, one of the greatest opponents of capitalism, is dismissed and misprized as being simply hungry for power. Yet as Frei Betto recounts, "Che was at peace with history. His critics claim that Che was motivated by his hunger for power. But in an unusual and surprising move, Che stripped himself of power and immersed himself anonymously in the Congo jungle and later Bolivia. He demonstrated his altruism and his radical consecration to Latin American liberation" (1997, p. 5).

LET'S GRAB THE WHOLE ENCHILADA: PLAYING HIDE-AND-SEEK WITH CLASS

Because capital has itself invaded almost every sphere of life in the United States, the focus of the educational Left has been distracted from the great class struggles that have punctuated this century and now rests almost entirely on an understanding of asymmetrical gender and ethnic relations. Although this new focus is important, class struggle is now perilously viewed as an outdated issue. When social class is discussed, class struggle is usually viewed as relational, not as oppositional. In the context of discussions of 'social status' rather than 'class struggle,' techno-elite curriculum innovation has secured a privileged position that is functionally advantageous to the socially reproductive logic of entrepreneurial capitalism, private ownership, and the personal appropriation of social production. This neoliberal dictatorship of the *comprador* elite has resecured a monopoly on resources held by the transnational ruling class and their allies in the culture industry. The very meaning of freedom has come to denote the freedom to structure the distribution of wealth and to exploit workers more easily across national boundaries by driving down wages to their lowest common denominator and by eviscerating social programs designed to assist laboring humanity. Territories that were once linked to national interests have given way to networks inscribed within world markets independent of major national political constraints, as history, the economy, and politics no longer bind together but operate within independent spheres.

Gangster politicians on the hustle, brokering a system of lap-dog democracy for private industry at the expense of public interest, of public service, of public rights, and—in many recent instances, such as California's Propositions 187, 209, and 227—of civil rights, are putting commercial interests before human dignity and social justice, dismantling the Keynesian welfare state with such a determinate fury that the concept of exploitation has been reduced to an empty abstraction separated from the idea of living, breathing individuals who suffer as a result of it. The seduction of capital is overwhelming even among the most well-intentioned groups of progressive educators. A small group of individuals can become big winners, and a vastly larger number will be guaranteed a place in the ranks of the big losers in an era made fierce by globalization, and at a time when markets are fragmented into submarkets by science and technology. The hidden curriculum, or 'pedagogical unsaid,' is nothing new, although the ideological state apparatuses have made it a more sophisticated enterprise. Its function is largely the same as it was during earlier phases of industrial capitalism: to deform knowledge into a discreet and decontexualized set of technical skills packaged to serve big-business interests, cheap labor, and ideological conformity. Ira Shor lucidly captures the entrapment of education in the web of capitalist social relations when he writes:

> The very economic dynamism of this society has had an impact on pedagogy, putting a lot of force behind individual empowerment, self-help, self-improvement, self-reliance, in the lower grades and in adult education. This emphasis on 'self' is the educational equivalent of the capitalist infatuation with the lone entrepreneur, that romantic and fading factor in an economy now monopolized by giant corporations. (Freire and Shor, 1987, p. 130)

In fact, at a time in which real wages are being steadily ratcheted downward, students are being prepared to become custodians of the capitalist state—a state destabilized by the constant deterritorialization and reterritorialization of capital and whose power is increasingly facilitated by the rapid movement of information that permits instant turnover times within financial markets.

While Marx maintained that the commodity, figured as a universal equivalent, is excluded from the relative form of value, it could be ventured—at least since the moment that the United States went off the gold standard—that the commodity now serves as its own equivalent by means of finance capital. Larry Grossberg (1999) suggests rather provocatively that this contemporary economic transformation is akin to a form of neomercantilism and a revision of and a return to a colonial organization of capital and capitalism under neoliberalism. The relationship between banking or finance capital and money is becoming more and more representational. Today, capital is most productive in creating more money, a development that is changing the ontology of value and creating money owed to itself in the form of perpetual debt. And while this unique situation within economic relations creates a new capitalist subject—primarily through the media deployment of commodities invested with a new auratic quality—I do not believe that this situation culminates in a complete rejection of labor power and the fashioning of proletarian subjectivity.

Labor is surely less valorized today, but I do not believe this means that subjectivity has become disposable or that the body no longer toils and struggles because of the exploitation of its labor. The working class has not disappeared but has undergone recomposition into core workers, temporary workers, and contingent workers (Perrucci and Wysong, 1999). As Robert Perrucci and Earl Wysong note,

> Only two of ten Americans (20 percent) control 92 percent of the financial wealth of the country, meaning ownership of stocks, bonds, and commercial real estate. The other eight out of ten Americans (80 percent) hold the remaining 8 percent of total wealth. This means that about 80 million families, or about 216 million people, work every day throughout their entire adult lives producing wealth that goes largely to others, while they receive a few "crumbs" from the pie themselves. (1999, p. 131)

EDUCATION AND THE MARKETPLACE:
SOCIAL CONTROL MASQUERADING AS SOCIAL CONTROL
IN A "WHO CARES?" CLIMATE

When evil can now disguise itself as evil—as itself—and not have to worry about it, then we can rest assured that we live in a strange universe. It was not always the case. About fifteen years after the Cuban revolution, when "Che Guevara became the *prototype of a new revolutionary generation*" (Petras, 1997a, p. 11, emphasis in original), U.S. educational scholars on the Left began fighting the destructive logic of capital through the development of what has been variously called radical pedagogy, feminist pedagogy, critical pedagogy, and, later, border pedagogy, postcolonial pedagogy, and revolutionary pedagogy. These were tumultuous times for the U.S. academy, fighting the complicity of anthropologists and social scientists in American foreign policy and the U.S. war machine (not that this complicity no longer exists—it does—but today it is so overt it goes unmarked). Anthropologists Eric Wolf and Joseph Jorgensen were reprimanded by the Executive Committee of the American Anthropological Association "for conducting inquiries within the discipline on the extent of anthropological complicity in clandestine military research on Southeast Asia" (Di Leonardo, 1998, p. 237). Wolf and Jorgensen revealed how social science, particularly anthropology, was used in numerous operations and initiatives by the military—such as "work on 'native administration' for the navy in Micronesia, military use of the Human Relations Area Files, the scandalous Project Camelot in Latin America, the Indian government's discovery of American military funding of a Berkeley anthropological project in the Himalayas, and finally documents on widespread anthropological involvement in American military counterinsurgery work in Thailand" (p. 237). As a result, they were investigated by an ad hoc committee of the American Anthropological Association headed by Margaret Mead.

Despite the revelations about the complicity of schooling with the military-industrial complex, school-reform efforts in the 1960s were fairly tame. They had primarily been about creating 'alternative' rather than 'oppositional' educative spaces, in the form of 'free schools' underwritten by a curriculum influenced by the human potential movement of Carl Rogers, Abraham Maslov, and others. Critical pedagogy followed in the wake of the human potential movement as a way of fostering a more oppositional position toward education and schooling practices. It began to be recognized in the academy by the late 1970s.

Critical pedagogy is a way of thinking about, negotiating, and transforming the relationship among classroom teaching, the production of knowledge, the institutional structures of the school, and the social and material relations of the wider community, society, and nation-state (McLaren, 1995, 1997a, 1997b; Giroux and McLaren, 1994). Developed by progressive educators and researchers attempting to eliminate inequalities on the basis of social class, it has sparked up to the present a wide array of antisexist, antiracist, and antihomophobic, classroom-based curricula and policy initiatives.

Though critics of critical pedagogy often decry this educational approach for its idealist multiculturalism, its supporters, including the late Paulo Freire, have often complained that critical pedagogy has too often been domesticated and reduced to student-directed learning approaches devoid of social critique and a revolutionary agenda (Freire, 1994). In my view, this is due partly to the educational Left's retreat from historical materialism and metatheory as 'outdated' systems of intelligibility that have historically run their course, and the dislocation of power, knowledge, and desire brought on by the New Left's infatuation with more conservative forms of fashionable apostasy as found in certain incarnations of French postmodernist theoretical advances. Some postmodern theorists (reactionary as opposed to critical postmodernists) and their poststructuralist bedfellows operate from a theoretical terrain built upon a number of questionable assumptions—they view symbolic exchange as taking place outside the domain of value; privilege structures of deference over structures of exploitation and relations of exchange over relations of production; emphasize local narratives over grand narratives; encourage the coming to voice of the symbolically dispossessed over the transformation of existing social relations; reduce models of reality to historical fictions; abandon the assessment of the truth value of competing narratives; and replace the idea that power is class specific and historically bound with the idea that power is everywhere and nowhere. Instead of challenging the organizational structures of the dominant society that perpetuate the advantaged positions, practices, and privileges of the superclass and its credentialed-class allies, they end up advancing a philosophical commission that propagates hegemonic class rule and re-establishes the rule of the capitalist class (Wenger, 1991; Wenger,

1993/1994). What this has done precisely is to continue the work of reproducing class antagonisms and creating a new balance of hegemonic relations favoring the dominant class and ensuring their continued possession of disproportionate levels of power and wealth.

GLOBALIZATION AND ITS CAPITAL SINS

Over recent years, neo-Marxist educationalists have articulated trenchant critiques of postmodernism and in doing so have reinvigorated the debates over revolutionary class struggle within the current crisis of globalization (Green, 1994; Cole and Hill, 1995; Hill and Cole, 1995; Brosio, 1997; Rikowski, 1997; Cole, Hill, and Rikowski, 1997; Hill, McLaren, Cole, and Rikowski, 1999). It is undeniably the case that the capitalist class is more odious and powerful today than when Che was struggling to cut it at its joints with the machete of armed resistance. One explanation for the strength of the capitalist class is that its predatory power is now fundamentally linked to the global, commercial media system. Capitalist discourses are coordinated by a small number of transnational media corporations that are mostly based in the United States. This is a system, according to Robert W. McChesney,

> that works to advance the cause of the global market and promote commercial values, while denigrating journalism and culture not conducive to the immediate bottom line or long-run corporate interests. It is a disaster for anything but the most superficial notion of democracy—a democracy where, to paraphrase John Jay's maxim, those who own the world ought to govern it. (1997, p. 11)

William Robinson is also worth quoting at length on this issue:

> Global capitalism is predatory and parasitic. In today's global economy, capitalism is less benign, less responsive to the interests of broad majorities around the world, and less accountable to society than ever before. Some 400 transnational corporations own two-thirds of the planet's fixed assets and control 70 per cent of world trade. With the world's resources controlled by a few hundred global corporations, the life blood and the very fate of humanity is in the hands of transnational capital, which holds the power to make life and death decisions for millions of human beings. Such tremendous concentrations of economic power lead to tremendous concentrations of political power globally. Any discussion of "democracy" under such conditions becomes meaningless.
>
> The paradox of the demise of dictatorships, "democratic transitions" and the spread of "democracy" around the world is explained by new forms of social control, and the misuse of the concept of democracy, the original meaning of which, the power (cratos) of the people (demos), has been disconfigured beyond recognition. What the transnational elite calls democracy is more accurately termed *polyarchy*, to borrow a concept from academia. Polyarchy is neither dictatorship

nor democracy. It refers to a system in which a small group actually rules, on behalf of capital, and participation in decision-making by the majority is confined to choosing among competing elites in tightly controlled electoral processes. This "low-intensity democracy" is a form of consensual domination. Social control and domination is hegemonic, in the sense meant by Antonio Gramsci, rather than coercive. It is based less on outright repression than on diverse forms of ideological co-optation and political disempowerment made possible by the structural domination and 'veto power' of global capital. (1996, pp. 20–21)

In a similar vein, Marxist educationalist Richard Brosio astutely asserts:

Presently, organized workers in the First World countries are forced to compete with those from areas only recently sucked into the vortex of globalizing capitalism. Furthermore, supra-national organizations created by capitalism can act with a free hand; threaten disinvestment or capital strike; narrow policy options of national governments; and even of democratic politics itself. Organized labor had learned how to deal somewhat effectively with the central states in their own countries; however, it has not yet figured out how to play defense against the latest offensive by capital. Because of titanic (and undemocratic) economic changes, the industries that best supported working-class cultures are being destroyed. (1997, p. 22)

The current trend of popular capitalism is a means of garnering public support for the move toward privatization. Offering the public a means of personal financial gain—as in offering shares of a formerly stated-owned and now privatized corporation at low prices or through employee stock ownership plans or tax deductions for those who use the private rather than the public sector—results in the disciplining of the working classes, the undermining of the trade-union movement, the erosion of the principles of universality and social right, and the revivification of the concept of deserving versus undeserving poor (Teeple, 1995).

In fact, what we are witnessing in countries such as the United States is the development of a capitalist culture underwritten by privileging hierarchies that resemble those of (so-called) Third World countries ravaged by Western imperialism. According to Alan Tonelson:

Observing the growing tendency of wealthier Americans to literally wall themselves off from the problems of their fellow countrymen with private schools, gated communities, and private security forces, writers as different as Robert Reich, the former labor secretary, and conservative military strategist Edward Luttwak warn that parts of America are starting to resemble chronically divided, class-ridden third world societies. (1997, p. 359)

Supranational institutions such as NAFTA help to promote the goals of transnational finance and production and increase the adverse relations between capital and labor. Here it is important to remember that global networks of financial markets have superseded national capital, labor, and technologies. And though most of the activities of transnational capital are still concentrated in the Triad (North America, Europe, Japan), more involvement has been taking place in Latin America. Here, the aim of corporate investments in lower-income countries is to gain access to growing markets and to cut labor costs.

Laurie Wallach and Michelle Storza report that after five years of NAFTA policies, the results have been devastating to the environment:

> Under NAFTA there has been a 37 percent boom in maquiladoras (where wages are 16 percent lower than at other Mexican factories). With 1,947 border plants now operating, maquiladora employment has skyrocketed 92 percent in Tijuana alone. Few of these factories properly dispose of toxic waste, which has compounded environmental and health problems. A twelve-year border study has found a correlation between maquiladora growth and severe birth defects. The neural-tube-defect rate for babies born in the Brownsville, Texas–Matamoros, Mexico, area has risen to 19 per 10,000 babies, almost twice the national average. (1999, p. 7)

The authors further underscore the brutal effects that NAFTA has had on expanding exponentially the poverty for Mexican workers and creating unimaginable wealth for the very few:

> Although their productivity is up 36.4 percent under NAFTA, wages have dropped by 29 percent. Indeed, five years into NAFTA, Mexican maquiladora workers earn on average $55.77 per week, not a living wage. Between 1984 and 1994, through several currency devaluations, the Mexican poverty rate remained at 34 percent. Now 60 percent of the Mexican labor force lives below the poverty line; 8 million Mexicans have been pushed out of the middle class and into poverty during NAFTA's first five years as 28,000 Mexican small business failed to compete with NAFTA multinationals. (p. 7)

BACKWARD-MOVING ADVANCED CAPITALISM: THE GLOBALIZATION OF MISERY

The situation in Latin America is growing more grim in the current era of globalization. For instance, Blanca Heredia notes that "developing countries today are a much more heterogeneous group than at the beginning of the postwar period. Globalization is not helping them become more equal; the poorest are not catching up the fastest. Instead, globalization is making the differences between developing countries increasingly deep and wide" (1997, p. 385).

It is likely that the growth of poverty in absolute terms since Che's time would have surprised even the most cynical critic of capitalism, including Che himself. As Heredia points out:

Since the 1980s, poverty has grown in absolute terms throughout developing countries and has increased in both absolute and relative terms in much of Africa and
Latin America. In the latter, after a sharp rise in the 1980s, the proportion of poor
people started to slowly decrease from the early 1990s onward, but in only two
countries: Chile and Colombia. In the rest of the region poverty has continued to
grow and, if current trends persist, will continue to do so in the next 10 years at the
rate of two more poor people per minute. (1997, p. 386)

Given all the tired and shopworn rhetoric about the success of NAFTA both
in North and South America that we have come to expect from U.S. politicians
in their slavish veneration of the new international economic order, it appears
tragically ironic that, in 1995, fifteen of South America's seventeen countries had
levels of income inequality exceeding those normally associated with their level
of development (Heredia, 1997, p. 386). Furthermore, social conditions in many
Latin American countries have deteriorated dramatically over the past decade
and have become, for many working-class Latin Americans, intractably grim
with little cause for optimism in the foreseeable future. Heredia writes: "In
much of the region, the globalizing 1980s and 1990s have brought more Mercedes and more homeless children to the streets; they have also brought more
Norwegian salmon, more youngsters involved in crime, more Nike sneakers to
dream about, and more violence in and outside the home. In the midst of growing poverty and inequality, life, even for those fully wired into the global mall,
has become much more harsh" (1997, p. 386).

What happens when struggling Third World countries request help from the
United States in their struggle for democratization? What happens when they
seek assistance in competing in the world economy? For many, they are forced
to accept regimens imposed by the International Monetary Fund that require
the slashing of tariffs, the laying off of state employees, and the selling of the
most profitable of their state-run industries to foreign corporations. If the country agrees to be 'rescued' by the market, we soon witness aggressive take-over
attempts by multinational corporations.

Bill Resnick warns, "When multinational corporations pay lower wages, take
their profits out of country, and support oppressive, kleptocratic governments,
then their investments just mean misery and destruction of natural resources"
(1997, p. 12). What multinational corporations often do (as in the case of Nike
in Indonesia) is to deny the host country the authority to regulate capital flows
or foreign investment, and to prohibit the requirement that investors transfer
technology and skills to domestic partners. Furthermore, foreign aid and bank
loans must be used to support private capital and private local assets, thus weakening public economic management while increasing private profits. Corporations also threaten to leave foreign cities or states unless they get tax and regulatory favors, including environmental surrenders from governments and wage
concessions from workers (pp. 13–14). Resnick reports that in the global super-

market, World Bank and 'free' trade policies strongly discourage food subsidies, so that producers everywhere sell at world-market prices and that all countries must compete for rice, grain, and milk at the same price (p. 13).

It is also exceedingly ironic that during the last twenty years, advanced capitalist countries have witnessed the emergence of sweatshops in cities such as New York and Los Angeles, as (so-called) First World working-class populations experience a steady erosion of whatever social power they once had and a drastic degradation of living standards. It is also worth noting that U.S. perceptions of Latin American sweatshops are professionally managed by corporate 'spin doctors' and news management, who frequently suggest that criticism of these sweatshops is hurting the unemployed and that what we perceive in the United States as the exploitation of workers is actually upward mobility in the host country (Fairchild, 1997).

In Malaysia, 80 percent of the operators on the shop floor in the FTZs are women. In the Philippines, most of the manufacturing occurs outside of the FTZs and relies on village home-sewers. Ananta Kumar Giri (1995) reports that outside the Mexican *maquiladora* zone, housewives operate a cottage industry as part of the low-level, segmented labor market indirectly controlled by industrial capital. In Malaysia and Mexico, companies prefer unmarried women employees, who are put to work under the managerial custody of male supervisors. Exhausted operators are routinely replaced by new crops of school-leavers. Giri further notes that for female factory workers assigned to microscopes, early exhaustion and deterioration of eyesight has resulted in companies limiting their employment to the early stage of their adult life so that fresh labor capable of sustained intensive work at low wages is ensured. New workers are often only employed on six-month contracts so that they can be released and rehired at the same, low, wage rates.

TREACHEROUS BALANCING ACTS

In July 1993, Left and progressive organizations around the world joined in a gathering known as the Fora de São Paulo (the forum began in 1990; the most recent meeting occurred in August 1997) and released a declaration urging the creation and implementation of development models that move toward sustained, independent, and environmentally balanced economic growth with an equitable distribution of wealth. The group also urged that economic development be accompanied by a strengthening of democracy. Daniel Ortego of Nicaragua's Sandinista Party as well as Cuauhtémoc Cárdenas, leader of the Revolutionary Democratic Party of Mexico and now Mayor of Mexico City, both urged economic policies that take into account the history, culture, and circumstances of individual countries (San Juan, 1998b). An eclectic group of Latin American politicians and intellectuals known as the "Buenos Aires consensus" (to counter the economic gospel group known as the "Washington consensus," comprised of czars of international finance who prescribe free-market reforms as a cure-all for the problems in Latin America) met recently for the fifth in a series of discussions about politics and economics in Buenos Aires, Argentina. Participants in the group included Cardenas; Vicente Fox, Governor of Guana-juato State in Mexico and a member of the center-right National Action Party; Richard Lagos, a public works minister from Chile; Luiz Inacio 'Lula' da Silva, leader of Brazil's Workers' Party; Carlos 'Chacho' Alvarez, leader of Argentina's Frepaso Party; former Salvadoran guerrillas; and others. A communique from the group unhesitatingly proclaimed:

> We are firm proponents of overcoming the "neoliberal" policies that have extracted the market from its condition as an instrument and elevated it to the sta-tus of a religion. . . . Unrestrained privatization, systematic reduction of taxes and deregulation of labor markets. . . have aggravated social tensions and conflicts, deepening the poverty of vast sectors of the population. (Rotella, 1997, p. 5)[8]

Within this new global scenario, moments of defeat—for instance, the demise of the Nicaraguan revolution in the late 1980s and the counter-revolution in Grenada half a decade earlier—have given way in later years to some splinters of hope such as the outbreak of Mayan peasant resistance in Chiapas, Mexico, and the working-class struggles in Santiago del Estero and other Argentine cities in late 1993 and early 1994. Yet in the United States, amid the current political quiescence and descending revolutionary wave and class struggle, Che's new socialist being exists furtively in the historical imagination of the educational Left, denuded of any critical potency, and even mocked by academic postmod-ernists as yet another 'modernist' form of outmoded phallomilitary 'totalizing' demagoguery. But for those of us on the Left who still yearn and struggle for a socialist alternative to the current transnational agenda, the example of Che's anti-imperialist actions, his political vision, and his life committed to revolu-tionary ideals needs to be vigorously defended. Along with the figures of Mal-colm X, Lenin, Freire, Marx, Luxemburg, and others, the example of Che can serve as a means of rethinking the possibilities of resistance to and transforma-tion of the new polyarchies of emergent global society. After all, it is capitalism that is currently in crisis today, and perhaps the temporary retreat of revolu-tionary struggle from the world stage can serve as a means of reorganization—assessing the relationship of class forces, rethinking global class alliances, and reconsidering measures for the anti-capitalist struggle ahead.

MILITANT UTOPIANISM AND THE PEDAGOGY OF CHE GUEVARA

The pedagogy of Ernesto 'Che' Guevara was as insistent as his Marxism and anything but domesticated. First and foremost, Che was a revolutionary teacher

and a teacher of the revolution, the exemplary internationalist pedagogue of revolutionary practice. Che's theories of the transition to socialism, his perspectives
on revolutionary war and the philosophy of the guerrilla, and his socialist humanism locate him securely within the Marxist tradition. A foreign correspondent
interviewing Che shortly after the revolution had taken over Havana asked him
if he were a Marxist. Detecting hostility in the tone and temper of the question,
Che replied: "I don't know enough to be a Marxist" (Löwy, 1973). Che's pedagogy was solidly linked to a Marxist problematic: the necessity of class struggle on
an international basis. In fact, it could be argued that he anticipated the postnational imperialism of capital co-ordinated by transnational corporate polyarchies
in his insistence on creating—by any means necessary—a proletariat internationalism. Che was animated by outrage at the casualness and detachment with
which capital destroys human lives—disproportionately the toilers of the world
and the dark-skinned populations—and insulates the rich against compassion and
accountability. Che saw U.S. capitalism as a deceitful and mocking consciousness
that has arrayed the rich against the masses; he characterized it as possessing an
inveterate need to divide the world, creating unblinkable and unbridgeable dis-
crepancies between the rich and the poor. Capitalism opens up a fissure between
those who assent to the new spirit of progress and competition and those who feel
social life is threatened by it and therefore resist it. A revolution against capitalism and its political affiliate, imperialism, was not perceived by Che as an aber-
ration but rather as one among a number of necessary periodic convulsions that
were never ending as long as social injustices continued to exist.[9]

According to Petras (1997a), there have been four distinct waves of revolutionary politics around the world since 1950 that can lay claim to being influenced by a Guevarista politics: 1959–1967, from the Cuban revolution to Che's
assassination; 1968–1976, popular uprisings in the Southern Cone and Andean
countries to the military coups; 1977–1990, the rise of popular movements in
Central America and the Sandinista revolution; and 1990–present, new sociopolitical revolutionary peasant and indigenous movements such as the Zapatistas
(El Ejército Zapatista de Liberación Nacional, or Zapatista National Liberation
Army) in Chiapas, Mexico. It is worth noting that fourth-wave revolutionary
movements such as the Landless Rural Worker Movement in Brazil and the
Zapatistas in Mexico, "*consciously* see themselves as inspired by Guevara, his
practice and teachings" (Petras, 1997a, p. 17).

To understand Che's pedagogy is not to dredge his corpus of writings for explicit
references to his philosophy of teaching. Che's pedagogy can be more produc-
tively viewed in relation to the way he was able to map his Marxist-
Leninist teachings onto his larger project of guerrilla military action designed to
expose the brutality of violent dictatorships and ruling oligarchies and to make it
possible for the oppressed and exploited toilers of the world to realize that victory
against government military regimes was possible. His pedagogy is in some ways

similar to the great revolutionary figure, V. I. Lenin, who asserted that objective and subjective historical conditions must determine the appropriate 'combat methods,' including educational mass mobilization and organization (Loveman and Davies, 1985, p. 6). Che's pedagogy was influenced by numerous events and relationships: his playing the screen-half position in rugby as a teenager has been attributed to constructing Che's personality in a profound way, since the majority of advances in the game depend upon who is playing this position (Harris, 1970); the philosophy of Che's parents, who rarely discussed religion at home, who created a very politicized household, with his conservative father and leftist mother both identifying with the Republican cause during the Spanish Civil War, who both took a strong anti-Nazi position during World War II, who worked in an underground movement to oppose the regime of Juan Perón, and who let Che and his brother go on a hitchhiking trip to the surrounding provinces for two months when Che was only fourteen; Che's home-schooling due to his frequent asthma attacks, which saw his mother taking great pains to teach Che to speak French and to read classical literature; his travels in Bolivia, in 1953, where he witnessed the extreme poverty of the peasants; his visit to Guatemala, where he witnessed the fall of Jacobo Arbenz's government (orchestrated by the CIA); the time spent in Mexico City with exiles from the Dominican Republic, Peru, Cuba, Colombia, and Venezuela; and especially his relationship with Fidel Castro (whom he met in July or August of 1955) and the Cuban refugees who belonged to the 26th of July Movement (named after the 1953 assault by Fidel's men on the Moncado Barracks in Cuba), whom he met in 1955 in Mexico City and with whom he helped plan the Cuban revolution; his personal admiration for Fidel, who shared many of Che's own traits and ideals (like Che, Fidel was an athlete and intellectual—in fact, Fidel was voted Cuba's best all-around athlete in 1943 and attended the best Jesuit schools in Cuba, instilling in him a legendary passion for learning; he was reported to have memorized entire textbooks while in school); his military training alongside Fidel in the mountains of the Chalco district (at Las Rosas Ranch) in Mexico under the leadership of Alberto Bayo, a former guerrilla fighter who had served as a general in the Spanish Republican Army, had waged numerous guerrilla campaigns against Franco's forces, and had gained experience in guerrilla warfare in Morocco against the Arabs; and Che's three years of combat against the forces of Cuban dictator Fulgencio Batista.

One cannot underestimate how decisive a moment it was for the history of revolutionary struggle when Che stepped aboard the yacht, *Granma,* with Fidel and a group of guerrillas as they traveled from Mexico to Cuba to start the revolution. On November 25, 1956, the *Granma* left Tuxpan in the Gulf of Mexico for Santiago de Cuba, and ran aground in the fishing village of Belio, Oriente province. Che was one of eighty-two guerrillas who came ashore from the *Granma,* and only one of twenty-two who regrouped in the Sierra Maestra mountains (although accounts frequently place that number at twelve—possibly to emulate the twelve apostles of Jesus) after Batista's troops ambushed the rebels. Che and Fidel believed—correctly—that they would gain the backing of the poor, since only a few Cuban farmers owned their farmlands (most of the best farmlands were owned by the United Fruit and West Indian Corporations), and most *guajiros* and *macheteros* were living in systematic poverty and destitution. And from the moment he began to struggle alongside the *precaristas* (landless workers of the land), Che became a pedagogue of armed struggle.

Che fervently believed that a guerrilla struggle would provide the means for viruliferous oligarchic regimes to unmask themselves. He possessed unflinching faith in the certainty of victory in the battle for revolutionary change, insisting that the duty of all revolutionaries was to make revolution—an act grounded in a larger socialist vision that took into consideration concrete historical and material conditions as well as existing social relations and that tried to vernalize them to hasten forth the revolution. Che considered guerrilla warfare a revolutionary war of the people in which the guerrillas, acting as the revolutionary vanguard, would win the support of the masses. He believed in creating revolutionary conditions rather than total victories, inspiring the popular forces, and utilizing the strength of student, peasant, and worker organizations so they would become subversive to the ruling establishment. Che also believed that guerrilla movements could emerge victorious by striking from anywhere, by maintaining constant pressure, by engaging in political consciousness raising, by becoming historical actors who determine the direction of the people's struggle, and by emphasizing tactical flexibility and protracted struggle. For Che, guerrilla warfare was only one method—but a critically important one—for furthering socialist revolution in Latin America (Loveman and Davies, 1985).[10] And though counterinsurgery programs in the United States and in Latin America crushed most of the guerrilla movements of the 1960s and 1970s from Central America, Uruguay, Argentina, and the Southern Cone, the Sandinistas carried Che's spirit of struggle into the streets of Nicaragua, while other guerrilla movements in El Salvador and Guatemala did the same.

Che's theory of *foquismo*—that rebels should engage in hit-and-run attacks and then retreat without engaging in a frontal battle against regular armies—was employed by Che in Bolivia in his attempt to control the Ñancahuazú area and to move in small groups to Cochabamba (west) and Santa Cruz (south). Bolivia in this instance seemed an ideal place to initiate a continent-wide revolution, since it shared borders with five of the other nine republics of South America (Peru, Chile, Argentina, Paraguay, and Brazil). However, when Che's guerrilla base was discovered by the army, his whole plan was accelerated such that he could not maintain contact with the urban base in La Paz and with those outside the country. One of the major problems faced by Che was a tactical decision he had made that resulted in dividing his forces on April 15, 1967; he was subsequently never able to reunite them. Che led one unit of twenty-seven men, and Cuban-born Juan Vitalio Acuña Nuñez (Joaquín, also known as 'Vilo') led a second group consisting of seventeen men and one woman (Tania). Joaquín's group was destroyed as it was crossing the Rio Grande at the Valdo de Yesso on August 31, and this fatefully marked the end of the guerrilla *foco*. Joaquín was betrayed by a farmer living near Masicuri River named Horatio Rojas, who notified Captain Mario Vargas Salinas that the *guerrilleros* were spending the night at his farm and would cross the stream the following day. Elsewhere, the army surrounded Che and the remaining guerrillas on October 8, 1967. After Che's execution, the surviving guerrillas, with Pombo in command and Inti Pardo as their guide, escaped to high ground. After subsequent skirmishes five escaped to Chile with the help of a Bolivian Indian named Tani.

It is important to note, following Petras, that Che saw theory and practice (what critical educators call pedagogical praxis) as a continuing process that represents "a living reinvention of the Marxist categories of 'class struggle' and 'class politics' in a changing context" (Petras, 1997a, p. 17). For Che (as for groups such as Mexico's Zapatistas), this meant a bold refusal simply to consolidate democracy within an overall strategy of modernization—something many ex-guerrillas and leftists who operate within a mechanical determinism and "stage" theory currently counsel and employ in a fidelity to their orthodox Marxist allegiances. Che believed that his work in Bolivia would inspire other guerrilla columns in the Southern Cone countries to take action, eventually provoking U.S. intervention and another 'Vietnam' situation.

ZAPATISMO: THE STRUGGLE IN CHIAPAS AND ITS GUEVARIAN POSSIBILITIES

Che came into contact with South American indigenous groups for the first time in Peru, when, as a young man, he witnessed how the Indians of the Peruvian altiplano were exploited and oppressed and led into an addiction to *coca*. We know, for instance, that in Yacay, he observed a procession of Incas honoring the Lord of Tremors and made inquiries about how they survived on a daily basis. Later on when Che was living in a *pensión* in Guatemala with Ricardo Rojo, he met a number of Peruvian exiles who were members of Peru's left-wing APRA Party, then under attack in Peru because of its opposition to the Manuel Odria regime (these exiles were later to introduce Che to Hilda Gadea, a young Peruvian exile whom Che would marry and have one child with) (Anderson, 1997). Yet it remains unclear how much serious knowledge Che had about the indigenous peoples of Peru and other Latin American countries. While in Bolivia he had hoped to conscript indigenous groups into his guerrilla movement, but he was unable to do so largely because Che was perceived as a white man from the outside who was trying to speak on behalf of a people who had endured a unique and contradictory history with the Bolivian army.[11]

El Ejército Zapatista de Liberación Nacional (Zapatista Army of National Liberation—EZLN) [named after Emiliano Zapata, the indigenous Mexican peasant leader who led a revolutionary army and was martyred in 1917 because of his struggle on behalf of the landless poor] declared war on the Mexican government on January 1, 1994. An offspring of the Fuerzas de Liberación Nacional (FLN)—a Maoist-inspired urban group of northern Mexican student radicals that was created as a result of the government's massacre of students in Tlatelolco in 1968—the EZLN is constituted both as an Indian and a *campesino* (peasant) movement. The EZLN was born on November 17, 1983, as a result of a meeting among three indigenous people and three *mestizos* (Harvey, 1998). Early in its development, it maintained loose ties with the Unión del Pueblo and the Linea Proletaria faction of Politica Popular. The EZLN adopts many of the characteristics of indigenous organizations, which are structured as non-hierarchical, decentralized, community-based social activity groups. The Zapatistas, composed principally of Mayan peoples (almost exclusively Tzetazal, Tzotzil, Chole, Mam, Zoque, and Tojolabal Indians) from Chiapas, have received a great deal of sympathetic international publicity, in part because they have not used armed force since the initial uprising, they have the enthusiastic support of many influential NGOs, and they offer the charismatic leadership of Subcomandante Marcos, a balaclava-clad insurgent who wears munition-filled bandoliers and an Ingram machine gun tucked into his belt, who writes poetry, smokes a pipe, speaks English and French, and in some ways appears to share the mystical aura that Che himself exuded. Unlike many revolutionary groups, the EZLN has adopted a "Woman's Law" that proclaims the right of all women to their bodies, political participation, wages, health care, and freedom from violence.

Many of today's indigenous-based revolutionary movements—including the Zapatistas—do not necessarily see a continuation of armed struggle as a viable strategy at this moment, but this does not make them any less indebted to Che's ideas and example. The Zapatistas did use armed insurrection at the beginning of their campaign (which coincided with the day that the North American Free Trade Agreement went into effect on January 1, 1994) but they are currently exercising other political options.

After the New Year's 1994 rebellion, a cease-fire was brokered with the help of Bishop Samuel Ruíz, who heads the Comisión Nacional de Intermediación (National Mediation Commission—CONAI), which is attempting to seek a negotiated solution to the conflict. Shortly afterward, the Mexican congress established a multiparty Comisión de Concordia y Pacificación (Commission for Concord and Pacification—COCOPA) and then passed a "Law of Dialogue" that guaranteed that federal soldiers would not be deployed while the peace talks were taking place. However, in February 1995, the federal army launched a surprise offensive in an attempt to capture the Zapatista leaders. This attack—which was in flagrant violation of the law established by congress—ultimately failed. On February 17, 1996, the government and rebels signed an agreement in the highland town of San Andrés Larráinzar (renamed San Andrés Sakam

Ch'en) that focused on the issue of human rights and the rights of indigenous peoples (Stahler-Sholk, 1998). The San Andrés accords on Indigenous Rights and Culture defends the collective as opposed to individual rights of indigenous peoples. The COCOPA initiative later defined 'community' versus 'people' very clearly, hoping to end the division of native peoples into small communities. The San Andrés accords—forty pages of agreements between government representatives and seventeen Zapatista leaders—granted limited constitutional autonomy to Mexico's indigenous communities. If the accords had been honored, Mexico's 800 Indian-majority municipalities or counties would have had local control over their own territory, natural resources, and justice and educational systems, in addition to employing traditional assemblies to legitimize the selection of officials rather than party politics (Ross, 1999a).

Nevertheless, the government has consistently and maliciously refused to concede the rights of the indigenous peoples to choose their own leadership and to control their own natural resources, and has blatantly—even defiantly—reneged on implementing the accords. The 'conflict zone' in Chiapas is continuing to spread, from the eastern jungle region to the northern zone and most recently to the central highlands.[12]

After the 1994 uprising, the Zapatistas built an amphitheater in the Tojolabal community of La Realidad, in the middle of the jungle, in order to invite democratic sectors of Mexican society to join them to discuss the future of Mexico in a National Democratic Convention. They called the location Aguascalientes, after the site of the constitutional convention of the 1914 Mexican Revolution. After thousands of people from across the country and beyond responded to the Zapatistas' call, the army marched in and quickly dismantled the locale. Not surprisingly, the Zapatistas responded by building five more sites and calling all five redoubts Aguascalientes, centers of cultural and political resistance (Stahler-Sholk, 1998).

For the Zapatistas, economic modernization is not a viable option in an age of cynical imperialism. They believe that the development of productive forces must be accompanied by an end to inequality and the eradiction of exploitation. The *caciquismo* (the maintenance of political power through support of a particular political party) of the appointed municipal authorities, the control of indigenous communities by the Institutional Revolutionary Party, the lack of regional autonomy of the *ejidos* (collectively held land awarded in land reforms), the ending of the inalienability of Indian lands in Mexico as part of NAFTA's requirement that all land be saleable, and the reneging on the San Andrés accords by the Mexican government (Poynton, 1997) can all be traced to 300 years of colonial rule, and all point to a prolonged state of tension between the government and the Frente Zapatista and pro-Zapatista supporters. This tension, in place for a long time, started to peak after the U.S. Congress's NAFTA vote. As Noam Chomsky points out, shortly after this vote took place,

workers were fired from Mexican Honeywell and GE plants for helping to organize independent unions. This is standard practice. The Ford Motor Co. fired its
entire Mexican work force at one plant in 1987, eliminating the union contract and
rehiring workers at far lower salaries. Brutal repression crushed protests. Volkswagen, with the backing of the Institutional Revolutionary Party (PRI), followed
suit in 1992, firing its fourteen thousand Mexican workers and rehiring only those
who renounced independent union leaders. These are central components in the
"economic miracle" that is to be "locked in" by NAFTA. (1995a, p. 179)

The PRI had historically ignored the protests of the Tarahumara, Tepehua-
nas, Yaqui, Mayos, and indigenous groups in Chiapas and had cunningly participated in massive dislocations of semisubsistence farmers cultivating their *milpa*
(cornfields) and of landless wage laborers who sought work in the towns. They
sought after the neutralization of the *campesino* bloc in favor of the agro-indus-
trial interests of the capitalist class. Who was to think that the new agent of revolutionary praxis would be the indigenous peoples rather than the industrial proletariat, the students, or the unemployed in the cities? As Subcomandante
Marcos—the *jefe maximo* of the Zapatistas—noted:

Who would have speculated before December 31, 1993 that it wasn't going to be
the proletariat leading the revolution? Then who? Who was it going to be? They
could have speculated that it would be the teachers, they could have speculated
that it would be the unemployed, they could have speculated that it would be the
students or some sector of the middle class, they could have speculated that it
would be leftist or democratic factions within the Federal Army or within the supposedly democratic faction of the PRI. They could have speculated many things,
including that the United States would become socialist and then they would
invade us and make us socialists [laughter]. This was the reasoning then. Even in
the university this idea had taken root. It didn't occur to anyone that the Indigenous peoples were going to play this role and they would manage to demand their
place in the nation, or that they would demand that the nation recognize that they
have a proposal, that they have a proposal for the nation. The same or better or
worse—it's open for discussion—as any other proposal that intellectuals or political parties or social groups have for this country. (Aguilera et al., 1994, pp.
295–296)

Michael Löwy reports that "Zapatism" is a "subtle mixture, an alchemistic
fusion, an explosive cocktail made up of several ingredients, several traditions,
each of them indispensable, each of them present in the final product" (1998, p.
2). The first "thread" in the "design" of Zapatism is, notes Löwy, Guevarism—
Marxism in its Latin American, revolutionary form. The second thread is the life
and legacy of Emiliano Zapata. Zapata led the struggle for agrarian reform and
redistribution of the land through his "commune of Morelos" but he also was an

internationalist whose rallying cry was "Land and Liberty." Another thread of Zapatism's overall design is liberation theology and the work of the Catholic catechists in Chiapas since the 1970s. However, Löwy notes that perhaps the most important thread of Zapatism is the Mayan culture of the native people of Chiapas, which "harks back to a community tradition of the past, a pre-capitalist, pre-modern, pre-Columbian tradition" (p. 3).

Any counter-hegemonic bloc in Latin America or elsewhere has to begin with indigenous movements. According to William Robinson:

A crucial social movement is constituted by the growth of indigenous struggles throughout the Americas, often intertwined with peasant and rural worker struggles. The indigenous form a majority of the population in Guatemala and in Bolivia, huge minorities in Ecuador, Peru, Paraguay and Mexico, and have a significant presence in most other Latin American countries. In Mexico, the Zapatista uprising is a largely Mayan movement. It has forced Mexico and the world to recognize the multiethnic and multinational character of the country, and has also focused a spotlight on the persistence of a *de facto* apartheid system in Mexico after 500 years. Tellingly, the Zapatistas launched their struggle on new year's day, 1994, the very day the North American Free Trade Agreement went into effect, as a highly symbolic way to protest neo-liberalism and globalisation in Mexico and Latin America. In Ecuador, the indigenous have formed the Confederation of Indigenous Nationalities of Ecuador (CONAIE), a powerful organisation that forced the resignation, in February 1997, of the corrupt neo-liberal president, Abdala Bucaram. It has continued at the forefront of that country's struggle against neo-liberalism and for social justice. In Guatemala, Rigoberta Menchú shone the global spotlight on indigenous struggles when she won the Nobel Peace Prize in 1992, and the Mayan majority is engaged in a renewed mobilisation, assertiveness and political protagonism that some say has not been paralleled since resistance to the Conquest. These diverse struggles have identified neo-liberalism and the local structures of global capitalism as the source of continued indigenous oppression. Therefore, as the indigenous fight for their own dignity, survival and liberation, they also represent and defend the interests of the entire poor majority. (1998/1999, pp. 123–124)

According to Andres Oppenheimer, in a ritual that occurred in December 1993, one month before the Zapatista uprising, deep in the Lacandon jungle near the border with Guatemala. Subcomandante Marcos stood before a thousand Indian rebels clad in military uniforms and was given the staff of command—a scepter made out of an ocote tree branch—by a dozen Mayan leaders. The Tzeltal leaders in their white shirts and black ponchos, the Tzotziles in their red ponchos, the Choles in their black slacks, and the Tojolabales in their all-white clothing, presented Marcos with seven symbols: emblems of combat that included a Mexican flag, a red-and-black Zapatista flag, a rifle, and a bullet; and symbols of life that included a container of human blood, a piece

Subcomandante Marcos (courtesy of Peter McLaren)

of corn, and a handful of clay. The ceremony began with the singing of "The Horizon," the Zapatista National Anthem (*Ya se mira el horizonte, combatiente Zapatista!*) and ended with a prayer in Tzeltal: "Seven words, seven forces, seven roads. Life, truth, men, peace, democracy, freedom, and justice. Seven forces that empower the staff of command. Take the scepter of the seven forces and hold it with honor" (Oppenheimer, 1996, p. 17). Though Marcos may be mestizo, and an intellectual from the middle class of northern Mexico, he undoubtedly has been transformed by the Mayan way of life. But this does not mean that he is no longer influenced by Che, or that Guevarismo and Zapatismo are incompatible. During a military purge (known as Operation Rainbow) of the Zapatista leadership, government troops raided the six-room rebel headquarters that Marcos had quickly abandoned in 1995 and found near his bed *History Will Absolve Me* by Fidel Castro and *Revolutionary Works* by Che Guevara—right next to Microsoft Windows manuals and a pipe (Oppenheimer, 1996).

Although the Zapatista revolutionary strategy has been one of improvisation, the Zapatistas' commitment to revolutionary praxis has been unwavering. Combining various forms of struggle may be the best strategy in certain contexts—

such as the building of legal organizations and the forging of social alliances. As Petras notes, "Political conditions favor different styles of politics even as the movements continue to develop in the revolutionary spirit of Che's practice" (1997a, p. 19). For instance, organizing peasant rebel groups in the rural areas of Cuba, Bolivia, and Colombia is a far different proposition from organizing today in cities such as São Paulo, Tokyo, Mexico City, or Los Angeles, whose populations range from eleven million to over twenty million.

POSTMODERNISTS IN MASKS?

Commenting on the Zapatista revolution in Chiapas, Daniel Nugent makes the important observation that Mexico remains a neocolonial society in that neither the Wars of Independence and the Wars of Reform during the nineteenth century nor the revolution of 1910 and the so-called reforms of the Salinastroika period from 1988–1994 amounted to a radical break with the colonial past. Intellectuals such as Pablo Gonzalez Casanova and Carlos Fuentes have called the Zapatistas the world's first postcommunist, postmodern insurgents who have broken from the old Sandinista-Castroite-Marxist-Leninist legacy (Fuentes, 1994, p. 5–6). In his book *Postmodern War*, Chris Hables Gray (1997, pp. 5–6) describes the Zapatistas as a hybrid, postmodern movement. However, Nugent is critical of postmodern theorists (typically those from the elite metropolitan precincts of the Western Academy) who attempt to locate neo-Zapatismo as a "postmodern political movement" because of the EZLN's use of modems, fax machines, and e-mail. Nugent writes:

> Do their [the EZLN] demands include a modem and VCR in every *jacal* or adobe hut in Mexico? No. Is their chosen name "The postmodern army of multinational emancipation" or "Cyberwarriors of the South?" No. They are the Zapatista Army of National Liberation. Emiliano Zapata (not a "free-floating signifier" but a specific historical subject), who led the peasants of Morelos, from 1911 until his assassination in 1919, in recovering control of the land and driving out the *caciques*/foreign political bosses is a very unlikely postmodern hero. (Nugent, 1997, p. 168)

Arguing that the language of postmodernity adds little or nothing to our understanding of Chiapas, Nugent adds that such a discourse "simply serves to underline the profound distance between postmodern intellectuals and the activists or supporters of the EZLN" (1997, p. 172). He concludes with the following admonition: "Something approximating, however remotely, the determinative power that postmodern intellectuals claim for their own discursive practices—the power to create reality itself—is, in the real world, possible for servants of a ruling class, with the power of the state underwriting their discourses" (1997, p. 173).[13]

THE EPR AND ITS FACTIONS

Mexico possesses the largest indigenous population in Latin America (estimated at between eight and ten million). Although there are twenty-seven known armed revolutionary groups throughout Mexico, it is unlikely that revolutionary struggle there can succeed with the support of mainly rural populations. Over the last decade, the EPR (Ejército Popular Revolucionario, or People's Revolutionary Army) of Aguas Blancas, Guerrero, has engaged in numerous armed skirmishes in Chiapas, Oaxaca (where they first appeared in 1996 and were engaged by the 28th Military Zone led by General José Ruben Rivas Pena), Guanajuato, and the states of Mexico and Tabasco; it has established a parallel political party (el Partido Democrático Popular Revolucionario—PDPR). The mainly *mestizo* leadership of the EPR is connected with a nationwide coalition of leftist groups, including radical peasant and teacher unions called the Construction of a National Liberation Movement (FAC-MLN).[14]

In June 1998, in the state of Guerrero, the Mexican army attacked the Mixteca community of El Charco (the puddle), located seventy miles west of Acapulco, and killed twelve members of the People's Revolutionary Army (and wounded five) who had spent the night in the Caritino Maldonado bilingual school. Some of those killed were apparently members of the ERPI (Ejército Revolucionario del Pueblo Insurgente or Revolutionary Army of the Insurgent People), a new, largely indigenous, *guerrillero* faction that recently split from the EPR (which is a front for fourteen radical organizations). In September 1996, in Loxicha, Oaxaca, the military launched a campaign against the EPR and took seventeen Chiapanecos to 'safe' houses and tortured them with electric shocks and the *tehuacanazo* (a bicarbonated soda cocktail that is shaken and blasted into the victims' sinus cavities). Weeks later, a dozen or more residents were similarly tortured. It is no surprise that Mexican authorities have targeted education groups in Oaxaca and Guerrero, where the EPR is most active. For instance, Local 22 of the country's independent teachers union, the National Education Workers Coordinating Committee, has been singled out for scrutiny, and two prominent union organizers have 'disappeared' (Schou, 1998).

One of the founding organizations of the EPR is the Party of the Poor (PDLP), which can be traced to Mexico's native tradition of armed peasant insurrection, Emiliano Zapata, Ruben Jaramillo, Gerraro Vázquez, and Lucio Cabañas (La Botz, 1996). It can also be linked to the Partido Revolucionario Obrero Clandestino—Unión del Pueblo—and to the Revolutionary Workers Clandestine Party "People's Union" (PROCUP), which became the urban arm of the PDLP and an extension of the Unión del Pueblo (People's Union). Yet the activities of the EPR are sporadic and its numbers are small. In response to the EZLN's 1994 call for armed uprisings outside Chiapas, PROCUP did explode several bombs around Mexico City, damaging an electrical tower. But for an armed revolution to succeed, a massive coalition would need to develop, one that included insurgent groups working in urban sectors.

TAKING ITS STOLL: BLAME THE GUERRILLAS AND DAMN THE COMMIES

As in Che's day, global economic strategy and U.S. interests continue the assault on poor, indigenous populations throughout Latin America. One need only witness the recent rodomotade of 'American First' rhetoric surrounding the recent attack on Rigoberta Menchú. Anthropologist David Stoll, who alleges that Menchú exaggerated and fabricated some of the events that she chronicled in her autobiography, *I Rigoberta Menchú*, wants to leave the impression that the Guatamalan revolution did not have popular support. In blaming the guerrilla movements for the lack of peaceful political and economic reform, he is suggesting that they are directly responsible for Latin American political violence and repression. As Greg Grandin and Francisco Goldman point out, Stoll is gravely mistaken if he thinks "that, if not for the guerrillas, the Guatamalan military might not have become the most bloodthirsty killing machine in the hemisphere" (1999, p. 27)— it exterminated between 70 and 90 percent of the Ixtil, a Mayan ethnic group. Stoll essentially blames the victims for the torture and destruction that the military visited upon them (Grandin and Goldman, 1999). Do commentators such as Stoll, who are hell-bent on discrediting guerrilla movements in Latin America, so easily forget how swiftly the United States reacted by pressuring the passing of Resolution 93? This resolution condemned Guatemala for being "communist-infiltrated" when the Jacobo Arbenz regime distributed to 100,000 Guatemalan peasants uncultivated land expropriated from the country's large feudal estates, including 11,000 hectares of uncultivated land belonging to the U.S.-owned United Fruit Company. Does social amnesia suddenly set in with a vengeance when confronted by the historical evidence that the CIA trained Guatemalan officers and commandos, prepared a mercenary invasion force in neighboring Honduras under the command of Carlos Castillo Arnas, supplied them with weapons and airplanes, and orchestrated the betrayal of the leadership of the Guatemalan army? Perhaps Stoll, in his slobbering desire to undermine Marxist revolutionary struggle and what he sees as a romantic Guevarismo, should consider the findings of the Commission for Historical Clarification, which in a meeting in Guatemala City in late February 1999, reported that the army permitted and participated in acts of genocide against Maya Indians for a period of thirty-five years (Forster, 1999). The government was found responsible for 93 percent of the 42,275 human-rights violations and the murder of 200,000 civilians, most of which occurred under the infamous leadership of Efrain Rios Montt, who presided over a 'scorched earth' policy from 1982–1983 with former Chilean dictator, Augusto Pinochet.[15] U.S. financial support helped the military target *campesinos*, labor, community and human-rights organizers, teachers, students, educators, and religious workers for torture and extrajudicial executions. Refugees fleeing death squads who sought sanctuary in the United States were often sent back. The U.S. government and corporations in Guatemala were accused of playing direct roles in prolonging the fighting. In other words, the U.S. government and its companies colluded in pressuring Guatemala to maintain its archaic and exploitative economic structures so that they could reap influence and profits (Darling, 1999). Stoll's pernicious attempt to blame the guerrillas for pre-empting the peace process and his self-righteous zealotry in condemning the Ladino leadership of the guerrillas for forcing themselves on Mayan Indian villagers in their recruitment attempts, has delighted right-wing anti-multiculturalists in the United States and justified their rabid anti-Marxism.

CHIAPAS UNDER SIEGE: NADA PERSONAL

The Mexican government's opposition to the Zapatistas can be explained not only by racist formations organized against Mexico's indigenous populations but also by the fact that Chiapas has the second-largest, untapped reserve of oil in the Americas and large reserves of forested areas.[16]

Chiapas produces vast quantities of petroleum, electricity, coffee, wood, and cattle. It also harbors major petroleum reserves that are second only to those of Venezuela in the Western Hemisphere. The estimated oil potential of Chiapas and Guatemala combined is greater than that of Saudi Arabia. Pemex, the national oil company, pumps out 92,000 barrels of petroleum and billions of cubic feet of natural gas a day out of the townships of Estación Juarez, Reforma, Ostuacán, Pichucalco, and Ocosingo. Despite this abundance, most houses are without electricity; over 50 percent of the work force earns less than U.S. $3.32 a day; and approximately 80 percent of the children suffer from malnutrition. Nearly 15,000 deaths occur each year from curable diseases. Sixty percent of children have little or no access to education, one in four Chiapanecos is indigenous but only one in every fifteen classrooms is located in an indigenous community and only four out of every 100 children receive formal education. Less than half of households have running water while two-thirds of the population lack sanitation facilities. Only 20 percent of Chiapaneco businesses are not experiencing a financial crisis and over one-third of Mexico's total armed forces are stationed permanently in Mexico (Fact Sheet, National Commission For Democracy in Mexico).

The lack of enforcement of environmental and health and safety regulations in Mexico makes Chiapas exceptionally attractive to corporations from regulated industrial nations. The Mexican government has business agreements with U.S. companies, Simpson Paper and Louisiana Paper, and it has been reported that one multinational company has a plan to plant 300,000 hectares of nonindigenous eucalyptus trees throughout Chiapas and surrounding territories and to sell them to International Paper. The lands in question are inhabited by indigenous people who have lived there for centuries. The Mexican government has already brokered a deal between Mexico's Federal Electricity Commission and a major Canadian corporation, Hydro-Quebec International, to develop natural gas resources throughout Chiapas. That Zapatista-controlled lands—not to mention the general 'unrest' in the region—pose an obstacle to foreign corporations has not been lost on the Mexican government, especially when foreign corporations complain that the Zapatistas pose a serious threat to investment in Mexico (Viviana, 1997). Consider the following description of the political context in Chiapas by Subcomandante Marcos:

> Welcome to San Cristóbal de las Casas, a "Colonial City" according to the history books, although the majority of the population is Indigenous. Welcome to Pronasol's huge market. Here you can buy or sell anything except Indigenous dignity. Here everything is expensive except death. But don't stay too long, continue along the road, the proud result of the tourist infrastructure. In 1988 there were 6,270 hotel rooms, 139 restaurants, and 42 travel agencies in this state. This year, 1,058,098 tourists visited Chiapas and left 255 billion pesos in the hands of restaurant and hotel owners.
>
> Have you calculated the numbers? Yes, you're right: there are seven hotel rooms for every 1,000 tourists while there are only 0.3 hospitals beds per 1,000 Chiapaneco citizens. Leave the calculations behind and drive on, noticing the three police officials in berets jogging along the shoulder of the road. Drive by the Public Security station and continue on passing hotels, restaurants, large stores and heading towards the exit to Comitán. Leaving San Cristóbal behind you will see the famous San Cristóbal caves surrounded by leafy forest. Do you see the sign? No, you are not mistaken, this natural park is administered by . . . the Army! Without leaving your uncertainty behind, drive on. . . . Do you see them? Modern buildings, nice homes, paved roads. . . . Is it a university? Workers' housing? No, look at the sign next to the cannons closely and read: "General Army Barracks of the 31st Military Zone." With the olive-green image still in your eyes, drive on to the intersection and decide not to go to Comitán so that you will avoid the pain of seeing that, a few meters ahead, on the hill that is called the Foreigner, North American military personnel are operating, and teaching their Mexican counterparts to operate radar. (1994, p. 32)

The Mexican government has undertaken shrewd reforms with respect to the privatization of *ejidal* lands (collectively held land usually for farming and provided for by Article 27 of the Mexican Constitution) and also formerly state-owned petroleum and natural gas industries. Eight important unexplored oil sites are located on *ejido* land currently under Zapatista control, and large petroleum and natural gas sources exist near Ocosingo. Consider the fact that the

Mexican government put up its oil reserves and the proceeds from Mexican crude oil, oil products, and petrochemical exports for collateral for a U.S. $50 billion bailout package from the United States (National Commission for Democracy in Mexico, n.d.), and it should come as no surprise that, for many guerrilla movements, there exists a significant political tension between military 'defense' and the practice of democracy. Zapatistas are currently living on the thin line produced by such a tension.

Within an economy dependent on liquid capital that would be weakened by capital flight at any sign of increased instability, the victor in a multifront struggle between the Mexican army and a congerie of other groups—including the Zapatistas, EPR guerrilla forces in Guerrero, peasants mobilized in Oaxaca, and trade unionists—is not clear to see (Petras, 1997b). According to a classified Pentagon report, the United States regards the present tension in Chiapas as a "medium range" destabilization risk, and the eventual deployment of U.S. troops to Mexico could be received favorably by the Mexican people if the Mexican government is faced with the threat of being overthrown as a result of economic and social chaos (Petrich, 1996). Petras writes that the tension between democracy and military defense

> can only be dealt with in the concrete situation of an occupied Chiapas, with helicopters hovering overhead and special airborne troops awaiting orders to strike. In the event of a government attack, the EZLN would be separated from their social base and the public image projected by the media would shift from a struggle between Indian communities and the one-party state to a military conflict between guerrillas and the armed forces. Such a polarization would weaken progressive urban support. (Petras, 1997b, p. 40)

An unvarnished focus on indigenous politics distinguishes the struggle of the Zapatistas from the universal proletarianism of Che. The Zapatista guerrillas identify their struggle with the tradition of indigenous resistance to colonization, domination, and exploitation (Churchill, 1995). The accusation by the Mexican government that the Zapatistas are really led by northern, white Ladinos (a term similar to 'mestizo' usually referring to individuals of mostly Spanish descent or linked to bourgeois Spanish culture) amounts to rank racism. The Zapatistas' method of military organization is not modeled so much after El Che as after the Mayan guerrillas in Guatemala. According to Arturo Santamaría Gómez:

> The Zapatistas are not *foquistas* (in the manner of Che Guevara); they do not advocate founding a small nucleus of armed fighters with the expectation of growing in the course of confrontations with the state. They appear to have followed a strategy of the "cold accumulation of forces," which was previously used by the Revolutionary Organization of the people in Arms (ORPA) in Guatemala. ORPA, which is now part of the National Revolutionary Unity of Guatemala (URNG) was founded in 1972 . . . and

spent "seven long years of silent work" . . . developing a guerrilla organization, one which was also made up largely of [Mayas]. (cited in Churchill, 1995, p. 145)

Some commentators have gone so far as to describe the Zapatistas as a revolutionary social movement and not a guerrilla army. Greg Ruggiero likens the Zapatista rebellion to the revolution advocated by Paulo Freire:

During the four years of their open struggle the Zapatistas have proved that they are NOT a guerrilla force seeking to seize power, but rather a revolutionary social movement seeking to activate and mobilize "civil society"—a truly subversive project in a global economic system that seeks to place corporate interest above democratic law, and redefine citizen power as consumer choice. In situating civil society at the heart of their project, Zapatista strategies of organization and outreach provide an inspiring example of radical social empowerment and movement building for grassroots organizers, community leaders, and activists worldwide.

The Zapatista approach is revolutionary because of its emphasis on communication and dialogue over authority and force. "We are the network," say the Zapatistas, "all of us who speak and listen." This is the revolution that Paulo Freire wrote of in *Pedagogy of the Oppressed*, a revolution that seeks not only to liberate the oppressed, but the oppressors as well; an empowerment struggle lead by a vision of humanity that supports localism and diversity, and increase in power through genuine dialogue and community participation. (1998, pp. 7–8)

When the Zapatistas first burst on the scene in 1994, they denied that they were linked to Central American *guerrilleros;* they also claimed to reject outdated Marxist ideologies, preferring to identify themselves as a national movement with indigenous roots. And they have reached out not to other guerrilla groups, but to Mexican civil society with its proliferation of peaceful social movements. Marcos has even written a children's book, *La Historia de los Colores,* a folk tale with mythical gods who created colors to brighten a dull, gray universe.[17]

The Zapatistas have also called on international organizations such as the Red Cross and other human-rights organizations to come to Chiapas to monitor the situation. Many nongovernmental organizations (NGOs) have voiced sympathy and support for the EZLN's struggle and, with the help of vast media networking capabilities, have helped to make Chiapas a global media event.

Although Subcomandante Marcos has emerged as the poet-warrior spokesperson of the Zapatistas and the symbol of "el otro Mexico,"[18] it is clear that the Zapatistas exercise collective decision making. Marcos initially came to Chiapas to help create self-defense groups to protect Chiapanecos from the "White Guards," who were hired by wealthy Chiapas landowners to drive the Indians off the ranchers' lands and to harass them. It was much later that Marcos and his compañeros decided to organize a rebel army and spark an uprising. He ended up subordinating himself to the collective decisions of the Mayans. Santamaría Gómez reports:

> In another break with the traditional model of guerrilla insurgency, the EZLN has apparently rejected the idea of leadership by a single charismatic *caudillo* (supreme leader of a political movement, especially a guerrilla). In the early days of the insurrection, the government appeared intent on creating a principal leader by singling out the commander of the EZLN's military operation in San Cristóbal de las Casas, Subcomandante Marcos [one of the very few non-Maya fighters]. However, the Zapatistas speak of a "committee" which makes decisions, rather than any individual. (cited in Churchill, 1995, p. 146)

Clearly, Subcomandante Marcos has a singular gift for resituating the struggle against capitalist exploitation in a performative mode. Guillermo Gómez-Peña writes:

> I've always regarded Marcos as a performance artist extraordinaire. I think that perhaps Marco's geniality lies precisely in his ability to understand the symbolic power of performative actions, the symbolic power of props and costuming. He also understands the importance of new technologies; the importance of staging press conferences-as-performance, and of course, the strategic use of poetics in a time in which political language is completely hollow and bankrupt. Performance artists are interested in exactly the same things. (Kun, 1999, p. 188)

While it may be true that Subcomandante Marcos has a creative gift for inventing himself as a romantic figure for the benefit of the media, it would be naive to reduce Marcos to a cyberspace superstar. True, the war in Chiapas has produced only twelve days of open combat but this has as much to do with the decision of the Zapatistas to respect the January 12, 1994, truce as it does with a political decision to abandon political insurrection by any means necessary in favor of cyberwar. At present, with more than 75,000 troops positioned within 66 of Chiapas's 111 municipalities, with paramilitary groups in 27 municipalities running amok, and with the expulsion of over 150 foreign human rights observers, an impasse exists with no foreseeable end in sight.

SALINAS, ALSO KNOWN AS "EL CHUPACABRA"

The Mayan communities—Tzotziles in the highland areas, Tzeltales and Tojolabales in the lower elevations, and Choles and Choltis in the flatlands—have endured a long history of struggling against neoliberalism *a la Mexicana* (Churchill, 1995).

President Salinas de Gortari's reform of Article 27 of the Mexican Constitution and the Agrarian Code took away the possibility of peasants acquiring land. Article 27 is especially troubling to the Mayan campesinos. It is a reform that allows campesinos to sell, rent, or share their land with private investors. Though *ejido* members can sell their land or maintain it as communal property, they have very little 'choice' in the matter because of the devastation caused by the economic policies aimed at the productive sector (García de León, 1995). This amounts to the cancellation of the right of campesinos to the land and protection to those who use *caciquismo* and exploitation to maintain their power. According to Antonio García de León, the reform of Article 27 gives legal support to the formation of new *latifundios* through stock investment and can divest the campesinos of their patrimony in favor of new, unjust concentrations of land and resources. Consequently, "land as commodity would end up replacing the old, but essential concept of earth as mother, and our inalienable patrimony to live from her" (de León, 1995, p. 214). President Salinas and his advisors had decided to drastically restructure Mexico's economy by removing the government's involvement in and support of 'antimodern' sectors. During the Miguel de la Madrid presidency (1982–1988), the international banking community forced Mexico into an austerity program in return for bailing Mexico out of its debt crisis, which dried up subsidies to the peasants for fertilizer and other chemical imputs and eroded price support for crops. Salinas's 'modernization' scheme, designed to increase the productivity of millions of peasant-held hectares used for crops that were not competitive on world markets, was the catalyst for the Zapatista struggle. The elimination of the transport subsidies that the Mexican Coffee Institute had negotiated with the Union of Unions in eastern Chiapas "galvanized peasant antagonism to the national state" (Collier, 1994, p. 85).[19]

MEN WITH GUNS

Yet as the Zapatistas move toward legal political solutions rather than armed struggle in their goal of agrarian reform and cultural and political autonomy in Chiapas, they are faced with the daunting reality that an average of two PRD (Partido de la Revolución Democrática, an official opposition party) leaders or activists are murdered every week in Mexico, and that over 250 have been killed since the election of President Zedillo (Petras, 1997b, p. 41).

At approximately midnight on December 22, 1997, a PRI-ista paramilitary death squad known as Máscara Roja (Red Mask) and armed with machetes and AK-47 assault rifles, massacred 45 Tzotzil Indian villagers near a small church in the village of Acteal, a tiny hamlet of the Tzotzil Maya village in the Chenalhó district of the state of Chiapas, seventy kilometers north of San Cristobal de las Casas. Twenty-one women and fifteen children were slaughtered, one of them a two-month-old infant. Nine men were also killed in this savage attack that lasted for more than four hours. One survivor of the massacre reported that the gunmen had said, "We need to finish off the seed!" and then proceeded to slice open the womb of a pregnant victim (Weinberg, 1998, p. 46). The gunmen followed the fleeing wounded and spent the afternoon hunting them down and hacking them to pieces. Another survivor reported,

I have an older sister who was pregnant, who was shot in Acteal. When she died in the shooting I personally saw how they opened her belly to take out the baby. They also killed my sister-in-law, also shot her, they carried her toward the stream. . . . The ones who were killing are the PRIista [ruling party] groups who carried guns, and all of them—the paramilitaries—escaped. (cited in Stahler-Sholk, 1998, p. 63)

Cutting fetuses out of pregnant women is a trademark of the infamous 'Kaibiles' of Guatemala. The Kaibiles are an elite counterinsurgerncy unit that reportedly have trained fifty high-ranking Mexican officers since the Zapatista uprising in 1994 (Cockcroft, 1998). All the victims of the Acteal massacre bore gunshot wounds caused by high-caliber arms and exploding bullets of the type that are almost exclusively used by the military. The victims were members or supporters of a nonviolent civic group called Las Abejas (the bees), which acknowledged support for land reform and autonomy demands of the Zapatistas. The massacre occurred just four days after the PRI delegation for local peace talks in Chenalhó had informed the CONAI (the National Mediation Committee headed by Bishop Samuel Ruiz) that they were breaking off the talks (Cockcroft, 1998). At the Reclusorio Norte Prison in Yanga, Veracruz, five men and two women accused of being Zapatistas are serving six years on charges of possession, fabrication, and transporting of arms. They represent seven of sixteen people who have been held captive for more than nineteen months with no trial or jury. Under such conditions, one has to question how realistic the move to transform the Zapatistas into a political party really is. How long, for instance, would the Zapatistas' Subcomandante Marcos last if he were to remove his mask, pump hands instead of shotguns, and kiss babies in the *zócalo* during public political forums? How long would it take for U.S. corporate propaganda machines to transform the warriors in battle fatigues who fight for justice for indigenous women (one-third of the Zapatista combatants are women, and women make up over half of the Zapatista logistical support base) into phallomilitary consumer rebels fighting over Guess jeans? How effective would be the actions of comandantes Ramona, Petra, Ana Maria, and Susanna—who led battalions into the war against the Mexican military—if they delinked their armed struggle from Article 39 of the Mexican Constitution and attended corporate negotiations wearing business suits and bow blouses? If PRI assassins would gun down a PRI presidential candidate, Luis Donaldo Colosio, or José ('Pepe') Francisco Ruiz Massieu, the general secretary of PRI, then they certainly would not hesitate to assassinate the Zapatista leaders.

Prior to the massacre, two truckloads of uniformed and fully armed military personnel had entered Acteal supposedly looking for weapons. They beat several peasants while searching a number of houses, ransacking them as they went. No weapons were found. It has been reported that police patrols in

Acteal at the time of the massacre heard gunfire for two hours but did nothing. After the massacre at Acteal, the police captured approximately fifty men in black uniforms who were led by an ex-army official. When the state police commander arrived, he ordered his agents to return the weapons to the prisoners and to set them free (Weinberg, 1998). It has been alleged that a state police commander, Felipe Vazquez Espinosa, had lent the killers police patrol cars to help them stockpile guns and ammunition (Weinberg, 1998). Because of the international uproar over Acteal, President Zedillo replaced the state governor and Secretary of Gobernación, Emilio Chuayffet, and arrested some low-level local officials.

More than 15,000 Zapatista sympathizers have left their lands since the massacre, victims of intimidation and further violence. In one incident in Chenalho following the massacre, Mayan women were beaten with batons by military police; and on January 12, 1998, in Ocosingo, state police opened fire on demonstrators who were protesting the Acteal massacre, and a Tzeltel Mayan woman was shot dead and her baby injured. Ocosingo is the traditional headquarters of wealthy landowners and ranchers and their private armies (*guardias blancas*).[20] Though the EZLN did not retaliate with armed force in response to Acteal, a group called the Justice Army of the Undefended People reportedly attacked a police command post in Guerrero (Cockcroft, 1998).

The municipality of Chenalhó is located in the region known as 'Los Altos,' or the highlands, of Chiapas. Like so many indigenous regions in Mexico and throughout Latin America, the local population's misery had been conveniently hidden from the public eye. There is a 51 percent illiteracy rate; 88 percent of villagers are without drainage or sewage systems; 78 percent are without electricity; 56 percent are without access to running water; and 91 percent of the homes have dirt floors. Approximately three-quarters of elementary school children do not finish the first grade. These are not unlike the villages visited by El Che as a young man in the Sierra Maestra when he had his first extended contact with peasant populations.

COUNTERINSURGENCY: GUNS, MACHETES, AND NO ROSES

For the last several years, the PRI government of President Zedillo has been arming paramilitary death squads—Red Mask, Brigada San Bartolome de los Llanos in Venustiano Carranza, Peace and Justice in Tila, Los Chinchulines in Chilon, the Indigenous Revolutionary Anti-Zapatista Movement—as part of Zedillo's strategy of low-intensity warfare. The United States has been eagerly assisting in such efforts. Chiapas's new governor, Roberto Albors Guillen—"a scion of the state's cattle oligarchy"—is the grandson of former Governor Absalon Castellanos Dominguez, who was briefly held by the EZLN during the 1994 uprising and charged with crimes against the Indian population of Chiapas by a

Zapatista tribunal [when Castellanos was an army general and commander in 1980, he had overseen a massacre of *campesino* squatters of possibly more than fifty Indians at a highland ranch (Weinberg, 1998, p. 48)].

The U.S. Army's School of the Americas at Fort Benning, Georgia, boasts a rogues' gallery of graduates who went on to glowingly distinguish themselves as fascist illuminaries and brutal sadists. The elite federal Airborne Special Forces Groups (GAFE), which occupied Chenalho and set up roadblocks throughout the highlands, has 'bragging' rights to being trained by U.S. Army Special Forces since 1996. In fact, approximately 3,200 Mexican officers have been trained by the Green Berets at Fort Bragg, North Carolina. Also overseeing the campaign in Chiapas are graduates of the U.S. Army's School of the Americas at Fort Benning, Georgia, where they receive expert instruction in the deep physics of torture and assassination. Fort Benning is the famous alma mater of Panama's Manuel Noriega and the late Roberto D'Aubuisson, charismatic leader of the Salvadoran death-squads. One of the urbane and blood-thirsty originators of the counterinsurgency movement in Chiapas is General Mario Renan Castillo Fernandez, commander of the 7th Military Region and a trained expert in psychological warfare; he received his training at Fort Bragg. Fernandez was present at a ceremony when the Chiapas government presented a half million dollar grant to the paramilitary terrorist group, *Paz y Justicia* (Weinberg, 1998). In the 1997 fiscal year, U.S. military aid to Mexico reached U.S. $37 million in helicopters and surveillance aircraft, and U.S. $10 million more for command-and-control electronics (Weinberg, 1998). More than fifty Huey helicopters have been sold to Mexico over the last few years.

Recently, progovernment paramilitary groups have been forming in the communities of Los Chorros, Colonia Puebla, La Experanza, and Quextic, all within the municipality of Chenalho. Violent confrontations erupt frequently. With the tacit approval of the state and federal governments, local PRI-ista bosses, the *caciques*—who control the indigenous communities as if they were personal fiefdoms—have provoked ongoing violence in the region, encouraging thugs to fire assault weapons into the communities, to burn down houses, and to destroy the belongings of Zapatista sympathizers. This counterinsurgery project on the part of the Federal Army has been active since 1995. The objective of this project is to displace the Zapatista war toward a conflict among the indigenous peoples by provoking tensions on the basis of religious, political, or ethnic differences. In order to carry out their counterinsurgency program, the government of the state of Chiapas has dedicated itself to financing equipment and armaments (with funds from the Department of Social Development) and giving military training (directed by officials of the Federal Army) to indigenous peoples recruited by the Institutional Revolutionary Party. The government has been accused by the Clandestine Indigenous Revolutionary Committee, General Command of the Zapatistas, of guaranteeing impunity to paramilitary death squads and facilitating their operation in the main rebel zones in the highlands of Chiapas. The paramilitary groups have been able to acquire AK-47s—superior to the EZLN's antiquated Mausers—because of assistance from the Mexican army.

After Bishop Samuel Ruíz—the principal mediator in the Chiapas conflict—resigned in protest over what he considered to be an exercise in bad faith on the part of the Mexican government, fighting broke out in the community of Los Plátanos and in the villages of Unión Progreso and Chabajeval. Innocent families were gunned down by the 'security' forces of the Federal Army, and houses were bombed. Not surprisingly, State Attorney General Rodolfo Soto, a PRI lackey, told reporters in the Chiapas state capital of Tuxtla Gutiérrez, that the Zapatistas had provoked the conflict. The police from the State Public Security, Federal Police, and the Attorney General's office, and members of Mixed Brigades and Operations routinely assault indigenous communities and are responsible for incarcerations and assassinations. El Bosque, Taniperlas, Amparo Aguatina, Nabil, and the municipality of Nicolás Ruíz are just some of the areas assaulted by police forces.

According to Captain Jesus Valles, who was stationed at the 30th military zone just across the Chiapas line in Villahermoso Tabasco, he was ordered by his commanding officer on the first day of the uprising to take no prisoners. Rather than carry out his orders against the Zapatista insurgents in the Lacandon jungle city of Ocosingo, he along with two of these fellow soldiers chose to protest the illegality and immorality of the orders. Captain Valles was transferred to a unit in Tehuacan, Puebla. Eventually he was warned that he would soon be 'disappeared.' When President Ernesto Zedillo ordered the Tehuacan unit to obliterate the EZLN leadership in 1995, Captain Valles and his wife fled across the border to Texas, where they were granted asylum. Valles claims that his commanding officer, Brigadier General Luis Humberto Portillo, ordered troops to exterminate suspected Zapatista rebels but to exercise caution if the press was in the vicinity (Ross, 1999a, p. 17).

Estimates places as many as 20,000 persons now in local 'campamentos' seeking refuge from the violence directed against them in their own communities. Approximately 7,000 Indians have fled Acteal and Chenalho's municipal center for the mountain hamlets of Palho, where thousands of them are refusing government aid, despite hunger and sickness (Weinberg, 1998).

The Mexican government is doing nothing to disarm the PRI paramilitary groups in the so-called peasant sanctuaries of Los Chorros, Pechiquil, Chenalho, and Tenejapa. Instead, the Federal Army is carrying out operations in communities with a strong Zapatista presence, such as La Realidad and Morelia. In the winter and spring of 1998, federal troops (sometimes accompanied by elite commandos, state security police, judicial police, and immigration officials) entered the municipality of Altamirano and invaded the communities of Nueva Esperanza, Morelia (in the autonomous municipality of 17 de Noviembre on the edge of the Lacandon rain forest), 10 de Mayo, and 10 de Abril; in the municipality of Ocosingo they invaded La Galeana and the new autonomous municipality of Ricardo Flores Magón; in the municipality of Las Margaritas they invaded the autonomous municipality of Tierra y Libertad, and soldiers took control of the municipality of Nicolás Ruíz. In many cases the soldiers harassed, beat, tortured, and imprisoned men, women (some of whom were pregnant), and children, as well as deported or imprisoned human-rights observers.

As Public Security police trucks patrol Taniperla to Monte Libano, accompanied by plainclothes government agents; and as PRI paramilitaries from the MIRA (Movimento Indígena Revolucionario Antizapatista, or Revolutionary Antizapatista Indigenous Movement) join soldiers from the Federal Army in setting fires around Lake Ocotal, burning coffee groves and cornfields, and placing barbed wire around the community school and cooperative store in Taniperla, the tormented figure of the resurrected Che hovers over the forces of destruction, announcing the moment of judgment to follow.

THIRDWORLDISM AND CAPITALISM: HA HA HA!

As I have mentioned, the Zapatistas are Guevara-inspired but not properly Guevarian in that they are grounded solidly in the politics of indigenous peoples. Arif Dirlik (1997) considers the "local" struggles of the so-called Fourth World indigenous peoples to have a profound importance in the current historical situation. Earlier national liberation struggles (such as that of Che) aimed at 'delinking' from the capitalist world system in order to achieve integrated national development that would provide peace and prosperity to the people within the nation. Such goals were considered impossible if incorporated into capitalism. Today, most so-called Third World states promote export-oriented economies, which attempt to assist national development figures but bring poverty and misery to the majority of their populations. To camouflage or to 'cover' for their internationalization of national economies and loss of economic sovereignty, these states now vigorously promote cultural nationalism, which only further incorporates them into global capitalism (Dirlik, 1997). According to Dirlik, "Third-Worldism has abandoned is earlier goals of national liberation . . . to turn into neo-Fascist reifications of national cultures and, rather than provide alternatives to the capitalist structuring of the world, not only legitimize capitalism but also contribute to a resurgence of Fascism globally" (1997, p. 157).

Dirlik argues that indigenous movements, in their repudiation of developmentalism in both its capitalist and socialist incarnations, promote the primacy of ties to the land and to nature as the source of both subsistence and identity and argue on behalf of a "vision of the world as a federation of communities" (1997, p. 159). He concludes:

The dream here is of people constituting and reconstituting themselves against capital and the state. If the indigenous vision in most cases also involves a reification of constructed pasts (which is not the case with Subcomandante Marcos, who draws on the future), unlike in the cases of nations and ethnicities, such reification aims at the creation of communities about whose fragileness and, therefore, need for identity, there is little question; the reification here, as it seeks to account for inherited inequalities, aims at liberation from rather than justification for such inequalities and oppressions. It represents, in other words, pasts that have been worked over already by visions of "liberty, justice, and democracy" for all. (1997, p. 160)

INDIGENOUS FORMATIONS: CONSTRUCTING THE ZAPATISTAS

Had Che been able to witness the extent of transnationalism that has taken place throughout the world, he surely would have appreciated and would have been influenced by the way in which the powerful indigenous political vision of the Zapatistas brings a new dimension to the dialectics of the local and the global, one that supports both a negative dialectics in relation to what exists at present (a language of critique) and a positive dialectics in relation to what does not exist as yet but what could possibly exist in the future (a language of hope and possibility.) The Zapatistas distinguish themselves from Che and his guerrilla movement by the fact they have not demanded to take power even though they are constituted as an army and are well-organized and based in over 300 communities. Rather, they urge civil society to become mobilized in order to secure a peaceful transition to democracy. As such, they serve not so much as the sword-arm of the oppressed but as the mirror that reflects back the Discourse of the Other. Hiding their faces in masks and bandanas so that the selfless and heroic purpose of their politics can be seen, and bearing arms so that they can be nonviolent, the Zapatistas have, as of this writing, not fired a single shot since January 8, 1994. Their goal is to create parallel communities of hope and struggle at the intersection of determination and self activity, and arising out of the historically specific forms of capitalist labor and new formations of subjectivity appearing within the social totality.

Clearly, the Zapatistas have broken with much in the Leninist, Guevarist, and Maoist traditions in order to follow the indigenous concept of "command obeying." According to Luis Lorenzano:

The practice of 'command obeying' clearly demonstrates the central difference [between the Zapatistas] and all former Latin American revolutionary experiences: the Zapatistas are not a 'guerrilla force' nor an 'armed party' with a particular social base, but rather they are the social base itself—the communities—in insurrection and structured as an army; this runs counter to both reformist and Leninist practices. And second, therefore, both warfare and politics are decided by the community. The 'leadership' (the members of the various Indigenous Revolutionary Clandestine Committees, federated by ethnic group and by community) hold their positions as long as they faithfully and effectively implement the mandates of the community. From the perspective of Western political tradition, the traditional indigenous-peasant community has undergone a metamorphosis to become the 'polis,' a community not just of land, language and culture, but a political community, with deliberative, legislative and executive capacities. (1998, p. 130)

Lorenzano sees the Zapatistas as an expression of the "new worker," creating the conditions for the revolution that avoid problems and risks associated with both vanguardism and reformism through its unique workers' communes of land and culture united through a federation with a collective, unified, political, and military command. According to Lorenzano, "They propose to society as a whole, not a program of purely peasant-indigenous demands, but alternatives within which the indigenous is an integral part of the radical democratic transformation of social life and of the state" (1998, p. 145).

John Holloway's description of the Zapatistas gives them a decidedly post-Marxist spin in which the concept of 'dignity' and not class struggle becomes the operative term. The Zapatistas create a "resonance" with the idea of "uniting the dignities" not by telling but by *preguntando caminamos,* or "asking we walk." This suggests a move from traditional revolutionary structures and objectives to a more experimental and flexible form of organization that recognizes "the validity of different forms of struggle and different opinions as to what the realisation of dignity means" (1998, p. 179). Holloway notes that orthodox Marxists have criticized the Zapatistas for abandoning the concept of 'class' or 'class struggle' and adopting a new language of struggle that appeals not to the working class or proletariat but to civil society. Some critics admonish this practice as an armed-peasant liberal reformism that speaks of dignity, truth, freedom, democracy, and justice rather than class struggle, revolution, and socialism. Holloway claims that whereas the Zapatista concept of dignity "detonates the definition of class," it does not "thereby cease to be a class concept" (1998, p. 182). Holloway argues that we do not belong to one class or another but that class antagonism exists in us, traverses us, tearing us apart to different degrees, and that this antagonism exists prior to and not—as often conceived by orthodox Marxists—subsequent to the constitution of classes. Holloway does not see class as a defined group of people and class antagonisms as existing between two groups of people, but in terms of the way that human practice is organized through daily work. According to Holloway, class struggle does not take place *within* the constituted forms of capitalist social relations but rather *is* the constitution of these social relations. From this perspective, all social practice is class struggle, and it permeates all of human existence. The conflict between labor and capital is really the antagonism between those who sell their creativity and those who appropriate and exploit it through the transformation of creativity into labor. As Holloway sees it, the most pressing and overarching conflict is between creative social practice (in other words, dignity, humanity) and subordination and alienation (or capital). He claims that the Zapatistas are right in focusing on "dignity" rather than class and positing it as the prime actor in the struggle against capital, since this serves as a way of improving upon the Marxist vocabulary of revolution, which is over-burdened by the concept of domination and its lack of an adequate lexicon of resistance. I do not share Holloway's position and I agree with Simon Clarke (1999) that we have to go beyond (what appears in Holloway's account as) a 'romantic anti-capitalism.' Labor cannot be reduced to "creativity"; Marx's theory of commodity fetishism reveals that the only force that can change the world is the self-organization of the direct producers.

RACISM: THE FRONTIER OF DISAPPEARANCE

Recently, in the villages of Taniperla and Amparo-Aguatinta, federal police attempted to dismantle pro-Zapatista town councils. Chiapas governor Roberto Albores Guillén has pledged to destroy them. Voodoo economics—Latin American style—currently devastating the region of Chiapas, courtesy of the North American Free Trade Agreement—has revealed that the 1992 Article 4 amendment of the Mexican constitution (which established Mexico as a pluricultural country that includes indigenous peoples) is little more than a political chimera, a multicultural *trompe l'oeil.* The neoliberal agenda of the Mexican ruling elite will do little to transform the indigenous population's enslavement to the capitalist landlords who run the coffee and cash-crop plantations and mahogany logging camps. The real agenda of Mexico's ruling elite is to transfer Mexico into an expanded manufacturing economy, and in the process to throw the peasants off their lands so that they have no means of subsistence and will be pliable fodder for capital's need for cheap labor. The deepening of social unevenness in Mexico is of little ethical concern to members of the U.S. investment community, as reflected by the call on the part of members of the Chase Bank of New York to "eliminate the Zapatistas" (Silverstein, 1995).

Chiapas is important geopolitically because "what is at stake is the rearranging of the material basis of U.S. hegemony in the world" (Ceceña and Barreda, 1998, p. 57). In Chiapas, like everywhere else, racism maintains the class structure through neoliberalism's industrial reserve army of workers. To achieve its goals, the capitalist exploitation of biodiversity and the accumulation of international capital relies significantly on racism directed against a group that historically has been shunned and marginalized. There also exists in Chiapas a purging of inefficient capital through the destruction of the indigenous labor force, which constitutes a dysfunctional surplus. According to Ceceña and Barreda;

> The best-known studies on racism have left out its economic dimension, which constitutes one of its most solid explanations. In the case of Chiapas, racism has become the principal element of justification for the plunder, subjugation and

extermination of the autochthonous populations. The cultural refinement of the Mayan groups that lived in the area was notably superior to that of their conquerors, who used racism as an ideological defence for the impunity and bestiality with which their weapons imposed the domination of European capitalism. We believe that the regime of cruel and predatory exploitation that continues to exist today in Chiapas is only possible through the justifying force of racism. (1998, p. 59)

This evidence of the economic dimension of racism bolsters my previous claim (McLaren, 1997a) that slavery was not a product of racism but that racism was and is a product of slavery and economic exploitation; that is, racism constitutes myths, systems of classification, and regimes of discourse that naturalize and legitimize the forced servitude of certain (different) groups whose labor can be exploited for the purpose of accumulation. The scorned and dominated indigenous populations of Chiapas suffer not because they are indigenous but because of their class position within the regional economic structure and level of development of the productive forces—and racism is the tool viciously used to maintain the class structure (Ceceña and Barreda, 1998).

ASSAULTS ON THE INFOSPHERE AND THE WAR AGAINST CYBOTAGE: THE U.S. ARMY COMPUTER NINJAS VERSUS THE ZAPATISTAS IN THE NEO-CORTICAL BATTLEFIELD

Now that the Cold War is over, the United States is targeting millennialist terrorists who attack the 'infosphere' in 'cyberwars' that involve such tactics as 'sustainable pulsing' and 'cybotage.' Is it any wonder that the Rand Corporation Arroyo Center's Strategy and Doctrine Program, sponsored by the U.S. Army, recently completed a study on the "netwar"—"The Zapatista Social Netwar in Mexico"—that focuses on the 1994–1996 period of the Zapatista movement's success in gaining international attention to its cause through the Internet. The Zapatistas figure here as less threatening than the "Arabs" but it is clear that the U.S. Army is not taking them lightly. The study distinguishes the social netwar of militant social activists—the Zapatistas and their NGO supporters—from the 'terrorist' and 'criminal' netwar of Islamic fundamentalist organizations such as Hamas. The report states:

Social netwar aims to affect what an opponent knows, or thinks it knows, not only about a challenger but also about itself and the world around it. More broadly, social netwar aims to shape beliefs and attitudes in the surrounding social milieu. A social netwar is likely to involve battles for public opinion and for media access and coverage, at local through global levels. It is also likely to revolve around propaganda campaigns, psychological warfare, and strategic public diplomacy, not just to educate and inform, but to deceive and disinform as well. It resembles a nonmilitary version of "neo-cortical warfare." . . . In other words, social netwar is more about a doctrinal leader like Subcomandante Marcos than about a lone, wild computer hacker like Kevin Mitnick. (Ronfeldt et al., 1998, pp. 21–22)

The report goes on to claim that "the world's leading example of social netwar lies in the decentralized, dispersed, cooperation among the myriad Mexican and transnational activist NGOs that support or sympathize with the EZLN and that aim to affect Mexico's policies on human rights, democracy, and other reform issues" (p. 22). NGOs are characterized as cross-border coalitions designed to wage an information-age social netwar through strategies such as "swarming," "sustainable pulsing," "packetization," and the "blurring of offense and defense" that, in effect, "would constrain the Mexican government and assist the EZLN's cause" (p. 3). According to the report:

> At the national level, the Zapatistas' netwar strategy succeeded in muddling the government's efforts to crush the insurgency, contrary to the fate of most previous armed rebellions against state authority in Mexico. The centralized state had difficulty dealing with this nonstate movement largely because of its transnational, internetted organization. Even tacit American support for a government crackdown on the EZLN in 1994 did not blunt the NGOs' effectiveness. (p. 102)

The Rand researchers warn that the Zapatistas may be able to destablize Mexico if certain conditions occur:

> At present, neither social (EZLN/Zapatista), guerrilla (EPR) or criminal (drug trafficking) netwar actors seem likely to make Mexico ungovernable or to create a situation that leads to a newly authoritarian regime. This *might* occur, if these netwars all got interlaced and reinforced each other, directly or indirectly, in conditions where an economic recession deepens, the federal government and the PRI (presumably still in power) lose legitimacy to an alarming degree, and infighting puts the elite "revolutionary family" and its political clans into chaos. (Ronfeldt et al., 1998, p. 104; emphasis in original)

What if such an unlikely scenario were to come about? Without a doubt, the U.S. Army is currently considering massive counternetwar offensives against groups such as the Zapatistas, the EPR, and their NGO allies. The Zapatistas are not about to fade forever into the rain forests. Jack Forbes writes that "the Zapatista War is here to stay" (1995, p. 195). Despite all the forces that are arrayed against them, "the indigenous people are ready to die" (p. 195). And if the U.S. and Mexican governments have their way, they will.

On March 21, 1999, the EZLN staged a national and international plebiscite or *consulta* called "Recognition of the Rights of Indigenous People and the End of the War of Extermination." The *consulta* asked if the Indians should be included in Mexico's national project and take an active part in the building of .

the new nation; if peace should be achieved by dialogue rather than military means (and the federal troops returned to their barracks); if the government should abide by *mandar obedeciendo*—governing by the will of the people; if indigenous rights should be recognized in the Mexican constitution in accordance with the interpretation of the San Andreas accords; and if Mexicans living outside Mexico have the right to participate and vote in Mexican elections (Ross, 1999a). The vote, destined for Mexico's nearly 2,5000 municipalities, was carried out in thirty countries on five continents. Ballots were gathered with the help of the Humanitarian Law Project, a United Nations–registered nongovernmental organization that has monitored elections in Mexico and other countries. At least one anti-*consulta* paramilitary group was trying to disrupt the process, even though the Law of Reconciliation is supposed to protect Zapatistas from detention. In response to the *consulta,* the PRI's Interior Secretary, Francisco Labastida, remarked, "Laws are not made in the jungle" (Ross, 1999, p. 24), and the governor of Chiapas continues to dismantle EZLN *autonomias.* The EZLN managed to get three million votes of support.

As of this writing, 5,000 indigenous Zapatista supporters are being forced to flee Zapatista base communities. They are being displaced to other communities and to the mountains of the Canadas. Three communities are being threatened by army troops and state police forces, including La Garracha of the Francisco Gomez Autonomous Municipality. And in Colombia's southern savanna, in the remote hamlet of La Machaca, another revolutionary group is on the move, the Revolutionary Armed Forces of Colombia. But here the move is as bizarre as it is disconcerting. Raul Reyes, commander of the FARC, met with Richard Grasso, chairman of the New York Stock Exchange, who explained to the guerrilla leader how markets worked. As the two figures embraced in this rebel-controlled area demilitarized by the government, Grasso told Reyes that Colombia would benefit from increased global investment and that he hoped that this meeting would mark the beginning of a new relationship between the FARC and the United States (*Los Angeles Times,* A20). Time will tell.

CHE AND INDIGENOUS STRUGGLE

Che was correct in asserting in the 1960s that the success of the revolution in Latin America lay with the *guajiros* and *macheteras* and other agrarian workers but he had a difficult time recruiting the indigenous population into his struggle. Bolivia was one of the most unstable countries in Latin America, and certainly the most poverty stricken. It had gone through 189 changes in government since it became an independent republic in 1825. In 1952 it had experienced a revolution based on popular participation, not unlike the situation in Mexico from 1910 to 1920 and, more recently, in Cuba. Bolivia was also next to Che's native Argentina and could have proved an important site for launching a peasant revolution in that country (a mission Che planned to lead sometime after his Bolivian campaign). Che had established an alliance with Inti Paredo, Bolivian chief of the National Liberation Army. Yet a rift developed between Che and a section of the leadership of the Bolivian Communist Party only a month after Che arrived at the guerrilla base on the Ñancahuazú River on November 7, 1966.[21] In March 1966, three guerrillas defected from Che's camp and one *chivato* (informer) betrayed the whereabouts of Che's *foco* to the CIA. While in Bolivia, Che did not sufficiently acknowledge the politics of postagrarian reform. He appears to have overlooked the fact that the Bolivian military had granted the indigenous peasants some land, that Bolivia's leader, General René Barrientos, spoke Quechua, and that the military had established relatively cooperative relations with the indigenous population—although it was, admittedly, a cooperation underwritten by military terror tactics. When martial law was declared in the mining area of Siglo XX (because the miners staged a strike that was also supported by the student movement), and army troops occupied the Huanuni, Catavi, and Siglo XX mines, Che and his guerrilla *foco* were separated from the miners by the Andes and more than a thousand kilometers, with no political ties or means of communication (Castañeda, 1997, p. 372).[22] Dozens of defenseless men, women, and children were killed and wounded, in part because the miners had agreed to donate a day's wages and some medicine to the *guerrilleros*. (The decision by the miners had been ratified at a congress of the Union Federation of Bolivian Mine Workers.) Clearly if Che had been able to win the support of the indigenous population, the outcome of his campaign could have been drastically different.

THE NEW SOCIALIST AGENT

> *Después le colocaron a Cristo Guevara una corona de espinas y una túnica de loco y le colgaron un rótulo del pescuezo en son de burla. INRI: Instigador Natural de la Rebelión de los Infelices*
>
> —Roque Dalton, *Credo del Ché*

Che modeled the role of the new revolutionary agent through his own interest in, if not devotion to, becoming a critical, self-reflexive agent of social transformation. Early in his life, and as a result of chronic asthma that restricted his school attendance up to sixth grade, Che experienced a home-based elementary education (his home had more than 3,000 books) at the tutelage of his adoring mother, Celia. What was remarkable about his early public school education in Alta Gracias during the waning years of the Argentine oligarchy was that he, a boy from a privileged background, had the opportunity to interact with students from a number of social sectors, classes, and ethnic groups—for example, pupils from *el campo* (rural area); urban *morochos* (dark-skinned people); and students of Italian, Spanish, and peasant origins (Castañeda, 1997). After seven years of elementary schooling, Che was enrolled in the Colegio Nacional Dean Funes of Córdoba, a public secondary school run by the Ministry of Education that was less exclusive than the Colegio Montserrat, which was usually attended by the children of the regional elite. Dean Funes National School was patterned after the French lycée and included rigorous classical training. Che was not an honors student but did distinguish himself. One of his teachers, Alfredo Pueyreddon, would later describe Che as "an outstanding student. He looked and acted much older than he was, and was clearly already grown up, with a definite personality" (Sandison, 1997, p. 19). Che remained intellectually risk-taking and curious throughout his life, a life in which his love of books played no small part.

Che worked as a clerk in a building firm, as a reporter for the nationalist newspaper *Acción Argentina* (Sandison, 1997, p. 19), and as a fieldworker in the grape harvests in Argentina; he served as a security guard in the northern mines of Chile, as a male nurse aboard Argentine ships *Florentino Ameghino* and *Anna G.,* in a leper colony in the Amazon region, and as a truck driver and dishwasher (Loveman and Davies, 1985, p. x). As a child, Che read the works of Robert Louis Stevenson, Jules Verne, Alexandre Dumas, and Jack London. Between the ages of eight and eleven, he was inspired by the heroic aspects of the Spanish Civil War. As a teenager, Che read Boccaccio's *Decameron* and Baudelaire in the original French. He also read Jose Ingenieros, Anatole France, Horacio Quiroga as well as Mallarmé, Zola, Lorca, Verlaine, Jung, Adler, Freud, Sarmientos, Machado, Steinbeck, Faulkner, Marx, Martí, Neruda, Engels, and Gandhi. Che belonged to the youth section of Acción Argentina, an antifascist organization founded by his father, and from 1945 to 1946 began to write a philosophical dictionary made up of seven notebooks containing general concepts in the social sciences and basic Marxist-Leninist categories (Cupull and González, 1997).

This background counters those who believe that Che began his study of Marxist economic theory in 1959, following his appointments to the head of INRA's Industry Department, president of the National Bank of Cuba, and as minister of industry; and following the arrival of the Hispanic-Soviet academic Anastasio Mansilla, professor of political economy. In fact, Che began his study of Marxism when he was sixteen years old, at which time he began to read Karl Marx, Friederich Engels, and V. I. Lenin. According to Carlos Tablada: "Among other works, he became familiar with *Capital* by Marx and the *Manifesto of the Communist Party* by Marx and Engels. . . .During the years of his university studies, he studied other works, such as *Anti-Dühring* by Engels and *Imperialism: The Highest Stage of Capitalism* and *The State and Revolution* by Lenin" (1991, p. 71).

Che traveled by a bicycle (powered by a Cucciolo engine) during his summer vacation to spend a few days at the Jose J. Puente leprosanium with his friend, Alberto Granado, in the town of San Francisco del Chañar. He was twenty-one at the time. Here Che would read Goethe's *Faust* aloud to the patients. In 1951 he is reported to have read Anibal Ponce's books, *Education and Class Struggle* and *The Wind in the World*. In 1952 (Che was twenty-four), Che and Alberto Granado visited five countries in eight months, a trip that began on a 500 cc, British-manufactured Norton motorcycle. On his travels, Che would hone his journal writing skills. And it was during these expeditions that Granado helped to establish Ernesto's nickname, "Che."[23]

While in Mexico City, on the eve of his departure aboard the *Granma*, Che hid in the house of Dr. Alfonso Bauer, a Guatemalan. Dr. Bauer has described the state of the room that Che occupied as

> a complete pandemonium—an unmade bed, a maté drinking straw here, a small cooking stove there, articles of clothing scattered about, and a half dozen books lying open as though they were all being read at the same time. Among them were *State and Revolution* by Lenin, *Capital* by Marx, a textbook on battlefield surgery, and a book of mine, *Cómo opera el capital yanqui en Centro América* [How U.S. capital operates in Central America]. (cited in Tablada, 1991, p. 73)

As a guerrilla leader in the Sierra Maestra, Che gave literacy classes to his peasant recruits and would occasionally read aloud to them from various sources such as Cervantes, Robert Louis Stevenson, and the poetry of Pablo Neruda (Gall, 1971). Che built schools in the Las Villas in the Sierra Maestra, and one of his first literacy students was Julio Zenon Acosta, who took care of Che during Che's malaria attacks in 1959 in Manzanillo.

During lulls on the battlefield, Che allegedly would retreat to this tent and read Proust, Faulkner, Sartre, and Milton (Markee, 1997). In the Congo, he would teach French and Swahili classes to the Congolese troops and also a class on "general culture" (Anderson, 1997). In Cuba during the revolution, members of Che's "Descamisados"—such as Israel Pardo and Joel Iglesias—were taught by Che how to read and write. And for those who did have some literacy skills, such as Ramon 'Guile' Pardo (Israel's younger brother), he initiated study circles. According to Anderson, "the study gradually evolved from Cuban history and military doctrine to politics and Marxism" (1997, p. 298). For Che, self-education through reading and diary writing became an important practice for the construction of socialist consciousness. Che is reported to have done some reading during the beginning of his Bolivian campaign, while resting from reconnoitering the Ñancahuazú and digging a tunnel to store food and supplies. He had with him Benedetto Croce's *History of the Story of Liberty*, Trotsky's *The Age of Permanent Revolution* and *The History of the Russian Revolution*, and Paul Rivet's *The Origins of the American Man*. Taibo notes that during this time he may have read Charles de Gaulle's war memoirs and those of Winston Churchill, and possibly Hegel's *The Phenomenology of the Mind* and something by Denis Diderot (1997, p. 474). When Che and his fighters were advancing on the town of Muyupampa, he gave Régis Debray some coded letters to send to Fidel and others as well as a shopping list of books he wanted the Frenchman to bring him when he returned, a list that included Gibbon's eighteenth-century classic, *The Decline and Fall of the Roman Empire* (Sandison, 1997, p. 133).

Decades after Che's death, Pombo (the code name of Harry Villegas Tamayo, Che's former bodyguard and fellow guerrilla) wrote about Che's influence on his own diary writing:

> Observations and comments written three decades ago in the heat of the struggle may appear harsh and full of passion. I am indeed struck by this today when I reread and relive some of the passages. At all times, however, the diary reflects the critical spirit, expressed in language that is frank and direct, straight to the point, in which we were educated by Commander Che Guevara. This was undoubtedly among the greatest lessons we received in his incomparable school. (1997, pp. 27–28)

In an interview with Mary-Alice Waters and Luis Madrid (1977), Pombo gives us at least some sense of what Che as a teacher was like:

> "Che was a lover of history," Pombo noted, "a tireless reader, a tireless student. The first thing Che did was try to get us to study. Do you understand? It was the very first thing! Che liked to surround himself with youth and force us to improve ourselves." (Waters and Madrid, 1997, pp. 8–9; emphasis in original).

Che outlined his educational vision for creating the new socialist man in his famous letter to Carlos Quijano, editor of *Marcha* (an independent radical weekly published in Montevideo, Uruguay) in 1965, published as *"El Socialismo y el Hombre en Cuba"* (Socialism and Man in Cuba). Here Che penned the now-famous words:

> I believe that the simplest way to begin is to recognize [humankind's] unmade quality: man is an unfinished product. The prejudices of the past are carried into the present in the individual's consciousness and a continual effort has to be made in order to eradicate them. It is a twofold process. On the one hand, society acts with its direct and indirect education; and on the other, the individual submits himself to a conscious process of self-education." (cited in Mazlish, Kaledin, and Ralston, 1971, p. 411)

Che's commitment to education in the forging of the "new man" was uncompromising. The key role of revolutionary education was the elimination of individualism. Paraphrasing Che's position, Anderson writes:

> At the heart of the revolution, then, was the elimination of individualism. "Individualism as such, as the isolated action of a person alone in a social environment,

must disappear in Cuba. Individualism tomorrow should be the proper utilization of the whole individual at the absolute benefit of the community." The revolution was not "a standardizer of the collective will"; rather, it was "a liberator of man's individual capacity," for it oriented that capacity to the service of the revolution. (1997, pp. 478–479)

Shortly after the revolution, Che voiced his concern that universities might become conservative flashpoints for reactionary action. He tried to convince students to join the plans of the revolutionary government. Chary of liberal arts degrees as useless in a labor market where there exists an extreme shortage of technicians and where the people had just witnessed an armed revolution, Che urged the University of Havana to develop an economics faculty. He asked the universities to permit students to continue their studies while still fulfilling their obligation to society. During the completion of an educational complex that was being built in Caney de las Mercedes and named after his friend and revolutionary hero, Camilo Cienfuegos.[24] Che broke rocks at the Estrada Palma quarry and on several Sundays came from Havana to spend eight hours of construction on the school (Taibo, 1997, p. 290). One of the central tenets of Che's revolutionary pedagogy was the importance of this type of work:

Che was a firm believer in productive work—of combining physical and mental tasks as key elements in understanding the everyday concerns of the people. He saw volunteer labor as an important ingredient in breaking down elitist outlooks among professionals and intellectuals—teaching them how the surplus that provided for cultural activity was generated. More basically, he saw this as a key element in creating bonds between manual and mental workers to avoid the emergence of a "new class" based on the superiority of the intellectuals. (Petras, 1998, p. 16)

For Che, there was no life outside of the revolution, and that life—lived in the practice of justice and truth—was grounded in a "love of a living humanity." The individual produces on a day-to-day basis his and her social duty to work. Che's new socialist being was forged within a dialectic of freedom and sacrifice, of moral duty and revolutionary need, and of the highest virtues of character—a new moral technology—and the incompleteness of the human spirit. This incompleteness of the human spirit allowed for the continual formation of "the new man who is glimpsed on the horizon" (Mazlish, Kaledin and Ralston, 1971, p. 418). As Che wrote, "The Revolution is made through man, but man must forge day by day his revolutionary spirit" (Mazlish, Kaledin and Ralston, 1971, p. 418). It is important to note that Che rejected in no uncertain terms the model of man developed in the Soviet model for the building of socialism. In fact, Che did not view Soviet society as qualitatively different from capitalist society, but rather as a "statized imitation of bourgeois consumer society" (Löwy, 1973, p. 66). In the Soviet Union, capitalism was still a "fact of consciousness" that needed, in Che's view, to be purged unconditionally. Che recognized that Soviet-style self-management, which treated individual enterprises and economic sectors as independent entities, would likely reinforce uneven development. Che's model, on the other hand, would allow the state to plan for the economy as a whole and promote a more balanced development (Markee, 1997). Rene Dumont reports a conversation with Che in 1960 in which it appeared that Che "did not think the Soviet Man was really a new sort of man, for he did not find him any different, really, from a Yankee" (cited in Löwy, 1973, p. 66). Che thought that communist morality should seek the elimination of material interest, an interest that Che felt was all too glaringly present in the Soviet Union. It is likely, however, that Che would have had to resign himself to an indefinite alignment with the Soviet Union if he had remained in Cuba.

Part of the forging of this new socialist being was, for Che, constituted by reading, writing, and the act of study. When Che was studying for his medical exams in Buenos Aires, he would frequently barricade himself behind a wall of books at his Aunt Beatriz's apartment or at his father's studio on Calle Paraguay, yet still make time to volunteer at Dr. Pisani's allergy clinic (Anderson, 1997). Che's political education took a major turn at the age of twenty-seven in Mexico in 1955 when he met Fidel and Raúl Castro and became involved in Cuba's 26th of July Movement, at which time he began a vigorous study of Marx. After the revolution, when Che became Director of the Cuban National Bank in October 1959, he would take tutorial classes in economics and mathematics (including a crash course on Marx's *Capital*) as a self-imposed measure to compensate for his lack of formal education in these subject areas (Löwy, 1973). In fact, Che's forms of relaxation while in Cuba were playing chess and doing mathematics. He is reported to have required his bodyguards to take literacy instruction, threatening serious sanctions if they did not attend with sufficient exuberance to their studies (Löwy, 1973). The importance of learning was so prominent in Che's itinerary of the revolutionary that among his last words before he was executed included the remark, "tell Aleida . . . to keep the children studying" (Castañeda, 1997, p. 401).

Here we can see reading, writing, and studying being deployed by Che as political and life-affirming acts. In Paulo Freire's terms, such literacy practices are "acts of knowing." Learning is inevitably and always a political act, and for Che, as for Freire, it also became a redemptive practice whose truth was struggled over in the theater of class warfare, and whose purpose was forged in the struggle for socialist democracy. The new socialist being is both critically self-reflexive and self-critical—in other words, is an agent of self- and social transformation. Self-transformation and social transformation were viewed by Che as well as by Freire as mutually constitutive, dialectically re-initiating acts resulting in revolutionary praxis—the creation of the new socialist being for decades to follow. At the moral apex of this vision of the new socialist being was a willingness to sacrifice to the extent of giving one's life. The new heroic agent of the revolution—exemplified by Che's own life and death—was willing to sacrifice his or her personal "need to live" for the greater cause of revolutionary freedom and justice. During a battle in Cuba's *Altos de Merino,* Che wrote:

> Upon arriving I found that the guards were already advancing. A little combat broke out in which we retreated very quickly. The position was bad and they were encircling us, but we put up little resistance. Personally, I noted something that I had never felt before: the need to live. That had better be corrected in the next opportunity. (cited in Anderson, 1997, p. 327)

According to Jorge Castañeda, for Che the new man

> is, in a sense, the Cuban Communist: the Veteran of the Sierra Maestra and volunteer work, of the Bay of Pigs and the missile crisis, of international missions and solidarity. In a word, he is very much like Che Guevara. Che never lacked a capacity for self-analysis, or a clear idea of his own destiny; indeed the fantasy of a chosen fate had obsessed him since his youthful nights in Chuquicamata and the Peruvian Amazon. (1997, p. 306)

Similarly, John Lee Anderson writes that when one reads Che's words on the new socialist agent, "it is difficult not to feel that Che was rendering his own truth, including others but above all else the account of his *own* revolutionary transformation. And this, really, was the essence of Che's philosophy: believing himself to have achieved the sublimation of his former self, the individual, he had reached a mental stage through which he could consciously sacrifice himself for society and its ideals. If he could do it, then so could others" (1997, p. 636). Alexander Cockburn further notes that "Che was profoundly romantic, in that he believed deeply in the possibility of absolute change. The concept of the 'new man' in Cuba's revolution was his, and his was the greatest impatience at the constraints of economic 'rationality.' As much as Pope John XXIII, Guevara could claim to be the inspiration of liberation theology as the vital current in radical social action in Latin America" (1997, p. 4).

According to Che, the most important leadership quality of the new socialist agent was love. In a passage now considered canonical, but in my opinion worth repeating, he wrote:

> Let me say, with the risk of appearing ridiculous, that the true revolutionary is guided by strong feelings of love. It is impossible to think of an authentic revolutionary without this quality. This is perhaps one of the greatest dramas of a leader; he must combine an impassioned spirit with a cold mind and make painful decisions without flinching one muscle. Our vanguard revolutionaries must idealize their love for the people, for the most sacred causes, and make it one and indivis-

ible. They cannot descend, with small doses of daily affection, to the places where ordinary men put their love into practice. (cited in Anderson, 1997, pp. 636–637)

Che believed that "the true communist, the true revolutionary is one who regards the greater problems of mankind as his own personal problem" (Löwy, 1997, p. 3). Che's Marxist humanism owes its greatest debt to Marx's *Das Kapital* and also to the young Marx of the *Economic and Philosophical Manuscripts* (written in 1844), especially in terms of Che's emphasis on the role of human consciousness in overcoming alienation. Che's pedagogy was in solid agreement with Marx's *Theses on Feuerbach,* which advocates a revolutionary education from below. It was important that the student be able to educate the teacher. Che wrote:

> The first step to educate the people is to introduce them to the revolution. Never pretend you can help them conquer their rights by education alone, while they must endure a despotic government. First and foremost, teach them to conquer their rights and, as they gain representation in the government, they will learn whatever they are taught and much more: with no great effort they shall soon become the teachers, towering above the rest. (cited in Löwy, 1997, p. 5)

What made Che singularly impressive—in any era—was his consistency and his highly developed sense of praxis. In fact, his political agency was such that it was wedded perfectly to his everyday thoughts and actions. Sinclair writes that:

> Che was an absolutist. He wanted to pursue everything to its just conclusion. His consistency was almost maddening in its effortlessness. There was no trace of hypocrisy in him. When he said that working for one's fellow man was the greatest joy a man could have, that was true for him. He thought it was fit for a revolutionary to go and die under the flag of a nation not yet born, and he did so, not making a great display of courage, but being brave and cheerful as if he were doing the most natural thing in the world. He said that no one was irreplaceable and felt that this applied to him as much as to anyone else. So he exposed himself and died. He was a complete man. (1998, p. 112)

Che's passion for learning mirrored that of Fidel, who, during his jail sentence on the Isle of Pines (where his hero Jose Martí had also been imprisoned), conducted classes in political history and philosophy. Che's love and compassion for others was partly due to his chronic asthma, which often went untreated during his guerrilla campaigns. It enabled him to empathize more fully with those who suffered from physical ailments (although he would never allow his fighters to use physical injuries as a means of excusing themselves from performing at their best). In his capacity as a physician, Che would routinely treat his own—and sometimes even enemy—soldiers and peasants. The constant ministrations of Che to the destitute and suffering extended on occasion to prisoners taken by the *guerrilleros*. Che managed to prevail against frequent and violent asthmatic attacks that wracked his entire body and severely scarred his lungs. In this respect, he was not unlike other famous historical figures who overcame physical handicaps. The famous socialist lecturer Helen Keller was deaf and blind; Ricardo Flores Magón of the Junta Organizadora del Partido Liberal Mexicano, and an intellectual progenitor of the Mexican Revolution, suffered from chronic diabetes; Antonio Gramsci was born a hunchback to a poor peasant family and was so sickly as a child that in the evenings over a period of several years his mother is said to have dressed him in his best clothes and put him to sleep in a coffin with the expectation that he would be dead by the morning (Csikszentmihali, 1990, pp. 234–235). Che's physical suffering was undoubtedly a defining factor in the formation of his revolutionary subjectivity, and helped to explain his internationalist struggle against suffering in all of its forms. Of course, what Che abhorred above all else was the type of needless suffering that was brought on by the greed of the capitalist class and the contempt its members held for the poor and downtrodden. Che's profound love of humanity, and his suppressed rage toward those who exploited others for their own advantage, created a warrior spirit bolstered by an intellectual labor that drove him ethically and politically forward. For Che, the body became the revolutionary's most severe teacher. But Che's physical strength and agility were not those of the phallomilitary mercenary of the ruling class, whose mindless athleticism serves the highest bidder, but rather that of the battle-tough warrior whose steely resolve pushes the body to its limits, yet never divorces it from critical, contextual analysis of the goals ahead.

What was most striking about Che's pedagogy was his teaching through personal example, what teachers often call 'modeling ethically and practically' what is to be taught. Petras concludes:

> Teaching by example was Che's guiding principle. In his active role in the guerrilla struggle, he suffered the same hardships, took the same risks, and asked no special favors despite his serious physical handicap (asthma). In fact, he overcommitted himself, worked longer hours, slept less, and was very critical of his errors and lapses. His pedagogical style was that learning was based on observing what one *did*, not only what one *said*. Too often the masses lost confidence in ideas because of the divergences between what leaders said and how they lived or practiced politics. Che considered trust essential in building a popular movement and creating a principled organization and to this end urged leaders to teach by example. (1998, p. 17)

MARXISM AS AN ANTIRACIST PRACTICE

Michael Löwy notes that, for Che, "the only pedagogy that is liberating is one that enables people to educate themselves through their revolutionary practice"

(1997, p. 5). In accepting an honorary degree from the University of Las Villas, Che warned students and faculty in attendance that the days when education was a privilege of the white middle class were over. He announced that "the university must paint itself black, mulatto, worker, and peasant" (Smith and Ratner, 1997, p. 43).

Manning Marable (1999) has noted that Cuba and black America share common historical experiences and social characteristics. First, both Cuba and the United States consist of racial formations developed out of slave economics, both are connected to the black Caribbean, and both share parallel struggles for political democracy and self-determination. The struggles of African Americans have inspired many Cuban progressives as illustrated by Cuban Mirta Aguirre's 1935 poem about the nine young black men who were framed for the rape of two white women in Scottsboro, Alabama:

Scottsboro en Alabama
Scottsboro en Yanquilandia.
Es un hierro puesto al fuego
y elevado en las entrañas de una raza.
Nueve negros casi niños, sin trabajo
Dos mujeres, prostitutas.
Ley de Lynch, capitalismo, burguesia,
Las tres K de la turbia historia
Y a los pies del monstruo enorme de mil garras,
Nueve negros casi niños.
Scottsboro en Alabama,
en la tierra imperialista: Yanquilanda
es un manto de martirio y es un manto
De verguenza
Que cobija las dos razas. (cited in Marable, 1999, p. 10).

In September 1960, when Fidel came to New York to speak at the opening of the fifteenth session of the General Assembly, the Cuban delegation stayed at Harlem's Hotel Theresa. Upon arrival, they were cheered on by thousands of black and Latino Harlemites. Malcom X dropped by to extend his personal greetings to Fidel whom Malcolm described as "the only white person that I have really liked" (Marable, 1999, p. 12). In the 1970s and 1980s, Cuba supported the Marxist influenced Popular Movement for the Liberation of Angola (MPLA) and sent 30,000 combat troops enabling the MPLA to defeat the South African-backed army of Jonas Savimbi (Marable, 1999). It sent 20,000 troops to Ethiopia to assist its Marxist regime in its conflict with Somalia. Throughout the black world, Cuba sent medical personnel, teachers, and technicians, from the social democratic government of Michael Manley in Jamaica, to the New Jewel Movement regime of Maurice Bishop in Grenada. Cuba's solidarity with anticolonial movements and radical governments throughout the black diaspora provoked a sharp decline in U.S.-Cuban bilateral relations (Marable, 1999). Today, Fidel emphasizes that "more than ever . . . we have to remember Malcom X, Che, and all the heroes of the struggle and the cause of the peoples" (cited in Marable, 1999, p. 15).

Marable notes that among African Americans, only Nelson Mandela of South Africa surpasses Fidel Castro in terms of moral authority and political credibility. Racial discrimination was outlawed in Cuba in 1959. Marable writes that

> The revolution's explicitly antiracist agenda was clearly stated by Fidel Castro in a televised speech on March 22, 1959. Outlawing racial discrimination in public accommodations, the workplace, and schools, Castro declared that "nobody can consider himself as being of a pure much less superior, race. (1999, p. 11)

Che was a great admirer of the courageous struggle of African Americans against the Jim Crow system of segregation that still persisted throughout the United States in the early 1960s. He especially admired Malcolm X. During Che's 1964 visit to New York, Malcolm invited Che to address a rally organized by the Organization of Afro-American Unity (OAAU) at the Audubon Ballroom in New York City. Mary-Alice Waters (1998, p. 22) reports that, two days prior to Malcom's invitation to Che, a group of *gusanos* (Cuban counter-revolutionaries, or 'worms') fired a bazooka shell from a U.S. rocket launcher at the United Nations building during Che's address, with the shell making quite an explosion but fortunately falling short of its mark and landing harmlessly in the East River. Consequently, Che was advised by his security advisors not to attend any public meetings, and thus he did not address the OAAU but instead sent heartfelt greetings of solidarity. After reading Che's message to those who were gathered there, Malcolm exclaimed:

> I love a revolutionary. . . . And one of the most revolutionary men in this country right now was going to come out here along with our friend Sheik Babu [the leader of the Zanzibar liberation struggle and pioneer of Tanzanian independence], but he thought better of it. . . . I'm happy to hear your warm round of applause in return, because it lets the Man know that he's just not in a position today to tell us who we should applaud for and who we shouldn't applaud for. And you don't see any anti-Castro Cubans here—we eat them up. (cited in Waters, 1998, p. 23)

Mary-Alice Waters finds a fitting comparison between Malcolm and Che:

> Che and Malcolm were bound by their utter contempt for the prerogatives of capital and the pretensions of its personifiers; by their respect for and openness to the integrity and intelligence of every human being who stood up and fought; and by their common refusal to compromise with the truth. They were bound by their unshakable confidence in the capacity of ordinary men and women to transform themselves in the process of fighting to transform the conditions of their existence

and change the world. And by their disdain for the rationalizations and cowardice of the misleaders of the toilers. (1998, p. 20)

Malcolm's and Che's struggles against racism were not burdened with today's fashionable notion that race is merely a refrangible discourse or 'social construction' or that racism is a shifting signifier that floats adventitiously atop the crust of culture, forever delinked from the law of value and the prison house of labor under capitalism. Like Tshembe, a character in Lorraine Hansberry's play, *Les Blancs,* Malcolm and Che emphasized racism's effects—its social effectuality—and struggled to create the social conditions that would refuse to nourish them. Tshembe dramatically captures this position in the following speech:

> I am not playing games . . . I am simply saying that a device *is* a device, but that it also has consequences: once invented it takes on a life, a reality of its own. So, in one century, men invoke the device of religion to cloak their conquests. In another, race. Now, in both cases you and I may recognize the fraudulence of the device, but the fact remains that a man who has a sword run through him because he refused to become a Moslem or a Christian—or who is shot in Zatembe or Mississippi because he is black—is suffering the utter *reality* of the device. And it is pointless to pretend that it doesn't *exist*—merely because it is a *lie*! (Hansberry, 1994, p. 92; emphasis in original)

Che recognized the importance of the African American struggle as the vanguard of the working-class movement in the United States, and he was also aware that, for many African Americans, Cuba after the revolution was an important role model for racial justice. In January 1959, Cuba's revolutionary government began to enforce a major ban on any forms of racial discrimination (Waters, 1998, p. 19). In his address to the General Assembly of the United Nations in December 1964, Che maintained, prophetically, that

> the time will come when this assembly will acquire greater maturity and demand of the United States government guarantees for the life of the Blacks and Latin Americans who live in that country, most of them U.S. citizens by origin or adoption. Those who kill their own children and discriminate daily against them because of the color of their skin; those who let the murderers of Blacks remain free, protecting them, and furthermore punishing the Black population because they demand their legitimate rights as free men—how can those who do this consider themselves guardians of freedom? . . . The government of the United States is not the champion of freedom, but rather the perpetuator of exploitation and oppression against the peoples of the world and against a large part of its own population. (cited in Waters, 1998, pp. 19–20).

Like Malcolm, Che was a great teacher. When Che lay wounded and exhausted on the dirt floor of the schoolhouse at La Higuera, he asked his captors to let him speak to the schoolteacher, Julia Cortez. In the final hours of his life, Che debated pedagogy. Taibo reports the following conversation between Che and Julia Cortez:

> "Ah, you're a teacher. Did you know that the 'e' in 'sé' has an accent in 'ya sé leer?'" he said, pointing to the chalkboard. "By the way, they don't have schools like this in Cuba. This would be like a prison for us. How can peasants' children study in a place like this? It's anti-pedagogical."
>
> "Ours is a poor country."
>
> But the government officials and the generals drive Mercedes cars and have a host of other things. . . . Don't they? That's what we're fighting against." (1997, p. 560)

REVOLUTION AND THE POSTMODERN CONDITION

It is certainly true that Che's new pedagogical agent of the revolution operates within an Enlightenment legacy that is currently under assault by the postmodernist academy. Many postmodernist scholars assume that liberation struggles, grounded as they are in Enlightenment rationality, are pernicious attempts to camouflage the subjugation of non-Western peoples. It is not so much the foolish insensitivity, impertinence, or impiety of the 'ludic' postmodernists toward the question of human suffering under capitalism that is the problem—after all, postmodernists do not have a monopoly on this—but they seem to have placed a virtual embargo on the concept of realism, even a realism that does not require a gods' eye view from Mt. Olympus or that is innocent of ideological mediation. Che's revolutionary politics need to be understood in its historical context. Che's politics were undeniably committed to equality and universalism and cannot be reduced to a mechanical economic determinism. His politics called for an equality that included men and women of different ethnic backgrounds. To what extent his world view constituted a 'metaphysics of presence' is a task I shall leave to other scholars more inclined to compare Che's ideas to contemporary theoretical trends. On this point I would somewhat hastily say that Che's Marxism would be inhospitable to both the vulgar economistic Marxism of the Second and Third International (represented by thinkers such as Bernstein, Kautsky, Plekhanov, and Bukharin) and to Althusser's structuralist Marxism with its notion of overdetermination. Nor would Che have felt comfortable with a Marxism without a subject (or with a subject as drunkenly decentered as the postmodernists have called for) at the center of history, such as the post-Marxism of Ernesto Laclau and Chantal Mouffe. As Ferraro writes:

> Having removed the subject from the center of history, structuralist Marxists were eventually forced to remove the structure itself. In the end there was nothing but

discursive analysis of the realm of "ideological misrecognition." Having been nurtured on the anti-humanism, anti-historicism, and anti-empiricism of the structuralist tradition, post-Marxist post-structuralists, once they had delivered themselves from structure as well, were, as Perry Anderson explains, left with a
"subjectivism without a subject" and a structuralism without a structure, or a
purely discursive reflexivity. All that such theories have been able to "accomplish"
is the "deconstruction" of all choices as a prelude to social inaction, and implicit
support of the status quo. Post-Marxist post-structuralism therefore is not only
post-Marxist but explicitly anti-Marxist as well. (1992, pp. 27–28)

Che's Marxism was grounded in historical materialism, in the idea of a self-
reflexive agent of struggle, and in the political choice both to understand history
and to change it. Che's vision of a new socialist agent is still indispensable in an
era that has witnessed the fragmentation of the educational Left. In our current
'postmodern' society that is a cross between Leviathan and Behemoth, between
absolutism and chaos, Che's vision is still relevant, perhaps even more so today.
Let me suggest here that by advancing Che's image of the new socialist agent I
am not at the same time arguing for the construction of a unified, homogeneous,
socialist agent of anticapitalist struggle premised upon a singular objective, an
antipode of the homogeneous, commodified agent of capital. Given the current
configurations and complexities of capital, and the stark reality that reveals the
paramountcy of capital in mediating the way that we apprehend our role as citizens, we need a vision with an emancipatory thrust that is dialectically self-
correcting and politically and ethically pertinent to the anticapitalist struggle
ahead—a struggle, by the way, that will depend as much upon creating new
organizations, programs, and institutional structures as upon the construction of
a new theoretical language (see McLaren 1999a, 1999b; Kincheloe and
McLaren, 1994). Yet it is necessary to raise further questions: Why has humanity not accumulated historical knowledge and developed into the kind of new
socialist being envisioned by Che? Why has this new revolutionary agent not yet
emerged? In fact, one could even ask if it is possible to resurrect this new social
agent in the context of an increasing internationalization of financial capital and
the uncoupling of the financial and productive circuits of capital. At a time when
the real economy of goods and services is no longer tightly bound to the symbolic economy of money, credit, and capital, and when speculative financial ven-
tures are increasingly separated from production, do conditions still exist for the
kind of revolutionary agency envisioned by Che? In retrospect, were the 1960s
the last opportunity for popular revolutionary insurgency on a grand scale to be
successful? Did the political disarray of prodigious dimensions that followed in
the wake of the rebuff of the post-1968 leftist intelligence by the European proletariat condemn the revolutionary project and the 'productionist' metanarrative
of Marx forever to the dustbin of history? Have the postmodernist emendations

of Marxist categories and the rejection—for the most part—of the Marxist project by the European and North American intelligentsia signaled the abandonment of hope in revolutionary social change? Would Ernesto Guevara be able to reinvent himself today as El Che?

Clearly, Che would have anticipated the power of an unchecked and unrestrained capitalism to continue to advance like a juggernaut into the new millennium and pillage the world's remaining resources for the benefit of the rich. As Mary-Alice Waters notes:

> The world of capitalist disorder—the imperialist reality of the twenty-first century—would not be strange to Che. Nor would he fail to recognize the weight, power, and political leverage of the Cuban revolution within this reality. Far from being dismayed by the odds we face, moreover, he would have examined this world with scientific precision and charted a course to win, turning toward the battles with the warrior's spirit he was imbued with. (1998, pp. 12–13)

One can only imagine what Che would make of the exploitative power embodied within new forms of today's transnational capital, especially in terms of the shift in the relation between nation-states and formerly nation-based classes, the scope of economic restructuring and its ability to erode the power of organized labor, and the extent to which global mass migrations pit groups in fierce competition over very scarce resources. In one sense, the situation certainly would not have surprised him and in fact would have confirmed his earliest warnings about U.S. imperialism. As Mary-Alice Waters affirms:

> Che understood, profoundly, the character of the enemy we face: that imperialism is a world system—the last stage of capitalism, a system ruled by the law of value—and that the world class struggle is an interrelated whole. Proletarian internationalism is not a luxury, or one among several effective choices; it is dictated by capital itself, by its inevitable national conflicts and its rapacious character. Che knew that proletarian internationalism is a precondition for the working class to surmount the competition among ourselves inherent in the condition of propertyless wage slavery, to rise to a level of discipline and culture necessary to win, and to transform ourselves in the process. (1998, p. 13)

When asked what Che would make of Cuba in the midst of contemporary global capitalist pressure, Orlando Borrego, who worked with Che in Cuba's Ministry of Industry, states:

> I picture him studying and obtaining a deeper theoretical understanding, doing a careful analysis of the phenomenon of globalization and all these backward ideas of neoliberalism. I picture him trying to give a practical solution to the extraordinary shortages and difficulties we have in Cuba, while avoiding concessions of prin-

ciple in the management of the economy that could bring disastrous consequences
to our revolutionary process, as happened in the former Soviet Union. (Terrero,
1998, p. 40)

But in another sense, the magnitude of the shifts in global capitalism, the
long-term deflationary crisis, the intensifying trade-currency conflicts, and the
structural contradictions they have brought about, would have, for Che, perhaps
eclipsed even his own worst fears. According to William Robinson, the transnational bourgeoisie now exercises class power through both a network of supra-
national institutions and relationships that can bypass formal states, and through
the utilization of national governments as "territorially-bound juridical units (the
interstate system), which are transformed into transmission belts and filtering
devices for the imposition of the transnational agenda" (1996, p. 19).

Robinson notes that the transnational elite has now been able to put democracy in place of dictatorship (what can be called the unbelievable state) in order
to perform at the level of the nation-state the functions of adopting fiscal and
monetary policies that guarantee macro-economic stability, provide the necessary infrastructure for global capitalist circuitry and flows, and allow social control for the transnational comprador elite as the nation-state moves more solidly
into the camp of neoliberalism, yet at the same time maintain the illusion of
national interests and concerns with foreign competition. In fact, the concern
for national interests is just an ideological ruse to enable authoritarian regimes
to move with a relative lack of contestation toward a transformation into elite
polyarchies. (Ellen Meiksins Wood and others would disagree with Robinson on
the contemporary role of the state within global capitalist relations, and I do not
attempt to deal with this important debate here.) More than likely, Che would
not be very surprised by the fact that so many of the literary practices in today's
schools—such as cooperative learning and creating communities of learners—
are functionally linked to this new global economy and promote a convenient
alliance between the new fast capitalism and conventional cognitive science.
While these new classroom measures are helping to design and analyze symbolic
economies, they are also being co-opted by and facilitating the new capitalism
(see Gee, Hull, and Lankshear, 1996).

What might perhaps have surprised Che about current conditions would be
the rapid internationalization of capitalist technology and the transmission of
social life in general into a single capitalist mode. William Robinson refers to this
process as "the accelerated division of all humanity into just two single classes,
global capital and labor (although both remain embedded in segmented structures and hierarchies)" (1996, p. 15). Che would perhaps be shocked by the
extent to which democratic control by people over the conditions of their daily
existence has become undermined by the commodification of all spheres of life
as the capitalist economy mutates into all regions of the social, including that

which produces our every self-consciousness of this process. Though it is true that the traditional working class is fragmented, and that inequalities in postmodern consumer societies have begun to be structured by patterns of consumption as well as patterns of production, "we are at different times and in various locations both beneficiaries and victims of a well-organized system of exploitation" (Ashley, 1997, p. 145).

Although Che did not desire investment to be guided by the law of value (profitability and the like), he did not deny the partial persistence of commodity categories for a short period—for instance, the commodity character of consumer goods sold to the public. In fact, he insisted that centralized planning (as opposed to the bureaucratic planning practiced in the USSR) utilize the law of value in a partial way in order to combat it on a larger scale. But could he have imagined the grand scale in which commodification works in today's era of globalization?

In Che's time there were precommodity spheres that could serve as buffers from the alienation of capital, and there was still a neater, more well-defined division between a property-owning class and a well-organized proletariat. Not all relationships had succumbed to the attack dogs of exchange value, and the working class could still (albeit, with some difficulty) construct its identity as a self-consciously revolutionary class. The dismantling of Keynesian welfare states in the North, and the extent of unbelievable structural adjustment in the South that helps to stabilize regimes of monopoly control for the transnational elite, would not have been a great surprise to Che, but he would surely be shocked by how much and how swiftly—nearly instantaneously—these regimes can operate through consensual mechanisms of control that occur with the creation of new structures of consumer subjectivity and the demand for new meanings (Ashley, 1997). The circulation of signs has become a strong factor in new modes of class domination, helping to replace older, more authoritarian measures of colonial rule. It's a different kind of imperialism that we face today, but imperialism nonetheless. What has happened is that commodity relations now provide the taken-for-granted basis for communicative interaction between people. In an economy of the commodity spectacle, commodity relations mediate the regime of both needs and desire. However, according to David Ashley, "even though consumerism is an increasingly important component of the circuit of capital, it does not, and cannot, absorb the totality of human material existence. . . . Capital, however, is still based on production as well as consumption, and is still driven by the desire for profit" (1997, pp. 211–212).

Today in the United States we are witnessing the emergence of a new dominant class constituted by a technological aristocracy and corporate executives who work in the interests of corporate share price (Ashley, 1997). Within this context, capital and the state are reconfiguring race and gender, as a white male comprador labor aristocracy is giving way to a more decentralized, local, and flexible means of using race and gender as divide-and-rule tactics, as global cap-

*Che speaking with sugarcane workers, 1963 (Economics and
Politics in the Transition to Socialism,* copyright © 1989 by
Pathfinder Press. Reprinted with permission.)

italism is relying more and more on Third World labor and on Third World labor
pools in First World spaces (Ashley, 1997).

It is suggestive to consider how Che might mount a revolutionary campaign
against what David Ashley (1997) refers to as the globalization of capital's circuit
and the culture of postmodernism, which include: the globalization and increasing abstraction of capital; the ascendancy of financial capital; the spatial organization of the division of labor; greater emphasis on the reproduction of the conditions of consumption; increasing production of semiotic privilege; new versions
of privatism; the displacement of reality in the name of the commodity; the pes-
simism associated with the belief that the world is objectively knowable; and the
current stress on identity politics over the internationalization of the proletariat.
In the face of the current fashion of dystopia and the postmodern assault on the
unified subject of the Enlightenment tradition, Che would have a difficult time
winning the sympathy of the postmodern Left. While he would agree with the
Foucauldians that discourse includes the social he would never agree that it can
be reduced to it, and he would probably find the theory of governmentality guilty

of providing conceptual ballast to the international division of labor. When one examines Che's vision of the necessary postnational journey toward socialism (and a profoundly dialectical journey at that) against the disillusionment and inertia of today's postmodern Left—sunk into a despair brought on by a Nietzschean perspectivism, the rehabilitation of antihumanism, and the political paralysis and semiotic inertia of a cultural politics that is rarely linked to the social relations of production—one has an overwhelming sense that perhaps too much ground has been lost in order to rescue the revolutionary socialist project. Che's emphasis on revolutionary consciousness would make him an intransigent adversary to those postmodernists who advocate local struggles underwritten by identity politics. While he would affirm the centrality of racial and gender justice in any politics of emancipation, he most assuredly would have little truck with the pallid apostasy of postmodern critique with its toothless liberalism and airbrushed insurgency that sets itself up against the grand internationalist narratives of liberation that Che made his lifework. For Che, revolution was an historical event of great amplitude that has to be constantly pushed forward and expanded until it encompasses the entire globe. The totalizing vision of Che remains compelling and instructive, and indeed is as urgent today as it was thirty years ago. Perhaps even more so.

What about analyzing Che from a postmodernist perspective? Will there be *The Specters of Che* and should we care if there is? I have decided not to put Che under erasure within the *il n'y a pas de hors-texte* provenance of Derrida or the "death of the subject" tropes of Foucault. But I will offer a brief commentary on Che's postmodern possibilities. How one can assume an effective revolutionary role with dead subjects is an issue that cannot be answered without recognizing how postmodernism can be functionally advantageous to global capitalism and the contemporary culture of commerce with its short-sighted mendacity and bloodless, corporate-backed policies for social and educational restructuring. Education's tropism toward entrepreneurialism is just one indication of this contemporary culture.

In many instances, postmodernist critique merely reproduces the very bourgeois structures of signification that it attempts to contest.[25] Though postmodernist critique might be able to dehierarchicize the notion of educational leadership, it may well serve to rehierarchicize the notion of leadership in yet another register, and in so doing simply serve to manage the crisis brought about by the postmodern culture of nominalist forms of subjectivity, fragmentation, pastiche, decentered monads, indeterminacy, and undecidability. Postmodernist critique can be simply a strategic deployment of reunderstanding educational leadership as a mode of aesthetic inquiry, majesterially delinked from (or at the very least, de-emphasizing) the reigning social relations of exploitation.

Attempts to 'postmodernize' Che and Guevarian leadership for today might in some ways be symptomatic of the structurally airbrushed contradictions and problematic assumptions within postmodern theory itself. The *haute politique* of postmodern theory valorizes the primacy of incommensurability as the touchstone of analysis and explanation; and though it has helped to usher in a more nuanced understanding of the politics of representation and the fictions of discourse, it has also diverted critical analysis from the sweep of advanced capitalism and the imperialist exploitation of the world's laboring class. Ironically, postmodernism has become the new doxology of the academic Left, only to impede our ability to understand the current historical conjuncture as inscribed in the uneven or unequal development of the capitalist world system. The bourgeois discourses of the imperialist metropole often decenter regimes of signification but then (often unwittingly) recenter them at yet another level of meaning. This is because the social relations of production are too often posited as merely contingent rather than historically necessary. Everyday life as a regime of discourse itself becomes antiseptically removed from the connections and the concrete internal relations that constitute the totality of its objective determinations.

Perhaps some post-Marxists would have preferred me to present a hypertext of Che, a Che who is merely a reflection of a reflection, a mimesis of a mimesis, a spectral presence haunting postmodern spaces (like the figure of Marx in Derrida's *The Specters of Marx*), an abstract sign, a structured absence. The more conservative incarnations of postmodernist critique can displace critique to a field of serial negation without grasping its prefigurative or emancipatory potential. The potential for emancipatory critique can best be grasped by a concept of totality and a dialectical approach to imperialism. Thus, I am not content with positing intelligibility internally or inside the texts of culture. Rather, I am concerned not only with the represented exterior of intelligibility—the external material relations that inform as well as deform knowledge—but also with their concrete determinations. The unsaid of post-Marxist critique is that postmodernism itself can become the naturalized vehicle for the transmission of dominant ideologies. In this regard, much post-Marxist critique appears to be subsumed under the meta-authority of postmodernism.

I believe that the best way to present Che's life and pedagogical work is from an historical, materialist perspective, rather than from an immanent or internal reading. The challenge is not to reveal the inconsistencies, *aporias*, or contradictions of Che as a text-in-itself (though surely this could prove to be an interesting exercise) so much as to grasp the significance of these contradictions and inconsistencies *by comprehending their necessity*.

The challenge in re-presenting Che is not so much a postmodernist unpacking of the text or mapping Che onto contemporary postmodern spaces, but an uncoiling of the political economy of the text by a remapping and relinking of systems of signification surrounding Che to the material and historical practices that constitute them. Postmodernists might like to put Che on a virtual stage with David Copperfield in the role of Derrida, placing Che under erasure and showing him to be little more than a pertuse tissue of signification folding back upon itself. Che suddenly collapses, freighted with the semantic debris left by attempts to purge him of his logocentrism or his "metaphysics of presence." In such a theoretical move, Che becomes little more than a play of rhetorical strategies—a matter of form—since, after all, historical actors are only the ahistorical effects of the immanent laws of language, or so the poststructuralists tell us.

The challenge for educators is to present a model of educational leadership that provides precisely what postmodern analysis all too commonly and suspiciously evacuates: dialectical critique and an attentiveness to political economy.

The question at stake—how do educators assume a model of leadership that can resist global capitalist exploitation and create a new social order?—is not adequately formable in the terms of critique that postmodernism provides, but it can be grasped in the dialectical thinking of Che Guevara, Paulo Freire, Antonio Gramsci, Amilcar Cabral, and others. Consequently, it is important to move outside (or perhaps at times alongside) the discourses of postmodernism in an attempt to relate the internal logic of the text of Che's life to the history of the present.

In sum, criticalists are dutybound to consider leadership roles as discourses, as rule-deploying texts. Correlatively, if we are to gain a more nuanced and measured grasp of these discourses, we need a theory of how these discourses came to be what they are as opposed to something else. And surely we could benefit from some postmodernist critique in this regard. But ultimately, I believe, we need an analysis of revolutionary leadership that enables us to see the social totality of capitalist social relations. Postmodernist critique too often encourages an examination of the cultural discourses of capitalism as open-ended sites of desire. A revolutionary model of educational leadership understands discourses as always an interpretation naturalized by the culture of commerce, and historically and socially produced in the arena of class struggle. A revolutionary leadership can only be achieved by examining the historical conditions of possibility for recognizing capitalist social relations and its blind fatalities, for framing them, for understanding them, and, most important, for transforming them.

E. San Juan (forthcoming) argues that

> from a historical-materialist perspective, the dynamic process of social reality cannot be grasped without comprehending the connections and the concrete internal relations that constitute the totality of its objective determinations. . . . Truth in this tradition comes from human practice, the intermediary between consciousness and its object; and it is human labor (knowing and making as a theorized synthesis) that unites theory and practice. As Lenin puts it, everything is mediated and connected by transitions that unite opposites, "transitions of every determination, quality, feature, side, property, into every other" so that "the individual exists only in the connection that leads to the universal." . . . (p. 10)

According to San Juan, what is required in the struggle to overcome alienation at the level of national struggle is the conquest by the colonized of full sovereignty.

In his "Notes on Man and Socialism in Cuba" (which drew heavily on Marx's early writing, including the *Economic and Philosophical Manuscripts*), Che exemplifies the politicization of translinguistics (San Juan, 1998b). His vision of the nation-state is both historically anchored and prophetic; the revolutionary as transformative agent is grounded in a translinguistic discourse. According to E. San Juan, Che views the individual as the central feature of the socialist state. The individual as a speaking subject is formed out of an ensemble of condensed mutualities. In this essay, Che is able to reverse the anticommunist charge that the socialist state subordinates the individual. Cultivating what Che refers to as an heroic attitude will enable subaltern domination to be transformed under the guidance of the vanguard party as epitomized by Fidel Castro and by the thematic topos of Cuba as the vanguard nation of the Americas. San Juan cogently and suggestively illustrates how, in Che's essay, the mutualities condensed in the speaking-subject of Che dissolved the gap between leaders and led in a process of rehumanization under socialism.

San Juan acknowledges a strong affinity between Che's discourse and the principle of ethical participation in the realization of a "concrete ought" that grounds the work of Bakhtin. In Che's essay, the superaddressee is communist society-in-the-making, a future immanent in the present (San Juan, 1998a). According to San Juan, the chronotype of nation mutates into a liminal space where the sociopolitical project of socialist hegemony—characterized as a mission of heroic sacrifice—displaces capitalist interest embodied in the 'other' of capitalist alienation. Describing the life of Filipino revolutionary figure María Lorena Barros, founder of the pioneer women's organization, Makibaka (Malayany Kilusan ng Bagong Kababaihan; Freedom Movement of New Women), E. San Juan notes how her life and death (Barros was executed by government soldiers in Mauban, Quezon Province, in 1976) transcended the categories of postcolonial theory—the "national allegory" of Fredric Jameson, the achievement of subjecthood beyond the interstices of the "Third Space" of Homi Bhabha, or the "imaginary homelands" of Salman Rushdie. In my estimation, San Juan's appraisal of Barros' trajectory as a feminist underground combatant also applies to Che's own revolutionary struggle in that it formed "an art of decision and risk-taking, an imagination sworn to determining accountability and articulating responsibility" (San Juan, 1998, p. 49) for the struggles of the disenfranchised. Borrowing from San Juan's brilliant analysis of Barros, C.L.R. James, and Rigoberta Menchú, we have in the example of Che a shining instance of performative identity—indeed, the performance of life's inventory through acts that surpass the past and valorize decision and accountability and historical retrospection. Here we have a life whose partisanship linked the 'I' and 'you' and the 'we' and 'they' through the determinate concreteness of everyday struggle, an intractable heterogenous and reintegrative impulse toward a diverse collectively, and a popular anticolonialism premised on narratives of belonging and solidarity. San Juan is worth quoting at length:

Che and Fidel Castro at airfield, 1959 (Che Guevara and the Cuban Revolution, copyright © 1987 by Pathfinder Press. Reprinted by permission.)

So instead of the in-between, we have transition and the interregnum as privileged sites of self-recognition via the community; instead of ambivalence, we have resolve, commitment, determination to face specific problems and crisis. Instead of the local, we have a striving for coalitions and counterhegemonic blocs to prefigure a universal public space. Instead of the syncretic and hybrid, we have creative demarcations and the crafting of the architectonic of the new, the emergent, the *Novus*. Instead of the polyvocal, we have the beginning of articulation from the silenced grassroots, the loci of invention and resourceful innovation. Here the trope of difference is displaced by the trope of possibilities, the binary impasse of reified hegemonic culture deconstructed by the imagination of materialist critique and extrapolation. Utterance is neither private nor solipsistic but an utterance of the mass line, not heteroglossic but triangulated; not contingent but charted by cognitive mapping and provisional orientations. (1998a, p. 51)

It is clear from the perspective taken in Che's *La Marcha* essay that the revolutionary agent of socialism exists dialectically as both individual and as collective membership, always in process, always beginning anew, as the future immanent in the concrete moment of revolutionary world-making. When Bolivia's Lieutenant Colonel Selich (later to become a general) was interrogating Che in the mud-walled schoolhouse in La Higuera, shortly before Che was executed, he was reported to have asked: "Are you Cuban or Argentine?" Che is said to have answered: "I am Cuban, Argentine, Bolivian, Peruvian, Ecuadorian, etc. . . . You understand" (Anderson, 1997, p. 734). Such a statement at once mocks and transcends the decentered speaking subject of postmodern discourse. Read in the context of Che's vision of the new agent of socialism, his remark to Lieutenant Colonial Selich embodies a radical postnational sense of locating the revolutionary agent in a discourse of mutuality that is inscribed by the call to struggle and to suffer as an individual for the greater good of the collective society-in-the-making. And though one must consider this statement in the context of the warning of President Gamal Nasser of Egypt, that Che could become "another Tarzan, a white man among black men, leading and protecting them" (Sandison, 1997, p. 90), Che's call for an internationalist struggle was not conditioned by a white missionary syndrome so prevalent in the history of Western imperialism, but by a desire for universal justice for the oppressed of the world. In this way it set itself against postmodern skepticism, with its resignation to political inactivity embodied in an "always already" preconstituted subject of history; in contrast, Che's was an heroic form of hope nourished by an anticipatory consciousness, one that offers to the collective society-in-the-making the blood of personal sacrifice. One thinks back to Mexico City in 1956, when Fidel appointed Che—known to most of Fidel's group at the time as "El Argentino"—as a leader of one of the *casa-campamentos* (safehouses). Some of the twenty or thirty Cubans in Che's safehouse challenged his leadership because he was not Cuban, but Argentine. Che was not the only foreigner in the group (there was a Mexican, a Dominican, and an Italian, among others) but Fidel wanted to keep the number of non-Cubans to a reasonable limit, as he didn't want a "mosaic of nationalities" to obscure the fact that this was a Cuban guerrilla movement (Anderson, 1997, p. 190). Yet Fidel unhesitatingly defended Che, since Che was ready to shed his blood for the group. According to Jesús Montané Oropesa, "though not a Cuban, [Che] was unconditionally ready to come with us and fight for our freedom, thus contributing to our revolution's inspiring tradition of internationalism" (1994, p. 17). Fidel adds that

> When one speaks of a proletarian internationalist, and when an example of a proletarian internationalist is sought, high above any other, will be the example of Che. National flags, prejudices, chauvinism, and egoism had disappeared from his mind and heart. He was ready to shed his blood spontaneously and immediately, on behalf of any people, for the cause of any people! (1994, p. 78)

It is worth noting that Che's Bolivian guerrilla force (excluding members of his network in urban centers) included one Argentine (Che), one German (Tania), three Peruvians, sixteen Cubans, and twenty-nine Bolivians. Motivated by similar concerns to those of Fidel, Che worked to increase the number of Bolivians. [On his mission to Bolivia, Che was accompanied by seventeen Cubans: a number of them were Sierra Maestra veterans, four were *commandantes* (the highest rank in the Cuban army); four were members of the highly respected Central Committee of the Cuban Communist Party; two were in their forties; and one was a Vice Minister and one was Director of Mines (Sinclair, 1998).]

Che's humanist vision of socialist society prompted him to break with the Soviet model of communism, which he saw as another form of state capitalism underwritten by a statist imitation of bourgeois consumer society (Löwy, 1973). Faced with Cuba's underdeveloped capitalist economy, Che supported a centralized budgetary system for the equitable allocation of resources between different sectors of the economy (Harris, 1998). Che did not envision an economy of marketization, material incentives, and enterprise financial self-management. He was vehemently opposed to Soviet state capitalism in which the division of labor remained intact, in which the hierarchical command structure of capital continued to be entrenched in the politico-economic system, and in which surplus labor and surplus value extraction were achieved through inflexible political regulation. Che considered the economic imperatives of the Soviet Union under Krushchev to be a "rightist" deviation from socialism (Harris, 1998, p. 28). Furthermore, he did not agree with the Soviet advice to the Cuban leadership that led to Cuba's renewed emphasis on sugar production, material incentives, and decentralized financial self-management at the production-enterprise level, since this constituted a blatant betrayal of the revolutionary regime's commitment to industrialization and the replacement of capitalist material incentives with communist moral incentives (Harris, 1998). Revolutionary consciousness in Che's mind had more to do with moral commitment than with material incentives. Even if we were to concede that, in the case of the USSR, a form of state capitalism was obtained, the USSR and the West were still competing within essentially the same paradigm. We have to acknowledge further that 'real existing socialism' has been more of an ideal than empirical fact. Che understood that socialism was something that has to be reinvented in the historical specificity of particular revolutionary conditions without the benefit of an historical blueprint.

For Che, the construction of communism occurred with the material base of society through the creation of the new man, the new socialist being. Che posited two pivotal points for this to occur at—the formation of a new moral agent and the development of technology (Löwy, 1973). He rejected the mechanistic view that material incentives will disappear because of the increased availability of consumer goods to the people. He also rejected financial self-management and the economistic perspective that views the raising of productive forces as the crucible for all social, political, and ideological transformations. Because Che recognized that spaces of autonomy exist within different levels of the social whole, he stressed the importance of political-moral motivation and the need for what he called multiform action in order to change the consciousness of the oppressed. Capitalism cannot be overcome with its own fetishes of material incentives but can be defeated only when the economic base is driven by a developing collectivist consciousness. Material incentives of a social character (such as hospitals, workers clubs, and the like) and of an educative character must be stressed (Löwy, 1973). In the transition period to socialism, Che favored regulating wages in accordance with the degrees of skill attained in order to stimulate the workers to study and to raise their cultural and technical level. However, Che argued that material incentives should eventually be replaced by moral incentives and by the social and political consciousness of the masses. Che was not interested in a communism without a revolutionary morality. According to Carlos Tablada:

> Che did not view economic development as an end in itself. Development of a society has meaning only if it serves to transform men and women, enhance their creative capacities, and draw them beyond self-centeredness. The transition to the kingdom of freedom is a voyage from "me" to "us." And socialism cannot carry out this transition with what Che called "the dull instruments left to us by capitalism." We cannot advance toward communism if life under socialism is organized like a competition among wolves, as in the previous society (1991, p. 70).

What does Che's historical materialist approach have to offer educators who work in teacher education? I raise this question at a time in which it is painfully evident that critical pedagogy and its political ally, multicultural education, no longer serve as an adequate social or pedagogical platform from which to mount a vigorous challenge to the current social division of labor and its effects on the socially reproductive function of schooling in late capitalist society. In fact, critical pedagogy no longer enjoys its status as a herald for democracy, as a clarion call for revolutionary praxis, as a language of critique and possibility in the service of a radical democratic imaginary, which was its promise in the late 1970s and early 1980s.

A nagging question has resurfaced: Can a renewed and revivified critical pedagogy serve as a point of departure for a politics of resistance and counterhegemonic struggle in the twenty-first century? And if we attempt to answer the question in the affirmative, what can we learn from the legacy and struggle of Ernesto Che Guevara? On the surface, there are certain reasons to be optimistic. Critical pedagogy has, after all, joined antiracist and feminist struggles in order to articulate a democratic social order built around the imperatives of diversity, tolerance, and equal access to material resources. But surely such a role, though commendable as far as it goes, has seen critical pedagogy severely compromise an earlier, more radical commitment to anti-imperialist struggle that we can associate with the life and death of Che.[26]

CRITICAL PEDAGOGY: WHAT IS TO BE DONE?

Educational goals and methods have always been characters in our national morality play, political archetypes representing order and stability and disorder and the breakdown of civilization. Against this backdrop, the issues of power and privilege have been effectively laundered from U.S. education under the ruse that education is an objective science. Lacking a political economy model, teachers are denied the opportunity to see and understand their own embeddedness in history, language, culture, and power. Schools have been a key locus for the production of the attributes and behavior of citizens and for giving legitimacy to the workings of Western officialdom and statecraft. Against a retooled culture of poverty arguments, Latinophobic policy initiatives that trammel the rights of Mexican immigrants and cavil against the unwillingness of the 'other' to assimilate, the repatriated rule of white makes right, and the mourning of white worlds lost to the multiculturalists, African Americans and Latino/as continue to fight an uphill battle under the shadow of forgotten imperialisms and the logic of empire. The current historical juncture marks a slide backward from civil rights won a quarter century earlier to a period where we are witnessing the consolidation of postindustrial corporate power, a war against a significantly Latinized labor force and the federal abandonment of their civil rights, and the triumph of capital over labor. In such a situation, progressive citizens look to the schools as sites where the struggle for justice can be waged in the hearts and minds of the young.

Sententiously self-described as the most progressive of the pedagogical approaches, and considered by many progressive educators to possess an almost ur-nature that is fantastically central to the practice of liberatory education, critical pedagogy has become in recent years so completely psychologized, so liberally humanized, so technologized, and so conceptually postmodernized, that its current relationship to broader liberation struggles seems severely attenuated, if not fatally terminated. Believing that it carried the potential to revolutionize our schools and create an insurgent revolutionary consciousness among our youth, conservatives have managed to transform critical pedagogy into a cynosure of political approbation and "America First" invective. Now critical pedagogy has become so depotentiated that it is no longer considered by the faint-hearted guardians of the American dream as a term of opprobrium. The conceptual net known as critical pedagogy has been cast so wide and at times so cavalierly that it has come to be associated with anything dragged up out of the troubled and infested waters of educational practice, from classroom furniture organized in a "dialogue friendly" circle to "feel-good" curricula designed to increase students' self-image. It has become, in other words, repatriated by liberal humanism and cathected to a combination of middle-brow, town-hall meeting entrepreneurship and Sunday School proselytizing. Its multicultural education equivalent can be linked to a politics of diversity that includes "tolerating difference" through the celebration of "ethnic" holidays and themes such as Black History Month and Cinco de Mayo. If the term 'critical pedagogy' is refracted onto the stage of current educational debates, we have to judge it as having been largely domesticated in a manner that many of its early exponents, such as Brazil's Paulo Freire, so strongly feared.

Many educationalists who are committed to critical pedagogy and multicultural education propagate versions of it that identify with their own bourgeois class interests. One doesn't have to question the integrity or competence of these educators or dismiss their work as disingenuous—for the most part it is not—to conclude that their articulations of critical pedagogy and multicultural education have been accommodated to mainstream versions of liberal humanism and progressivism. Although early exponents of critical pedagogy were denounced for their polemical excesses and radical political trajectories, a new generation of critical educators has since that time emerged who have largely adopted a pluralistic approach to social antagonisms that attempts to reknit what the 'culture wars' of the 1980s tore asunder. Their work is marked by a flirtation with but never full commitment to revolutionary praxis; it celebrates the "end of ideology," and a critique of global capitalism is rarely, if ever, brought into the debate.

Some reasons for the domestication of critical pedagogy have been mentioned above, but I would like to elaborate here on what I consider to be some of the most important reasons. There has clearly been a strong tendency among many critical educators infatuated by postmodern and poststructuralist perspectives to neglect or ignore profound changes in the structural nature and dynamics of U.S. late capitalism. Carl Boggs captures the seriousness of this situation when he writes:

> In politics as in the cultural and intellectual realm, a postmodern fascination with indeterminacy, ambiguity, and chaos easily supports a drift toward cynicism and passivity; the subject becomes powerless to change either itself or society. Further, the pretentious, jargon-filled, and often indecipherable discourse of postmodernism reinforces the most faddish tendencies in academia. Endless (and often pointless) attempts to deconstruct texts and narratives readily become a façade behind which professional scholars justify their own retreat from political commitment. . . . [T]he extreme postmodern assault on macro institutions severs the connections between critique and action. (1997, p. 767)

Why should political economy be a concern to educators in this era of post-Marxist sympathies and multiple social antagonisms? Precisely because we are living at a particular historical juncture of unregulated capitalism with an overwhelming income reconcentration at the top. There currently exist seventy transnational corporations whose revenue is greater than Cuba's—seventy privately owned economic nations. Millions are unemployed in First World economic communities and millions more in Third World communities; three-quarters of the new jobs in the

THE MAN IN THE BLACK BERET

capitalist world are temporary, low paid, low skill, and carry few, if any, benefits. Latin American economies are in the thrall of a decade-long crisis. In the United States in 1989, the top 1 percent earned more collectively than the bottom 40 percent. As Charles Handy surmises in the case of England, although the government recently stated that 82 percent of all workers are in "permanent" employment, in fact 24 percent of the labor force are part-time, 13 percent are self-employed, 6 percent are temporary, and 8 percent are unemployed, making a total of 51 percent who are not in a full-time job. Furthermore, the length of a full-time job is approximately 5.8 years. So capitalism is really about employability, not employment (Handy, 1996). Overconsumption—the political subsidization of a sub-bourgeois, mass sector of managers, entrepreneurs, and professionals—has occurred at a time when we are witnessing a vast redistribution of wealth from the poor to the rich, as corporations are benefiting from massive tax cuts and the reorientation of consumption toward the new middle class. Overconsumption is also accompanied by a general retreat of the labor movement (Callinicos, 1990). The globalization of capital has unleashed new practices of social control and forms of internationalized class domination. This is not to suggest, however, that certain cultural institutions do not mediate the economic or that there do not exist relative decommodified zones.

There has been a shifting of positions among many North American critical educators from earlier Marxist perspectives to liberal, social-democratic, neoliberal, and even right-wing perspectives. We have occasionally seen on the theoretical front the conscription of some Marxist writers, such as Antonio Gramsci, into the service of a neoliberal political agenda. In all, we have witnessed the evisceration of a Marxist politics in current educational debates and the accommodation of some of its positions into the capitalist state apparatus. Discussions of political and ideological relations and formations are being engaged by many North American leftist educators as if these arenas of social power exist in antiseptic isolation from anti-imperialist struggle. Part of this anti-imperialist struggle means acknowledging acts of aggression committed by the United States against Guatemala (1954), Lebanon (1958), the Dominican Republic (1965), Vietnam (1954–1975), Laos (1964–1975), Cambodia (1969–1975), Nicaragua (1980–1990), Grenada (1983), Panama (1989), and Yugoslavia (1999). Public discussions of U.S. imperialism are virtually shut out of the mainstream corporate media, which have been successful in convincing large segments of the U.S. public that centrist perspectives are "far left" positions. Journalists today operate as little more than stenographers of the state. As adept with smoke and mirrors in the rhetorical arena of the newsroom as David Copperfield is on a Las Vegas stage, newscasters transform lies into truth. Wizards of Officialdom, newscasters and journalists shape the imagination of the public, convincing the citizenry that what they perceive has not been prefabricated but corresponds to the "way it is."

It is clear that a renewed agenda for critical pedagogy must include more than the postmodernist goal of voguishly troubling the fixed notions of identity and difference, or unsettling the notion of a bounded, pregiven, or essential 'self.' The 'ludic' postmodernist position is profoundly undialectical, remains tethered to the arena of cultural representation, does not sufficiently address issues of economic distribution, capitalist exploitation, and acts of imperialist aggression, and is a position that Che would have likely found risible. Not to identify globalization with its project—globalism—and to link both the process and product to imperialism, is merely to airbrush capitalism and give it a shining face, a situation to which Che was unstintingly opposed. According to A. Sivanandan:

> Globalisation is a process, not a concept, globalism is the project. And the project is imperialism. To dismiss globalisation as a right-wing thesis, to traduce it as 'globaloney' and saddle it with post-modernism and/or identity politics is not to dismiss capitalist triumphalism, but to evade it—to retreat, in fact, to the safety of the old barricades and throw stones at capitalism like some intellectual intifada. (1998/1999, p. 6)

CRITICAL EDUCATION FOR THE NEW MILLENNIUM

In order to follow in the revolutionary footsteps of Che, both critical pedagogy and multicultural education need to address themselves to the adaptive persistence of capitalism, and to issues of capitalist imperialism and its specific manifestations of accumulative capacities through conquest (to which we have assigned the more benign term 'colonialism'). In other words, critical pedagogy needs to recognize when educational reformers are acting in unreflective accord with the interests of world capitalism and to establish a project of emancipation centered on the transformation of property relations and the creation of a just system of appropriation and distribution of social wealth. Marxist and neo-Marxist accounts have identified clearly imperialistic practices in recent movements toward global capital accumulation based on corporate monopoly capital and the international division of labor. The West has seen a progressive shift in its development that some liberals clearly would champion as the rise of individuality, the rule of law, and the autonomy of civil society. Yet from a Marxist and neo-Marxist perspective, these putative developments toward democracy can be seen, in effect, as

> new forms of exploitation and domination (the constitutive 'power from below' is, after all, the power of lordship), new relations of personal dependence and bondage, the privatization of surplus extraction and the transfer of ancient oppressions from the state to 'society'—that is, a transfer of power relations and domination from the state to private property. (Wood, 1995, p. 252)

Since the triumph of European capitalism in the seventeenth century, the bourgeoisie has acquired the legal, political, and military power to destroy virtually most of society in its quest for accumulation (Petras and Morley, 1992). Capitalism in advanced Western countries must be dismantled if extra-economic inequalities— such as racism and sexism—are to be challenged successfully (McLaren 1997a, 1997b, 1998). Although it is true that individuals have identities other than class identities that shape their experiences in crucial and important ways, anticapitalist struggle is the best means to inform educators how identities can be conceived and rearticulated within the construction of a radical socialist project. Ellen Meiksins Wood lucidly captures the totalizing power of capitalism in the following remarks:

> Capitalism is constituted by class exploitation, but capitalism is more than just a system of class oppression. It is a ruthless totalizing process which shapes our lives in every conceivable aspect, and everywhere, not just in the relative opulence of the capitalist North. Among other things, and even leaving aside the direct power wielded by capitalist wealth both in the economy and in the political sphere, it subjects all social life to the abstract requirements of the market, through the commodification of life in all its aspects, determining the allocation of labor, leisure, resources, patterns of production, consumption and the disposition of time. This makes a mockery of all our aspirations to autonomy, freedom of choice, and democratic self-government. (1995, pp. 262–263)

We need not accommodate ourselves to the capitalist law of value, as István Mészáros (1995) reminds us. The challenge ahead is to work toward the expropriation of the capitalists but also to ensure the abolition of capital itself. The abolition of capital, it should be noted, is intractably linked to the struggle against racism. Critical educators need to consider how racism in its present incarnations developed out of the dominant mode of global production during the seventeenth and eighteenth centuries of colonial plantations in the New World, with slave labor imported from Africa to produce consumer goods such as, among others, tobacco, sugar, and cotton (Callinicos, 1992; McLaren, 1997b). How the immigrant working class has been divided historically along racial lines is a process that needs to be better understood and more forcefully addressed by multicultural educators. How, for instance, does racism give white workers a particular identity that unites them with white capitalists (Callinicos, 1992)?

Critical pedagogy as a partner with multicultural education needs to deepen its reach of cultural theory and political economy and expand its participation in social-empirical analysis in order to address more critically the formation of intellectuals and institutions within the current forms of motion of history. Critical pedagogy and multicultural education need more than good intentions to achieve their goal. They require a revolutionary movement of educators informed by a principled ethics of compassion and social justice, a socialist ethos based on solidarity and social interdependence, and a language of critique that is capable of grasping the objective laws of history (San Juan, 1998b). Given current U.S. educational policy, with its goal of slavishly serving the interests of the

corporate world economy—one that effectively serves as a *de facto* world government made up of the IMF, World Bank, G-7, GATT, and other structures—
it is imperative that critical and multicultural educators renew their commitment to the struggle against exploitation on all fronts (Gabbard, 1995). In
emphasizing one such front—that of class struggle—I want to stress that the
renewed Marxist approach to critical pedagogy that I envision does not concep-
tualize race and gender antagonisms as a static, structural outcome of capitalist
social relations of advantage and disadvantage, but rather it locates such antagonisms within a theory of agency that acknowledges the importance of cultural
politics and social difference. Far from deactivating the sphere of culture by see-
ing it only or mainly in the service of capital accumulation, critical pedagogy and
multicultural education need to acknowledge the specificity of local struggles
around the micropolitics of race, class, gender, and sexual formation. A critical
pedagogy based on class struggle that does not confront racism, sexism, and
homophobia will not be able to eliminate the destructive proliferation of capital. Che's example of leadership calls for a radical distribution of global
resources, a revitalized socialist politics in this age of the new global robber
barons, and a transnational connectedness that is both capable and willing to
create new channels of internationalist solidarity and strategic commonalities
among left constituencies. Such new channels of internationalist solidarity can
be created in sites where political activism is not restricted only to the public
sphere but occurs at all sites of production and reproduction.

Critical pedagogy must assume a position of transmodernity. Enrique Dussel
describes transmodernity as one

> in which both modernity and its negated alterity (the victims) co-realize them-
> selves in a process of mutual creative fertilization. Trans-modernity (as a pro-
> ject of political, economic, ecological, erotic, pedagogical, and religious libera-
> tion) is the co-realization of that which it is impossible for modernity to
> accomplish by itself: that is, of an incorporative solidarity, which I have called
> analectic, between center/periphery, man/woman, different races, different
> ethnic groups, different classes, civilization/nature, Western culture/Third
> World cultures, et cetera. For this to happen, however, the negated and vic-
> timized "other-face" of modernity—the colonial periphery, the Indian, the
> slave, the woman, the child, the subalternized popular cultures—must in the
> first place, discover itself as innocent, as the "innocent victim" of a ritual sacri-
> fice, who, in the process of discovering itself as innocent may now judge moder-
> nity as guilty of an originary, constitutive, and irrational violence. (1993, p. 76;
> emphasis in original)

The critical pedagogy to which I am referring needs to be made less informa-
tive and more performative, less a pedagogy directed toward the interrogation of
prepackaged curricula than a corporeal pedagogy grounded in the lived experi-

ences of students. Critical pedagogy, as I am revisioning it from a Guevarist and Freirean perspective, is a pedagogy that brushes against the grain of textual foundationalism, ocular fetishism, and the monumentalist abstraction of patrician theory that characterizes most critical practice within the academy's multicultural classrooms. This is not an argument against theory. Far from it. Theoretical underdevelopment and anti-intellectualism is a major problem, especially in an era of ethnic name-calling that has become fetishized into a counter-revolutionary species of identity politics. I am arguing that theory must organically connect to a vision and a practice of revolutionary politics. It must be a theory of flesh and bones. I am calling for a pedagogy in which a revolutionary multicultural ethics is performed—is lived in the streets—rather than simply reduced to the practice of reciting simplistic formulae from the cultural thesaurus of the bourgeois academy. Teachers need to displace the textual politics that dominate most multicultural classrooms and engage in a politics of bodily and affective investment grounded in both theoretical and relational knowledge. A critical pedagogy for multicultural education should quicken the affective sensibilities of students as well as provide them with a language of social analysis, cultural critique, and social activism in the service of cutting the power and practice of capital at its joints (McLaren, 1997a; Kincheloe and Steinberg, 1997). Knowledge is not only contemplative but practical, sensuous activity, and through such activity human beings can navigate between fatalism and romantic idealism in order to create history with a purpose. Opportunities must be made for students to work in communities where they can spend time with ethnically diverse populations in the context of community activism and participation in progressive political alliances. Students need to move beyond simply knowing about criticalist, multiculturalist practice. They must also move toward an embodied and corporeal understanding of such practice and an affective investment in such practice at the level of everyday life such that they are able to deflect the invasive power of capital and the defrauding, ideologically self-interested reporting on national and international events by the mainstream U.S. media that serves to protect through its journalistic-industrial complex the corporate interests of the state. As such, critical pedagogy should have as its center of gravity the practice of ideology-critique.

Ideological processes are those that are connected to the production and representation of ideas, values, and beliefs and the manner in which they are lived or 'taken up' at the level of everyday life. Without ideological frameworks—or pre-existing discourse communities—we could not interpret or fabulate experience or make sense of the world at all. However, we need to remember that ideology has both positive and negative functions. While on the one hand ideology provides us with systems of intelligibility, vocabularies of normalization or standardization, and grammars of design in order to make sense of everyday life, on the other hand such frameworks, grammars, and architectonics of design are always selective, partial, and positional. They enable sense-making but constrain other ways of making meaning. Ideology can be institutionalized, of course, and we need to remember that dominant ideological relations are carefully occulted and thus silently motivate individuals to misrecognize their complicity in establishing or maintaining asymmetrical relations of power and privilege within the dominant sociocultural order. Ideologies do not work with the unappeasable frenzy of the political fanatic intent on blowing up abortion clinics but rather barricade themselves within the realm of common sense and insinuate themselves within the discourses of everyday life as fundamental components of ordinary thinking. Critical pedagogy ruptures or destabilizes the dominant ideological imperatives of white, patriarchal, capitalist society through strategies of demystification and decolonization (McLaren, 1995, 1997a, 1997b, 1998).

Critical educators would do well to possess those qualities of the intellectual about which Edward W. Said has written so eloquently. According to Said, the intellectual must possess an "unbudgeable conviction in a concept of justice and fairness that allows for differences between nations and individuals, without at the same time assigning them to hidden hierarchies, preferences, evaluations" (1996, p. 94). Said also notes that intellectuals possess "an alternative and more principled stand that enables them in effect to speak the truth to power" (p. 97). "Yes, the intellectual's voice is lonely," Said reminds us, "but it has resonance only because it associates itself freely with the reality of a movement, the aspirations of a people, the common pursuit of a shared ideal" (p. 102). In other words, the social role of the intellectual is more than a question of intellectual probity; rather it is an issue of critical self-reflexivity leading to sociopolitical praxis. It is in this sense that critical educators need to adopt the distinction made by Said between the professional and amateur intellectual:

> The professional claims detachment on the basis of a profession and pretends to objectivity, whereas the amateur is moved neither by rewards nor by the fulfillment of an immediate career plan but by a committed engagement with ideas and values in the public sphere. The intellectual over time naturally turns towards the political world partly because, unlike the academy or the laboratory, that world is animated by considerations of power and interest writ large that drive a whole society or nation, that, as Marx so fatefully said, take the intellectual from relatively discrete questions of interpretation to much more significant ones of social change and transformation. . . . [T]he intellectual who claims to write only for him or herself, or for the sake of pure learning, or abstract science is not to be, and must not be, believed. (1996, p. 110)

Clearly, the figure of Che fits Said's model of the amateur intellectual, the intellectual freed from the political interests of the bourgeois academy. In fact, the Guevarian intellectual in many respects exceeds the model outlined by

Said and is closer to Gramsci's organic intellectual than to Said's diasporic, postcolonial intellectual, whom San Juan criticizes as "the declassed intellectual of the metropolitan literary circles" (1998, p. 30) and dismisses as a type of middleman negotiator between "the bourgeoisie-comprador nationalism of neocolonized nation-states and the cosmopolitan 'high culture' circuit of academic celebrities" (San Juan, 1998, p. 32). The organic intellectual, by contrast, does not wallow in a "directionless or aleatory ambivalence," but employs a "pedagogical and agitational role," is aware of uneven capitalist development, and incorporates the demands and needs of the peasants into its national-popular program of action (San Juan, 1998). The Guevarian intellectual is not content to participate in the low-intensity democracy of Western neoliberal regimes but is singularly focused on the high-intensity democracy that only a socialist politics can hasten forth. In this respect it is closer to what Gustavo Fischman, Silvia Serra, Estanislao Antelo and I have called the "committed intellectual" (see McLaren et al., 1998). As in the case of Gramsci's organic intellectual, Guevarian intellectuals do not separate civil society from its internal relations with political society, but rather these relations must be grasped within a framework of differentiated and dynamic totality—a complex framework that is historically determined. Within such a framework, the broader terrain of culture is not considered to be divorced from political economy (San Juan, 1998). Guevarian intellectuals do not call for an acephalous revolutionary force; there is a vanguard leadership, but it is a vanguard that encourages intellectual growth and development from below. Guevarian intellectuals are universalizing and class rooted in their calls for a unified front of Third World, anti-imperialist struggle and in this respect bear a further affinity with organic and committed intellectuals.

What I have attempted to underscore in rethinking critical pedagogy in the age of globalization has been made quite clear in the writings and life of Che but remains nonetheless urgent: that the struggle over education is fundamentally linked to struggles in the larger theater of social and political life. The struggle that occupies and exercises us as political activists and educational researchers should entertain global and local perspectives in terms of the way in which capitalist relations and the international division of labor are produced and reproduced. Though I am largely sympathetic to attempts to reform school practices at the level of policy, curriculum, and classroom pedagogy, such attempts need to be realized and acted upon from the overall perspectives of the struggle against capitalist social relations, undertaken in the spirit of El Che and Paulo Freire.

THE ONCE AND FUTURE REVOLUTIONARY

What does Che's pedagogy teach us about how to respond to developments in global capitalism? The first answer to this question is that Che does not see globalization as a natural phenomenon. It should not be accepted as a necessary universal occurrence. Petras writes:

> Che's description of the expansion of capitalism in terms of political and social power relations is in sharp contrast with contemporary theorists' babble about "globalization." Whereas they describe the expansion of capitalism as impersonal, universal, and irreversible because it is the product of "natural" economic processes, Che recognizes that political power is the source of world capitalist expansion and focuses on imperialism. The globalization theorists have no general theory apart from references to technological and market relations that fail to explain exploitation and inequality. (1998, p. 10)

The second answer is that Che does not see globalization or capitalism as a process that bespeaks an internal logic that is necessarily self-perpetuating. Che views 'subjectivity' as the determining factor in globalization, and the struggle against capitalism in essence becomes the struggle to create resistant subjectivities through ideology critique and counterhegemonic praxis. These subjectivities can work collectively to smash capitalist structures and prevent them from consolidating their greed-motivated practices of exploitation. Petras notes:

> The globalists describe globalization as an objective structure that spreads through its internal logic, rejecting the possibility of its transformation by some social or political agency. Che conceptualizes imperialism as a contradictory historical phenomenon whose expansion creates class and national conflicts that lead to its decline. In contrast, globalists hold a linear conception of capitalist expression that leads to its consolidation into a new world order. The most extreme of them conceive of capitalism becoming a self-perpetuating world system in which the only changes that take place are countries' rising and declining, becoming cores or peripheries. (1998, p. 10; emphasis in original)

The third answer to this question is that Che links globalization to practices of imperialism that must be eradicated through class struggle. Unlike the postmodernists, who believe that both the question and the practice of imperialism have largely been resolved, Che puts class struggle at the center of his revolutionary agenda:

> Whereas for Che the big questions of state power, imperialist domination, and class relations remain at the center of political debate, among contemporary globalists the big questions have been resolved. For them the only politics possible is negotiating the terms of surrender to imperialism. In a word, Che challenges world imperialism by organizing resistance at the micro level of the villages of Africa and Bolivia and in international forums. The globalists argue that local activities should operate in the interstices of the capitalist system. (Petras, 1998, p. 11)

While postmodern intellectuals might not feel that socialism has an adequate historical reference outside of its location in imperial Western discourse, it was clear to Marxists such as Che that socialism was not just a discursive term, but one that had concrete meaning in the lives of the toilers of the world. The *haute politique* and academic brigandism of postmodern intellectuals has diverted critical analysis from the global sweep of advanced capitalism and the imperialist exploitation of the world's laboring class. Ironically, postmodernism has become the new doxology of the Left only to impede our ability to understand the current historical conjuncture as inscribed in the uneven and unequal development of the capitalist world system. It has been transformed on occasion into the ventriloquism of the comprador elite, replacing a language of critique and hope with an epistemological necrophilia that feeds on universalist discourses of emancipation.

Che is militantly optimistic about overcoming capitalism. His perspective is unwavering and heroic. Che is not about to counsel revolutionaries to be content with reforming capitalism so that it becomes more user friendly. His redoubtable revolutionary pragmatism betokens no unraveling of loyalties to Marx and his heirs. The development of the productive force does not oblige workers to remain passive and to promote the maturing of capitalism, thus postponing the revolution until the working class is more consolidated and coherent. The central issue for Che is not to modernize the economy, reform the state, or decentralize the government, but to challenge capitalism and cut it off at its knees. As Petras opines:

> Che's political perspective evokes a Promethean image of humans struggling to change their world. Contemporary globalists evoke Schopenhauer's pessimism regarding the prospects of transforming capitalism. Today the fundamental theoretical and political conflict is precisely between Che's Promethean perspective and the globalist Schopenhauerian pessimism and/or its euphoric Panglossian counterpart, holding that this is already the "best of all possible worlds." (1998, p. 11)

For Che, exploitative class relations cannot characterize the social formation at any cost, nor can an imperialist polarization exist within the basic units of production. This is absolutely clear. The question is not which variety of capitalism one should choose, or how to accommodate the bourgeois imperative of participating in the global economy while providing for the welfare of the people largely through a reformed electoral politics. Rather, the challenge for Che is to surmount both capitalism and capital through the creation of class solidarity and anti-imperialist revolutionary struggle.

It is important to remember that Che was a postnational guerrilla who struggled on behalf of the world's peasants and workers. He owed no final allegiance to one country, only to the revolutionary struggle for freedom. In this sense he tactfully (and sometimes brazenly) demurred at the advice of Soviet leaders who

were not happy with Che's attempts to expand the revolution into other countries. Che has become the revolutionary antipode to the capitalist pinstriped
warrior in Gucci loafers who also owes no allegiance to any one country but is
committed to establishing the law of profit and to promoting the greed-driven
struggle to exploit most of humanity in the name of democracy.

Smith and Ratner reflect upon the cruel irony surrounding the death of Che
and the triumph of capitalism when they report:

> Today, there are 60 million more poor people in Latin America than when [Che]
> died. Then, the gap separating the richest 20 percent form the poorest 20 percent
> was 60 to 1. In 1990, it was 150 to 1. These poor can only wonder what their lives
> would have been like under Che's vision of the "new man" living in a society of
> abundance in a world without exploitation. (1997, p. 44)

In sum, the pedagogy of Che Guevara and the new revolutionary movements is
a form of practical Marxism that is situated in the contextual specificity of class
struggle and speaks of a universal vision of anticapitalist struggle. Petras elaborates:

> Neither Che nor the new revolutionary movements operate with an elaborate and
> intricate theoretical framework, nor are they merely improvisers of ideas in the
> course of taking action (action first, theory later). Rather they start with certain
> basic tools of class analysis and then apply them to the concrete realities of the
> countries in the course of developing social action. The "applied Marxism" thus
> has a very strong empirical content (not Utopian visionary or abstract) built on the
> concrete nature of the social groups (Indians, peasants, etc.,) with which the move-
> ments are engaged. (1997a, pp. 17–18)

THE UNCERTAIN CHALLENGE IN NO UNCERTAIN TERMS

Che was in no way a perfect human being, and an honest recognition of his
imperfections makes his accomplishments all the more impressive.[27] Che was
not given over to anodyne comments when it came to revolutionary justice. He
could be impetuous and inflexible and could exact harsh punishment on those
who did not live up to his impeccable and uncompromising standards. Yet he did
not demand conduct from others that he was not willing to put into practice himself. Richard Harris writes that

> Che was not an insane fanatic, and he did not have a pathological love of blood-
> shed and human cruelty. However, he was not a normal and contented man. If he
> had been, he would never have become a revolutionary. He was a dreamer, an
> adventurer, and a rebel against the established order of things. He was a man
> deeply incensed by the social injustices which he saw all around him, and moti-

vated by a sincere desire to rectify them. He was the perfect revolutionary—the super-idealist who insists on bringing heaven immediately to earth. Moreover, his willingness to die for his ideals indicates that he possessed far more courage and conviction than the ordinary man. (1970, p. 40)

Each of Che's many guerrilla campaigns carried the promises of the commonweal of humankind and the dreams of an entire generation of the world's dispossessed. To assume that Che was blithely unaware of this was to underestimate Che's grasp of the world-historical magnitude of his revolutionary struggle. To have Che leave a permanent presence in your thoughts meant you were baptized in discipline and responsibility to others. His chiding advice to his guerrilla followers—often grave and portentous—could chafe the ego and disassemble pride and was designed to win the dominion of critical insight and not the praise of those comrades who craved affirmation, who possessed little forbearance in the face of criticism, or who sought instant clemency for their faulty behavior. Yet even taking into account his all-too-human side, Che continues

to be a seminal figure in revolutionary circles. The Berlin Wall may have fallen, the Soviet Russian empire may have crumbled and the monolithic socialist states it sponsored may have turned themselves into desperate dollar-hungry tourist traps, but there are still many in whom the fire of revolution blazes and for whom the legend—and the life—of Che Guevara represents a shining example of what can be achieved with little more than a dream and the energy and force of will to make that dream become reality. (Sandison, 1997, p. 152)

For Che, as for Marx, the educational struggle of the proletariat carried with it the politico-ethical warrant not only to understand the world but also to change it. Refusing to resign himself to the material conditions to which the working class was condemned, and refusing to be controlled by capital or capitalism, Che forged a vision of what change was possible and where it would lead. Certainly such an understanding is reflected in the phrase "Socialism or Death!" that the communists in Cuba have added to their banners in recent years. At a recent Latin American summit in Porlamar, Venezuela, Fidel remarked: "In Cuba there was, there is, and there will be a revolution based on principles that are not for sale" (*Los Angeles Times,* November 9, 1997, A4). Frei Betto talks about the bitterness of those "who fear that utopias may become reality. That is why it is easier to talk about Che's defeat than Fidel's victory" (1997, p. 5). He concludes that "utopias, thankfully, are like Che—stronger than those who would bury them" (p. 5).

Critical pedagogy read in the light of Che Guevara offers us a serious challenge to certain trajectories of postmodern education with their enthrallment toward open endedness, their resistance to fixity, and their quest for flexible identities. It calls attention to the bourgeois outlawry, fashionable philistinism, and aristocratic ironizing that characterizes those forms of postmodern criticism that betray a civil inattention to issues of relations of production and a motivated amnesia toward history.

Few revolutionary movements have been immune to Che's influence even when they have been pockmarked by distortions of Che's thoughts, by concepts that bear little kinship to Che's original meaning, or by conceits and tropes that may not have been Che's at all. The banderole inscribed "!Hasta la Victoria Siempre!" may have become bleached by age and the million tears of heartbroken rebels but it is still proudly unfurled wherever Che's revolutionary offspring take up the struggle for liberation. Che's chiseled personality, his proverbial courage, and the fierce equilibrium of his political project that he measures against one gauge only—how it brings about the revolution—continues to rankle the swelling constituencies of reactionaries and neo-conservatives precisely because they are scandalized by the truth that Che lived on a day-to-day basis. It remains to be seen, however, whether the current contradictions of capital will create the revolutionary potential to move the popular classes toward the political struggle that Che saw as the motor of history, or toward a defence of the inevitability of capital.

The question that poses a powerful challenge for critical educators is: How can the Left protagonize a process of structural change that goes beyond state intervention to achieve internal redistribution and a tacit acceptance of the neoliberal model of free-market integration into the global economy? To answer such a question, we need to learn from the important contributions of organized left parties such as the Sandinista National Liberation Front in Nicaragua, the Workers Party in Brazil, the Farabundo Liberation Front in El Salvador, the Party of the Democratic Revolution in Mexico, the Broad Front in Uruguay, the National Solidarity Front in Argentina, the Lavalas Family Party in Haiti, the Causa-R in Venezuela, the Communist Party in Cuba, and the Communist Party in Chile. But one also has to recognize the importance lessons of grassroots social movements that operate outside of state structures and organized left parties such as Christian base communities, solidarity groups, the Landless Workers of Brazil, revolutionary groups such as Mexico's Zapatistas (Robinson, 1998), and the Intersindical in Mexico that brings together leftist organizations and community groups and independent unions into a collective oppositional front. There are also the Cocaleros in Bolivia and the Peasant Syndicate and sectors of the mining unions in Bolivia, the National Peasant Federation of Paraguay, the Colombian Revolutionary Armed Forces, the National Federation of Indian and Peasant Organizations in Ecuador, the National Indian and Peasant Coordination in Guatemala, the Democratic Peasant Alliance in El Salvador, and the Revolutionary Force in the Dominican Republic (Petras, 1998). How can these new revolutionary movements mediate between the state and the popular masses? How can these struggles waged by the Left—including those by militant trade unionists, left-wing socialists, unsectarian anarchists, de-Stalinized communists, undogmatic Trotskyists (Löwy, 1998a)—be made within a transnational space that can challenge and contest the hegemony of the transnational elite and their local counterparts? How can a transnationalism from below—from the civil society as well as from the political society—occur that seeks to challenge the power of the global elite?

These are not the most propitious times for the cultivation of Guevarian revolutionary sensibility and a proletarian internationalism, especially when political activism migrates from the fields and the mines to the chic salons of the haute bourgeoisie, who luxuriate in their ironic toping of everyday life and whose preferred revolutionary activity consists of meditating upon the limitless excess of meaning and the eternal deferral of commitment. As humankind limps toward the millennium, its "minority of the opulent" huddles in a moment of congratulatory bliss within its gated communities and high-tech boardrooms, having staved off once again attempts by the people to make their own history. Democracy—the loyal creature that it is—has protected once again the interests of the few against the needs of the many.

It is clear that if educators are to follow Che's example, there must be a concerted effort to construct a social order that is not premised upon capital. In this regard I agree with Petras when he argues that "to approach revolutionary political action today requires that one adopt the Guevarian perspective" (1998, p. 11). As Kovel warns:

> Therefore capital must go if we are to survive as a civilization and, indeed, a species; and all partial measures and reforms should be taken in the spirit of bringing about capital's downfall. Nothing could seem more daunting than this, indeed, in the current balance of forces, it seems inconceivable. Therefore the first job must be to conceive it as a possibility, and not to succumb passively to the given situation. Capital expresses no law of nature; it has been the result of choice, and there is no essential reason to assume it cannot be un-chosen. Conceiving things this way is scarcely sufficient. But it is necessary, in both a moral and a practical sense. (1997, p. 14)

Samir Amin puts the challenge before us in no uncertain terms, and in terms that I am confident Che Guevara would have appreciated: "More than ever humanity is confronted with two choices: to let itself be led by capitalism's unfolding logic to a fate of collective suicide or, on the contrary, to give birth to the enormous human possibilities carried by that world-haunting spector of communism" (1998, p. 11). In the current information age of corporate power, how is it possible to contest the systemic logic of transnational capitalism with the power of social movements? The key, according to William Robinson, is to "fuse" political and social struggles:

> The challenge for popular social movements is how to fuse political with social struggles through the development of political instruments that can extend to political society (the state) the counterhegemonic space currently being opened up in civil society through mass mobilization. The Left has espoused a commit-

ment to the autonomy of social movements, to social change from the bottom up rather than the top down, to democracy within its organizations and to non-hierarchical practices over the old verticalism. These commitments need to be demonstrated in the actual practice of renovated Left and etched into the organizational forms of a counterhegemonic project. (1998/1999, p. 126).

Che's thought and life have renewed a commitment to the industrial proletariat of classical Marxism—not in historical-teleological terms, most certainly, but in the ethico-political terms by which Che committed himself to the oppressed of the world. His commitment was such that he gave up power, glory, family, and security for the cause of the revolution. According to Eduardo Galeano, Che "never kept anything for himself, nor ever asked for anything. Living is giving oneself, he thought; and he gave himself" (cited in Markee, 1997).

Che articulates our deepest aspirations and set of human ideals, and as such he serves as a bridge to both the past and the future. Che's example of sacrifice and struggle can still assist us, this time in an anticapitalist struggle within postnational contexts and what have been described as postmodern cultures of hybrid positionalities. Taibo announces that "thirty years after his death, his myth hovers over neoliberalism's delusions of grandeur. Irreverent, a joker, stubborn, morally stubborn, unforgettable" (1997, p. 587).[28]

Sinclair writes that

History will probably treat Guevara as the Garibaldi of his age, the most admired and beloved revolutionary of his time. The impact of his ideas on socialism and guerrilla warfare may be temporary, but his influence, particularly in Latin America, must be lasting. For there has been no man with so great an ideal of unity for that divided and unlucky continent since Bolívar. (1998, p. 113)

ARMED RESPONSE

One might object to admiring a man who intentionally killed other human beings. Yet it is important to remember that Che forbade torture and was involved in executions only when the victims themselves were torturers or murderers. As Petras notes:

In Cuba's Sierra Maestra he forbade his comrades to use torture to secure information. He argued that the use of torture would defeat the purpose of the revolution, which was to abolish inhumane treatment, and would corrupt the revolutionaries practicing it. Likewise, he frequently liberated common soldiers during the revolutionary war, recognizing that they too were victims of the system; only torturers and officials involved in assassinations were summarily executed. (1998, p. 16)

Revolutionary pedagogy needs to confront the issue of armed struggle, as did Che and as do Mexico's Zapatistas. For those of us committed to critical pedagogy and revolutionary praxis, this is not an easy issue with which to grapple. Since, as Lewis Gordon notes, "oppression is the imposition of extraordinary conditions of the ordinary upon individuals in the course of their effort to live 'ordinary' lives" (1995, p. 41), revolutionary pedagogy must sometimes undertake extraordinary action. Revolutionary pedagogy does not advocate "only the gun," but neither does it rule out armed resistance entirely:

> The important issue in every struggle is the question of relevant action. One doesn't know in advance what will be most appropriate for the achievement of a people's goals, nor will one know their potentials, whether violent or not, in advance . . . struggle can take many forms, and its scariest one—armed resistance—should never be ruled out. In fact, it must be used for its impact of making the colonizer appreciate the gravity of the situation. (Gordon, 1995, p. 79)

Armed struggle should be considered as a viable option only when other strategies and tactics have been exhausted, when no other alternatives can be found. As Rubén Zamora asserts, "People turn to armed struggle when they do not see an alternative. Of all the people I have known who went down that path, none did so because they wanted it. They didn't spend time debating the ethics of it because to them it was obvious. Ending violence means resolving the situation which gives rise to it" (cited in Chomsky, 1995a, p. 2). In deliberating how to react to violence, Che demands that we raise the types of questions that Chomsky raises. Referring to the massacre of the indigenous peoples of Guatemala by the military, Chomsky asks:

> Who created the "situation that gives rise to violence"? Who refused to listen to the screams of children being brutally murdered or dying from starvation and disease, because there are pleasanter things to do? Who paid taxes quietly and unthinkingly, helping to ensure that torture, massacre, and indescribable suffering continue, while doing nothing to end these crimes—or worse, justifying and abetting them? Who joined in the torrents of self-praise that pour forth in sickening abundance, keeping eyes carefully averted from what we have actually done with our huge resources and incomparable advantages? Who are the real barbarians? (1995b, p. 27)

In his role as "supreme prosecutor" in the trial of Batistianos accused of war crimes, Che acted with unflinching determination in presiding over their executions. And yet in battle he often revealed compassion and mercy.

Within our century we have witnessed successful revolutionary struggles largely premised on a commitment to nonviolence, from Gandhi to Martin Luther King to Cesar Chavez, to cite but a few examples. Nonviolence can change the heart of the oppressor as well as the oppressed. It is the preferred measure. However, one cannot remain passive when military or paramilitary assault teams bulk large on the horizon, or when death squads enter into defenseless communities. We cannot remain idle observers when our brothers and sisters in struggle starve in the streets. We must defend against life-threatening tyranny at all costs. Armed struggle has been used successfully in Vietnam, Cuba, Nicaragua, China, and Mozambique, and in other contexts. Armed struggle may be necessary in some countries today. According to Petras:

> Che spelled out the conditions under which armed struggle was necessary: dictatorship (Batista's Cuba, Barrientos's Bolivia), imperialist invasion (Vietnam, Guatemala), colonial/neocolonial dictatorship (Congo). Some of these conditions are present in some countries of Latin America today. Colombia, for example, despite its electoral façade, is a terrorist state in which death squads and the military rule vast regions of the country, and Mexico's Partido Revolucionario Institucional is a party-state dictatorship that assassinates rivals and steals elections. Further, Che recognized the limits of capitalist democracy and questioned the willingness of the bourgeoisie to accept electoral outcomes that went against their fundamental property interests. He doubted that imperialism would respect democracies that opposed foreign investment, debt collection, and market opportunities—here anticipating the U.S. military overthrow of the democratically elected Allende regime. (1998, p. 18)

ICON AND REVOLUTIONARY ICONOCLAST

Che's life was an exercise in revolutionary armed struggle, and his death was a death in fidelity to the demand for liberation, a demand that history has shown us often involves martyrdom in the case of exceptional leaders. Whether we should consider Che a martyr remains a *quaestro disputata*.[29] Kunzle (1997) reports that upon arriving at the Rio Grande during a training mission in Bolivia, Che appealed to Inti Paredo to baptize him. Che himself baptized the young Communist Party youth leader, Loyola Guzmán, with the name "Ignacia" after the famous sixteenth-century saint. An imposing statue of Che dominates the largest square in the Cuban city of Santa Clara, a city that was captured by Che's guerrilla forces on December 31, 1958, forcing Batista to flee the country the following day. The twice-life-size statue portrays a man of the people brought to life again not as a *jesucrístico* Man of Sorrows, but as a warrior and protector of the people. Fidel writes:

> Che did not fight for glory, for material possessions, or ambition. He never fought for fame. He was a person who right from the outset, from the very first battle, was ready

to give his life; who could have been killed as just one more soldier. If he had died in the first battle, he would have left behind the memory of his person, the personality and characteristics we knew him by, and nothing more. (Castro, 1994, p. 105)

Yet it is clear that while Che was a man of history rather than a man of God, he reproduced in his life and death a central element of martyrdom: a readiness to lay down his life for the cause of love, freedom, and social justice and for teaching humanity the wages of responsibility. He died for those who died the most inhumane of deaths, who died slowly, painfully, day after day; he died for the unprotected masses who were massacred by the forces of fascism and imperialism. Through the example of Che, the crucified peoples of the world are offered hope. Harris remarks that Che "was truly a man who died for his beliefs, and because of his almost mythical self-sacrifice for his revolutionary ideals he has been the single most important 'figure of veneration' for revolutionaries and guerrilla fighters around the world" (1998, p. 30). He expands eloquently on that statement by noting that Che

continues to be the 'herald' of a Latin American revolution that is the more necessary the more impossible it seems. His spirit lives on in the minds of people all over the world, and his revolutionary myth has grown. The revolutionary ideals that he lived and died for have transcended the gap in generations and cultures, and the familiar slogan of the late 1960s and early 1970s, "¡Che Vive!" (Che lives!), appears to have as much meaning now as it did then. His revolutionary legacy continues to influence not only those of us who were inspired by him then but also those who are discovering him today. (1998, p. 31)

Freire compares Che to another famous Christian martyr and revolutionary figure, Camilo Torres:

Guevara's unmistakable style of narrating his and his comrades' experiences, of describing his contacts with the "poor, loyal" peasants in almost evangelical language, reveals this remarkable man's deep capacity for love and communication. Thence emerges the force of his ardent testimony to the work of another loving man: Camilo Torres, "the guerrilla priest." (1993, p. 152)

Freire emphasizes Che's singular ability to engage in communion with the people. Communion, after all, is the root of communism, the principle of a way of life grounded in the praxis of collective struggle: "at no stage can revolutionary action forgo communion with the people. Communion in turn elicits cooperation, which brings leaders and people to the fusion described by Guevara. This fusion can exist only if revolutionary action is really human, empathetic, loving, communicative, and humble, in order to be liberating" (Freire, 1993, p. 152).[30]

Though some may lament the violent path of the guerrilla—the sword arm of justice—or prefer to cram Che into the modal Western folk category of the fanatical 'terrorist,' Che will live on in public debate for generations to come. Che helps us to deepen our understanding of love, a love that animated his resolve to live as a revolutionary, a resolve so strong that life takes on meaning only when it is willingly sacrificed for the dignified survival of the world's vanquished and immiserated peoples.

Michael Löwy (1997) concludes: "Bullets may kill a freedom fighter, but not his ideals. These will continue to live on, provided that they take root in the minds of those generations who will resume the struggle. That is what the wretches who slaughtered Rosa Luxemburg, Leon Trotsky, Emiliano Zapata and Che Guevara discovered much to their frustration" (1997, p. 6).

Fidel embellishes on Löwy's theme when he eulogizes:

> A combatant may die, but not his ideas. What was an agent of the U.S. government doing there, where Che was wounded and held captive? Why did they believe that by killing him he would cease to exist as a combatant? Today he is not in La Higuera. Instead, he is everywhere; he is to be found wherever there is a just cause to defend. Those with a stake in eliminating him and making him disappear were incapable of understanding that he had already left an inedible mark on history; that his shining, prophetic vision would become a symbol for all the poor of this world, in their millions. Young people, children, the elderly, men and women who knew him, honest persons throughout the world, regardless of their social origin, admire him. Che is waging and winning more battles than ever. Thank you Che, for your personal history, your life, and your example. (1998, p. 30)

One of the great heralds of the Latin American revolution, Ernesto Che Guevara was an incomparable figure of the twentieth century. An indefatigable thinker, a tireless worker, a brilliant strategist of guerrilla warfare, a courageous warrior, a master storyteller, a gifted teacher, and a person of unexcelled moral character, Che embodied all the virtues of the revolutionary subject of history. Perhaps more than any revolutionary who preceded him, Che understood that nothing quite shaped history as much as class struggle, the soil of revolutionary praxis. Che's utopianism was not naive, nor was it impractical. His was a critical utopianism that became animated only when hope was conjugated with struggle, and love was brought into the compassionate orbit of tireless service to humankind. Of course, we all serve something and someone, but it was Che the visionary who helped us to become less ethnocentric and more self-critical, to take stock of who we are, to recognize the gods of capital to whom we owe our allegiance, and to evaluate, sadly, what we have become as citizens of Western democracy. It was Che more than anyone else who taught us the often painful lesson that under the cover of democracy, the U.S. ruling elite commits acts of terrorism around the world and works against the liberation of the wretched of the earth. Che dedicated himself to combating dictatorships wherever they arose and in whatever guise they took. He bequeathed to us a lesson of unimaginable importance, both in his contribution to socialist thought and in the way that he lived his life. Che continues to symbolize a principled attachment to armed revolutionary struggles as a means of resisting capitalist exploitation and enabling humanity to realize the ideals of political freedom and social justice. For those of us who are preparing the socialist struggle for the coming millennium, the ideals, the strategies, and the example of Che Guevara give us much to ponder. Che's story is not merely graven on plaster memorabilia and bookstore posters, but lives on without visible symbol, woven into the richly textured fabric of daily human struggle, wherever justice beckons.

Che's struggle encapsulated a transgressive moment and instantiated an historical restoration of the meaning of sacrifice; his struggle as a revolutionary was intraveined with hope and determination and provided him with a point of unity outside of everyday, discontinuous existence. He taught us that the breach one institutes with capitalism can only be repaired through a revolutionary love. When such a breach in the name of liberation is not initiated out of love, then liberation casts a lethal shadow over hope, under a black sun. Che's struggle was not traduced by his ego but was born of a will to re-create the world, to make perceptible to others the point at which love and violence must coexist in the service of an order of being that transcends everyday cynicism and despair without at the same time leaving the world of flesh and bone. His struggle was not burdened by the rapturous emptying out of ego and the blissful union with transcendental being; nor was it constrained by the horn-rimmed apostasy or cool rage wrapped up in black Armani suits that creeps out of the postmodern academy in its revolt against the fixed universe of normative compulsions and its commandeering of the function of the intellectual. Che's struggle was grounded in the material world. His struggle for revolutionary subjectivity was irradiated by a power that shines through the eyes and moves trippingly within the hearts of the dispossessed. Addressing the main ceremony marking the thirtieth anniversary of the death in combat of Che Guevara, during which the remains of Che and six others of Che's *foco* were interred, Fidel Castro panegyrized:

The more that abuses, selfishness, and alienation exist; the more that Indians, ethnic minorities, women, and immigrants suffer discrimination; the more that children are objects of sexual trade or forced into the work force in their hundreds of millions; the more that ignorance, unsanitary conditions, insecurity, and homelessness prevail—the more Che's deeply humanistic message will stand out.

The more that corrupt, demagogic, and hypocritical politicians exist anywhere, the more Che's example of a pure, revolutionary, and consistent human being will come through. The more cowards, opportunists, and traitors there are on the face of the earth, the more Che's personal courage and revolutionary integrity will be admired. The more that others lack the ability to fulfill their duty, the more Che's iron willpower will be admired. The more that some individuals lack the most basic self-respect, the more Che's sense of honor and dignity will be admired. The more that skeptics abound, the more Che's faith in man will be admired. The more pessimists there are, the more Che's optimism will be admired. The more vacillators there are, the more Che's audacity will be admired. The more that loafers squander the product of the labor of others, the more Che's austerity, his spirit of study and work, will be admired. (1998, pp. 29–30)

Fidel's encomiastic remarks capture the full range of Che's character that continues to provide inspiration to those who choose to revisit his life and legacy. The figure of Che both disrupts and disturbs because he was at the wrong place at the right time, banging his shins against the ruling elite. The revolution as an archetype created Che as much as Che created the revolution. Through the example of his life, Che was successful in unearthing the primordial symbol of the revolutionary, a symbol that through his unsatisfied yearning was able to rise up from the collective imagination of humanity. As such, Che was a vehicle for something larger than himself. Che gave up his government post in Cuba for a life devoid of creature comforts because his revolutionary office was something far greater. True, he was a man of iron will, but what gave him greatness was that he allowed a larger, collective dream to work through him—the dream of liberation. Che was a great teacher in that he educated the spirit of his age, he taught us to live in harmony with the symbol of revolutionary struggle.

Che was executed in a schoolhouse, and his death stands synecdochically for generations of U.S. youth who have been betrayed by public education's vassalage to finance capital and global corporatism, whose spirits have been snuffed out by everyday state fascism and the *esbirros* (henchmen) of capital in the United States, whose collective agency has been replaced by privatized space, and whose dreams find asylum only in their parks and shopping centers and their corollary regimes of consumer fantasy. The pedagogy of Che Guevara is a pedagogy of hope and struggle, and until its revolutionary ethos is felt in the classrooms of schools and universities throughout the globe, the promise of emancipation for future generations remains bleak. Emancipation and its distillate, education, are realized only with courage, critical analysis, *firmeza,* and a knowledge of history. The pedagogy of Che Guevara not only shatters the welter of illusions and delirious and paranoiac fantasies of the bourgeoisie, but also sets the stage for the kind of intellectual labor and formation of political will that can unify theory and practice in the service of social justice. It is a powerful candidate for creating revolutionary agency—an agency that helps to forge among the oppressed themselves a sense of the authority to act concretely and with specific social outcomes in mind, a praxis that connects power to meaning, thought to action, and self-empowerment to social empowerment, and that joins the confidence of controlling one's own destiny to a larger collective project of reclaiming history for the poor and the powerless.

The legacy of Che will always be multireferential and uncontained. The meaning of Che will forever be a palimpsest, populated by the meanings of past generations and in need of re-examination by present and future generations. There is no master code, no set leitmotif, no grand narrative, no runic code or hallucinated certainty that can capture the meaning of Che Guevara de la Serna. The meaning of Che is neither predetermined nor panhistorically undecidable, but it has to be read in the context of the historical struggle of suffering humanity throughout the world to break the chains of capitalist exploitation. No matter how much the language of history presses its claims to offer a clear and comprehensive understanding of Che, there will always be a surfeit of meanings spilling over into the realm of both ambiguity and possibility. As a symbol of hope, some will look to the resupinate Che of Vallegrande who died for our capital sins, others to the resurrected Che of contemporary revolutionary movements who lives again in all of those who struggle against oppression. One thing, however, remains clear. No historical figure has, through ideas and through action, done more to undo the natural bond that is presumed to exist between capitalism and freedom. He achieved this by showing us how the meaning of democracy has been worn smooth by conventional acceptance and postrevolutionary complacencies.

As María Teresa León wrote:

> He died according to his principles, close to the poorest, most forsaken America, deprived of everything but his hope. Where they assassinated him, two fountains will spring: the fountain of freedom, and the fountain of justice. The Bolivian Indians, the pariahs of the continent, will whisper his name, say that he is alive, that he knocks at their doors because he is thirsty, and they will leave a pitcher of water on their windows so Che can drink when he passes by. And pass by he will, and he will cross an entire continent, and his name will be the force of the future, the high star of the Southern Cross, that will summon America to rise and fight for its political and economic independence against all foreign domination. (as cited in Cupull and González, 1997, p. 357)

Is Che simply the product of a 'nobler' era, as Henry Butterfield Ryan (1998) suggests? Is universal liberation à la Che by a small *foco* of *guerrilleros* an oxymoronic goal in a world now obsessed with local, site-specific struggles centering around the politics of identity? Did his image resonate with the U.S. counterculture chiefly because he was perceived as a 'dedicated enemy of everything they considered wrong with the United States" (1998, p. 162)? Was he simply the archetypal 'unfettered rebel' struck by 'wanderlust' or was he "a Lord Byron of the twentieth century, an intelligent, highly literate revolutionary fighting far from home?" (1998, p. 163) Did he owe his success, as Ryan claims, to a public primed by a "renewed interest in Glastonbury's lore to say nothing of the

Che talking to youth in 1960 (Che Guevara and the Cuban Revolution,
copyright © 1987 by Pathfinder Press. Reprinted by permission.)

Camelot myth" (1998, p. 163)? Can he be faithfully portrayed as a Marxist
Gawain searching "for his own kind of grail: a Marxist justice for the world's dispossessed and downtrodden" (1998, p. 163), or guerrilla Parsifal or Lancelot in
search of a Marxist Round Table? Would a sixties counterculture obsessed with
hedonism have been turned off to Che had they really known his unyielding devotion to discipline and selfless struggle on behalf of the revolution? Does Che symbolize the Grail in each and every one of us, our ability to perceive the spectacu-
lar wonder of our own lives? Is Che the Left's best candidate for uniting diverse
peoples across continents through the 'myth of the eternal return'? The figure of
Che may in fact work amongst us through some type of archetypal mechanism
but more important is his concrete role in the struggle for socialist democracy in
world historical terms. Che did not wander about in the mantle of Merlin, teaching humankind the wonder of everyday peace and harmony. Instead, he used his
critical faculties to uncover and expose the mechanisms of oppression used by the
global ruling class to keep the poor from taking up arms against their oppressors.
He used his skill as a fighter to overturn fascist dictatorships. Of course nature,
brotherhood, sisterhood, discipline, loyalty, and character were important to Che

in the struggle to remake human agency into revolutionary agency. To say that the Jungian shadow figure for Che was capital, an enemy who took on the guise of the imperialist aggressor and who had to be defeated before a new order could prevail, does little to further our understanding of how Che's teachings and his example are still so urgent in the world today.

In the end, Che gave his life in order to put his vision into practice, and it was within a concrete politico-educative praxis that his dreams took root, where they were dialectically nourished by struggle and hope, and where they were harvested by an undaunted faith in the oppressed. Che will continue to inspire revolutionary hope and struggle as long as misery and exploitation exist. Che's spirit is reborn each day in the lives of those who toil and struggle, in the daily acts of those whose suffering goes unnoticed and whose plight is ignored. His spirit is best reflected in his "Message to the Tricontinental," where he paid tribute to guerrilla commanders dead in action[31]: "Whenever death may surprise us, let it be welcome if our battle cry has reached even one receptive ear, if another hand reaches out to take up our arms, and other men come forward to join in our funeral dirge with the rattling of machine guns and with new cries of battle and victory" (cited in Villegas, 1997, p. 55).

NOTES

1. Terán quotes Che as saying: "Take it easy, you're going to kill a man." (Taibo, 1997, p. 561). Cupull and González (1997) note that Félix Rodríguez, Bernardino Huanca, Mario Terán, and Carlos Perez Panoso—all of them trained by North American advisors—shot Che. Another account had soldiers drawing lots to see who would kill Che (Castañeda, 1997). Jorge Castañeda presents Che's last words (according to Colonel Arnaldo Saucedo Parada, head of intelligence of the Eighth Division) as follows: "I knew you were going to shoot me; I should never have been taken alive. Tell Fidel that this failure does not mean the end of the revolution, that it will triumph elsewhere. Tell Aleida to forget this, remarry and be happy, and keep the children studying. Ask the soldiers to aim well" (1997, p. 401).

2. He also had been promised a wristwatch and a trip to West Point to take part in a course that would officially qualify him as a Sergeant Major (Taibo, 1997). The promise was never honored.

3. According to Anderson (1997) and Cupull and González (1997), El Chino and Willy were executed prior to Che's death. Che was killed by a bullet that entered his thorax, causing his lungs to fill with blood. It is worth noting here that when Che was captured, his Garand rifle had been damaged by an enemy bullet and no longer worked, and he had lost the magazine of his pistol (Villegas, 1997, p. 273). Here is the description from Richard Harris's account of Che's capture:

> Captain Prado watched the guerrillas disperse and run for cover through his field glasses and ordered Sergeant Bernardino Huanca and his men to descend in pursuit. A few minutes later, Sergeant Huanca fired a burst from his submachine gun at a guerrilla moving through a thicket of thorn bushes. One bullet sent the guerrilla's black beret flying off his head, while two others tore into his leg and forced him to the

ground. The fallen guerrilla was Che. As he lay helpless the Rangers began to concentrate their fire on the area where he had fallen. But Willy (one of Moises Guevara's recruits, whom Che had begun to regard as a potential deserter) rushed to his side, and helped him out of the line of fire and up one side of the ravine. As the two scrambled upward, they ran into four Rangers who were positioning a mortar. The Rangers ordered them to surrender, but Che, supporting himself against a tree, fired his carbine in answer. The soldiers returned the fire. A few seconds later, a bullet hit the barrel of Che's carbine, rendering it useless and wounding him in the right forearm. At this point, Che reportedly raised his hands and shouted: "Stop! Don't shoot! I'm Che Guevara, and I'm worth more to you alive than dead." A few yards away, Willy threw down his rifle and also surrendered (1970, p. 131).

4. Terán had been told by CIA operative Félix Rodríguez not to shoot Che in the face but from the neck down so that his wounds would appear as if they occurred in battle (Anderson, 1997). According to Richard Harris (1970), Terán drew the shortest straw in a lottery, and that is why he was chosen to execute Che. When Che, who was propped up against one of the walls, realized why Terán had come to see him, he asked for a moment to stand up. Terán was so frightened that he began to tremble, and then ran from the schoolhouse, only to be ordered back to shoot Che without further delay by Colonel Selich and Colonel Zenteno. Terán fired a burst from his carbine without looking at Che's face.

5. It should be noted that Castañeda claims that it was Gustavo Villoldo who objected to Che's head being severed, not Rodríguez, the less senior CIA operative (1997). Che's hands later surfaced in Cuba, where they remain stored in the Palace of the Revolution. According to Sandison (1997, p. 11), a government minister in La Paz wanted a cast made of Che's hands for use as a desk ornament. It was Bolivian Interior Minister Antonio Arguedas who smuggled Che's amputated hands and a microfilmed copy of Che's diary to Cuba. The rapid disposal of Che's body was in part due to the arrival of Che's brother, Roberto Guevara, a lawyer, who arrived to claim Che's body on October 12. He was told that Che had been cremated the day before. Roberto was refused permission to view his brother's severed hands. Later, Argentine police experts were allowed to see the hands and confirmed that they were those of Ernesto Guevara de la Serna (Harris, 1970).

6. The details of Che's history are well known. Let's pause here to recount some of the central events in his life. Ernesto Guevara de la Serna was born on June 14, 1928, to an affluent bohemian family in Rosario, Argentina's third-largest city and an important trading port located on the bank of the Paraná River. The family of his mother, Celia de la Serna, can be traced to Spain, while the family of his father, Ernesto Guevara Lynch, immigrated from Ireland. At twenty-three months of age, young Ernesto was diagnosed with bronchial asthma stemming from pneumonia he had suffered as a baby. When Ernesto was five, his family moved to Alta Gracia, a highland town nineteen miles from the city of Cordoba, hoping Ernesto's asthma would improve. At twenty, Ernesto travelled on a bicycle equipped with a small motor across Argentina's twelve provinces, and upon his return took part in his family's anti-Peronist activities. At twenty-three, Che and his friend, Alberto Granados, journeyed by motorcycle throughout Latin America. Their motorcycle eventually broke down and they ended up working at odd jobs until they finally arrived at Caracas, Venezuela. Alberto stayed on to work in a leper colony while Ernesto returned to Argentina to study to become a physician. After qualifying as a doctor in 1955, Ernesto returned to the leper shelter to visit Alberto and ended up undertaking some anthropological studies in Bolivia with a young lawyer, Ricardo Rojo, where

they observed the effects of the Bolivian revolution. Ernesto and Ricardo travelled through Colombia, Ecuador, and Panama, and arrived in Guatemala in January 1954. There Che met a Peruvian refugee, Hilda Gadea (whom he eventually married), and exiles from other Latin American countries. Che watched with dismay the purge of the Arbenz regime. During the early stage of the purge, Che organized resistance. With support from the United Fruit Company, the CIA, and the U.S. State Department, Colonel Carlos Castillo Armas and his forces eventually overthrew President Jacobo Arbenz. After Arbenz's forced resignation, Ernesto escaped by train for Mexico City accompanied by Hilda and other refugees. In Mexico City he met Fidel and Raúl Castro and joined their Movimiento 26 de Julio organized to overthrow President Fulgencio Batista's regime in Cuba. While in training, Ernesto came to be know as "Che." After his famous voyage on the yacht *Granma*, as part of a force totaling eighty-two fighters, Che was wounded in the chest and neck shortly after landing in Cuba. Che and a handful of survivors of the *Granma* contingent hid from Batista's 30,000 strong force in the mountains of the Sierra Maestra. Eventually, Che was elevated to the rank of commandante, a position held by only a few select members of the guerrilla army, including Fidel, Raúl, Juan Almeida, Delio Gomez Ochoa, and Camilo Cienfuegos. In the summer of 1958, Che commanded a column of 230 men that ventured into the Escambray Hills in the central province of Las Villas, and captured the city of Santa Clara in only six weeks, outfighting and outmaneuvering government forces numbered in the thousands. During the Las Villas campaign, he met Aleida March de la Torre, a Cuban combatant whom he would marry in 1959 after divorcing, but remaining close friends with, Hilda. In Santa Clara, Che captured an armored train equipped with anti-aircraft guns, machine guns, and ammunition. After the revolution was won and Fidel Castro set up a revolutionary government, Che was granted Cuban citizenship rights and served as Chairman of the National Bank of Cuba. He trained a force of 250,000 men who defeated a counterrevolutionary force of 'gusanos' sponsored by the United States at a battle known as the Bay of Pigs or what the Cubans call Playa Girón, Bahia Cochinos. Che spoke at the United Nations Assembly, became a charismatic ambassador of the Cuban revolution throughout the world as well as a roving diplomat and economic envoy. After the Cuban Missile Crisis, Che began to favor the rural revolution of China's Mao Zedong over Soviet-style communism. In 1965 he renounced his Cuban citizenship (in order to distance Fidel from responsibility for Che's guerrilla activities outside of Cuba) and in April travelled with a small Cuban force to Africa to join the struggle of ex-Belgian Congo guerrillas against Moisé Tshombé. Che led a contingent of approximately 100 Cuban fighters to support the forces of Patrice Lumumba, founding leader of the independence movement in the former Belgian colony of the Congo. (In September, 1960, Lumumba was ousted by a U.S.–backed coup led by army chief of staff Joseph Mobutu [Mobutu Sese Seko]. Lumumba was murdered in January 1961 by imperialist-backed forces loyal to Moisé Tshombé.) Che and the Cuban contingent fought with Laurent Kabila's pro-Lumumba forces in Rwanda and the Congo but withdrew from Africa in November 1965, when Congolese resistance was shattered by the troops of the U.S.–backed Congolese regime and South African mercenary troops. Mobutu Sese Seko consolidated a dictatorship that lasted until 1997. Che went to Tanzania in order to prepare to open a guerrilla front in Bolivia. He did further planning for this new expedition in Prague and in Cuba. On September 3, 1966, he journeyed to Bolivia where he met Roberto (Coco) and Guido (Inti) Peredo, and developed a strategy to create a number of insurrectionary 'fronts' in Latin America. Che set up a base camp in southern Bolivia in the Ñancahuazú Canyon. Problems ensued with Mario Monje,

Secretary of the Bolivian Communist Party, who worked against Che's success in Bolivia. Che commanded a guerrilla force of twenty-five, while seventeen served under Joaquin's command. On July 6, Che and his column captured the town of Samaipata with such skill and poise that the Bolivian High Command began to panic. Che's success was felt all the way to the White House, where efforts by the United States to destroy Che and his fighters were redoubled. Che was eventually joined by Moises Guevara, the communist leader of Bolivia's miners who had split with Monje. On August 31, Joaquin's column was ambushed and massacred by a new Ranger battalion trained by the Green Berets. On October 8, Che's column was engaged and Che was captured. He was executed on October 9. A handful of fighters from his column escaped to Chile: three Cubans, Leonardo Nuñez Tamayo (Urbano), Dariel Alarcón Ramirez (Benigno), Harry Villegas (Pombo); and two Bolivians, Guido Peredo Leigui (Inti), and David Adriazola Veizaga (Darío).

7. With the capture of Che at 1:15 p.m. on Sunday, October 8, and his execution at midmorning the following day, the CIA closed one of its "thickest" files in the agency's global records (Smith and Ratner, 1997). In fact, when, twenty-eight years after Che's execution, Bolivian General Mario Salinas told journalist Jon Lee Anderson where Che and his *compañeros* were buried, Salinas was placed under house arrest. Such was the impact of Che's legend, already freighted with decades of rumors, secrets, and mythology.

The United States spent a great deal of effort on helping the Bolivian army capture and murder El Che. The first installment of U.S. military equipment took place on April 1, 1967, when an Air Force C-130 cargo plane arrived in Santa Cruz. Shipments included light arms, ammunition, communications equipment, and helicopters, at a total cost of about $5 million. A training camp was set up at the site of a former sugar mill, named La Esperanza, near Santa Cruz. A unit of Bolivian Rangers were trained by U.S. Green Berets fresh from battle in Vietnam (Ratner and Smith, 1997). Fifteen U.S. Green Berets under the command of Major "Pappy" Shelton were sent to train a new regiment of the Bolivian Rangers called Manchego No. 2. Most of the Green Berets had served in the Special Forces garrison in the Panama Canal Zone. Before they were deployed in the Vallegrande–La Higuera area, the Bolivian soldiers were ordered to spend hours a day shouting "I'm the toughest!" and "I'm the best!" (Harris, 1970, p. 181). Shelton was a guitar-playing major from Mississippi who sent his soldiers to do good works or "civil action" such as giving medical treatment to peasants as part of the United States counterinsurgency strategy. Shelton would play his guitar at local bars as a way of gaining intimate information from local peasants and townspeople (Ryan, 1998, p. 94). A defector in Che's guerrilla *foco* sold information on Che's whereabouts to the CIA. Washington sent counterinsurgency aid in the form of newly developed aerial infrared photographic sensors that detected human body heat (this fact, however, has been disputed). The Pentagon set up a counterinsurgency camp at La Esperanza.

8. The group acknowledged that privatization and deregulation have weakened many public institutions within Latin American society. The group called for more regulation of speculative foreign capital and for more efforts at regional integration (Rotella, 1997). Latin America's second poorest country, Nicaragua, has a $6 billion external debt, and under a neoliberal agenda its teachers are paid $70 a month. Kevin Baxter notes that it would take a teacher "two months' pay to rent a room for one night at Managua's refurbished Hotel Intercontinental" (1998, p. 22).

9. Che would have seen through the recent NATO justification of the bombing of civilian targets in Yugoslavia as an attempt to launch a cover for its own war crimes and a rationalization for its imperialist mission.

10. Che's main theoretical work, *Guerrilla Warfare*, has been compared to Sergei Nechayev's work on the catechism of the revolutionary (Hodges, 1973, p. 18). Both proclaimed that the revolutionary is a Jesuit of warfare, and like a priest "he must be ready to endure any sacrifice including his life in the effort to overcome human oppression and exploitation" (Hodges, 1973, p. 18). Che has also been compared to Bakunin who wanted to create "two, three, many Polands" and was an internationalist who directed numerous armed uprisings in Bohemia, Germany, Poland, France, and Italy (in fact, some have suggested that Bakunin is actually the author of the notorious *Catechism of the Revolutionary* attributed to Nechayev; see Hodges, 1973, p. 19). Che himself has made references to Bakunin. Che's work also resembles that of Abraham Guillén, the famous Spanish theorist of the revolution (who was born in 1913, was sentenced to death for his anti-Franco activities, and escaped to Uruguay). Guillén's work also represented serious differences from Fidelista and Guevanista insurrectionary techniques. Whereas Che believed that there were two possibilities for Latin America—a socialist revolution through armed struggle or increased dependency on the United States—Guillén sought a third alternative: a national, as distinct from a social, revolution that represented as much as 80 percent of the population (that included not only workers, peasants, and intellectuals, but also the petite bourgeoisie and the new professional middle class inclusive of bureaucratic workers, students, and segments of the Catholic clergy). According to Guillén, Che underestimated the tactical importance of the daily urban struggles of workers for higher wages and full employment. And while Che excluded the petite bourgeoisie as a potential ally of the revolution, Guillén did not. Che stressed the encirclement of the cities from the countryside; in contrast. Guillén stressed the subversion of the countryside by the cities (Hodges, 1973, p. 25).

11. In Guatemala in the early 1970s, remaining members of Fuerzas Armadas Rebeldes (the Rebel Armed Forces, or FAR) created two additional groups, Organización del Pueblo en Armas (Organization of the People in Arms, or ORPA), and the Ejército Guerrillero de los Pobres (Guerrilla Army of the Poor, or EGP) both of which were inspired by the example of Che Guevara. The groups worked primarily in the western highlands with Indians and poor ladinos (Zimmerman, 1986).

12. Richard Stahler-Sholk notes that the Partido Revolucionario Institucional (what Stahler-Sholk refers to as "oxymoronically named") is "justly famous for multilayered mechanisms of political control that rarely require overt application of massive coercion—the 'perfect dictatorship,' in the felicitous phrase of conservative Peruvian novelist Mario Vargas Llosa, with a 69-year record of apparently one-party rule" (1998, p. 65).

13. Deborah Root (1996) describes how the "Mexico of the Western imagination" (p. 51) has entrapped Western intellectuals and artists (examples include Sergei Eisenstein, Georges Bataille, and Antonin Artaud). She warns of the dangers of colonial desire and the ambivalence of exoticism, which serves as a blind spot that prevents us from acknowledging the extent to which Western culture is underwritten by violence and death. North American and European radicals looking to the Zapatistas for redemptive thrills need to caution against their own mythologizing fantasies about the "Other," which often camouflages a hidden affinity for the *conquistador*. The Zapatistas did not come into being in order to redeem Western intellectuals from the wretched histories of European and North American genocide and imperialism.

14. The Mixtec Indians are shorter and darker-skinned than many other Mexican indigenous groups and have suffered many abuses both in Mexico and as part of a new wave of immigrant labor in San Diego County, California. In the United States they are often stuck in the lowest-paying agricultural jobs.

15. These revelations flatly contradict the Cold War assessments by the U.S. State Department.

16. The Mexican government, bolstered by North American corporations and multinational elites such as International Paper, is planning to clear-cut the rain forest in Chiapas. Present-day Guevarian groups such as the Zapatistas face a complex and uncertain future.

17. Interestingly, William J. Ivey, chairman of the National Endowment of the Arts, canceled a $15,000 grant to Cinco Puntes Press in El Paso, Texas, to translate the book into English, even though the book passed through a lengthy review process. Ivey feared some of the money might be funneled to the Zapatistas. The book still made it into publication.

18. Marcos is the official spokesperson of the EZLN's military wing under the Clandestine Revolutionary Indigenous Committee-General Command and is not Indian but one of three *ladinos*, a person of mixed descent, who came to Chiapas in 1983 and who was chosen spokesperson because of his facility with Spanish, English, and French.

19. In May 1993, there were reports that the army had raided an EZLN garrison in the remote colony of Corrlachen that was equipped with underground bunkers and a scale model of the municipal headtower of Ocosingo. The report was downplayed so as not to endanger the chances of the U.S. Congress voting for NAFTA (Collier, 1994).

20. Ironically, there now exists a taxi cooperative of the civil Frente Zapatista de Liberación Nacional (FZLN) whose members drive through the streets in Volkswagen bugs (Stahler-Sholk, 1998).

21. Some Bolivian Marxists were split between the Bolivian Communist Party (which was pro-Moscow and headed by Mario Monje) and the New Bolivian Communist Party (which was pro-Peking and headed by Oscar Zamora). Others belonged to a number of factions of the Trotskyite Workers' Revolutionary Party: the Revolutionary Party of the Nationalist Left, the Party of the Revolutionary Left, and the National Revolutionary Movement (Harris, 1970). There were extreme tensions between Mario Monje and Bolivian students, who wanted to adopt armed struggle, over Che and his mission in Bolivia. Monje did not want Bolivians to be subordinate to a Cuban-directed guerrilla movement. Bolivian students wanted to support a Marxist-Leninist movement, but outside of the Bolivian Communist Party's control. They sent a representative to Cuba to talk to Che and Oscar Zamora, who supported armed struggle in Bolivia. In addition, when a modicum of cooperation between Monje and the Cubans in La Paz had been established and the Ñancahuazú farm had been selected in the southwest as a base camp, Monje received reports that Régis Debray was looking for a site to start a *foco* group with the help of Chinese communists. (This fact is significant because it demonstrates the tension among orthodox communists after the Sino-Soviet split in 1964. Monje would not accept the influence of any Chinese communist in Bolivia.) Pro-Moscow leaders, Monje and Jorge Kolle, worked to ensure the quick demise of Che and his men by selling information to the CIA and by giving the Bolivian intelligence service information about Che's presence in Bolivia (Harris, 1970). Fidel accused Monje of actively sabotaging Che's guerrilla movement in Bolivia. According to Fidel,

Monje bears a certain responsibility, but historically it would be unjust to blame the Communist Party as a whole. A number of Communists joined Che. These included the Paredo brothers, excellent people who proved to be very fine cadres. They joined and supported Che and gave him a great deal of help. And important cadres in the party leadership differed with Monje and wanted to help Che. So when responsibility is assigned, it should be given to Monje; but you cannot accuse the entire Communist Party or blame it for the way events developed. (1994, p. 123)

It was no secret that Che admired China over the Soviet Union, preferring the *Pekinistas* or *Maoístas* and not the pro-Moscow line of Monje and Kolle, and in a meeting with Mao he received extremely encouraging news that Mao would support Che's idea to export the revolution if Che would stay in Cuba to counteract the influence of the Soviet Union. Che felt that it had been a mistake for Lenin to apply the New Economic Policy in the Soviet Union but that he had been pressured by the historical circumstances at the time to do so. Had Lenin lived longer, he most likely would have corrected this situation. Of course, Che always defended autonomy, and his major preference for an ally was Latin American countries. Che was not pleased with Fidel's relationship with the Soviet Union, and members of the Central Committee of the Soviet Communist Party opposed Che's dedication to armed struggle. Che did not accept the rigid positions of the Communist Party, referring to himself as a "pragmatic revolutionary" (Harris, 1970). Because Che believed that socialist revolutions would be carried out without the official sanction or direction of the orthodox Communist Party, Che became a prime target of pro-Moscow communists in Cuba, who thought he was a fanatic. Che anticipated assistance from Peru, because a *foco* had been formed there that had offered to send men to support the Bolivian effort. Inti Paredo offered to support Che after Tania's death at the hands of the Bolivian military. (Thanks to Jayne Spencer, personal communication, for some of this information.)

22. In May 1987 one hundred and twenty unemployed miners and their families camped out in the Alto region that surrounds the La Paz international airport. In April 1989 twenty of these *relocalizados* (out of three hundred) occupying the grounds of the University of La Paz crucified themselves on the gates and flagpoles of the university, declaring: *'Nosotros no hemos venido a pedir limosna sino justicia en la nivelación de nuetras liquidaciones!* These crucifixions took place amidst the rise of the new entrepreneurial class—the *cholaje*—or the cholo bourgeoisie (Sanjinés, 1996) and the proliferation of neoliberal economic policies in Bolivia. It is to the new entrepreneurs that Bolivia looks in its struggles for social justice, a rather cruel irony that would not have been lost on Che.

23. "Che" is an Argentine slang form of familiar address, loosely translated as "mate" or "buddy," and it has been entymologically linked to a Mapuche Indian word meaning "man." It is also similar to an Andalucian expression and a Guarani Indian word for "my" (Sandison, 1997). The syllable "che" is often used as a casual speech filler or punctuation and possibly derives from the Indian word "cioe," meaning "that is." It functions much like the English "right" or "so" (Kunzle, 1997, p. 54).

24. At twenty-seven years of age, Camilo disappeared on October 28, 1959, in an old Cessna helicopter during a tour of inspection (the pilot did not want to take off from Camaguey because of inclement weather, but Camilo insisted that he had to be flown back to Havana; it is speculated that they flew out to sea to avoid the storm and crashed).

25. Although I have been roundly critical of postmodernist theory I need to be clear that I am not making a blanket condemnation. For instance, there exist precincts within cultural studies where issues of political economy are carefully addressed and investigated. I am thinking of the work of Stuart Hall, Larry Grossberg, Doug Kellner, Henry Giroux, Joe Kincheloe, and others. Yet it is undeniable that many who have joined the ranks of postmodernist scholars at most pay lip service to issues of capitalism and class

128

struggle. They are wont to theorize connections and linkages among cultural representations, social formations, and productive relations.

26.   Postmodern feminists have been critical of Marxist approaches to pedagogy. On this issue Aijaz Ahmad remarks:

> Marxism is today often accused of neglecting all kinds of "difference," of gender, race, ethnicity, nationality, culture, and so on. But it is not Marxism that recognizes no gender differences. These differences are at once abolished by capitalism, by turning women as much as men into instruments of production. These differences are also maintained through cross-class sexual exploitation, not to speak of the differential wage rate, in which women are paid less than men for the same work, or the direct appropriation of women's labor in the domestic economy. (1998, p. 22)

Patti Lather (1998) articulates a post-Marxist, postpolitical critical pedagogy, assailing an historical materialist approach as antithetical to feminism. In her joking description of herself as a "neon Marxist," she fails to notice that historical materialism has learned a great deal from feminist theory, and her critique suffers from a crippling knee-jerk response to Marxism as a patriarchal totalizing narrative. Her hidebound anti-Marxist, anti-essentialist feminism suffers from its own suffocating reductivism since, in the words of Carole A. Stabile, historical materialism, "instead of examining only one form of oppression—like sexism, racism, or homophobia—would explore the way they all function within the overarching system of class domination in determining women's and men's life choices" (Stabile, 1997, p. 142).

Joanne Naiman argues that the retreat from class among many left feminists has had deleterious consequences for the struggle for social justice. Fear of "prescriptivism" and an attempt to distance themselves from Marxist analysis have often resulted in a "straw Marxist argument" and abstract calls for unity in diversity—all of which have led toward isolated struggles for emancipation and away from collective struggles necessary for the weakening of the power of capital. Left feminists who argue that class is simply one of the many oppressions experienced by individuals within capitalism are correct in asserting that various inequalities and oppressions are dialectically interrelated. Nevertheless, a full understanding of gender equality demands "a close examination of the objective characteristics of social systems, as well as their connection to individual behavior" (Naiman, 1996, p. 16). Naiman posits that "any demands for gender equality within the current arrangement of class relations can only meet with limited success. Full gender equality will never be possible in capitalist societies" (p. 26).

For powerful developments of Marxist feminist approaches, see the work of Teresa Ebert (1996), Rosemary Hennessy (1993), and Carol A. Stabile (1997). See also McLaren (1998a).

27.   Though he suffered terrible bouts of asthma (often relieving its worst symptoms by smoking the dry leaf of the clarin plant), he rarely complained, having disciplined himself as a result of his disease from a very young age. Suffering from festering bullet wounds and poisonous cysts from mosquito bites, Che expected his fellow guerrillas to bear their own physical agonies with the same silent tenacity and fearlessness that Che himself displayed.

28.   Just pronouncing the name "Che" in public can provide a wide array of responses. At an international conference on Che at the University of California, Los Angeles, a number of us on a panel (including Maurice Zeitlin and Jorge Casteñeda)

faced an angry crowd of Cubans, one of whom accused Che of personally executing his father at La Cabaña. Recently, in Porto Alegre, Brazil, while walking through a public market with a former student, Nize Maria Campos Pellanda, Nize immediately began to reminisce about the one meeting she had with Che and Fidel while she was a teenager attending a reception for them in Rio de Janeiro. Smiling broadly, she remarked: "I held at the time this image of a revolutionary as an angry man. I was surprised at how kind Che was. There was a type of sweetness surrounding him. He was a beautiful and charming man and I was pleased when he complimented me about the size and color of my eyes. My meeting with Che, although brief, helped to form my own politics over the years." Internationally renowned social theorist, Professor Maurice Zeitlin of the University of California, Los Angeles, recalls his three-hour meeting with Che in the summer of 1961. At the time Zeitlin was gathering data for his dissertation at the University of California, Berkeley. He notes: "He spoke softly. You had to lean over to hear him. He was self-effacing. Here he was, one of the two major leaders of the revolution, and he sat and listened and talked, man to man, as an equal, with this young student radical from Berkeley" (Zeitlin, 1997, p. 13).

29. When the Pope visited Cuba in 1998, he was reported to have said that though Che was certain that he wanted to serve the poor, he will still have to face the tribunal of God one day.

30. An illuminating comparison can be made between Che's views on the 'new man' and revolutionary love and the liberation theology that originated in Latin America in the 1960s. This fulcrum period of revolutionary philosophy continues to be prominent today among progressive Catholic theologians, priests, intellectuals, and the oppressed, who also embraced many Marxist and neo-Marxist revolutionary ideals. According to Harris (1998), liberation theology established close links with revolutionary movements throughout Peru, Brazil, Nicaragua, El Salvador, and Guatemala; and, in Bolivia, it influenced a revolutionary guerrilla movement comprised of members of the Christian Democratic Party. Led by the younger brother of Inti and Coco Peredo (both of whom had served under Che in his unsuccessful mission in the Ñancahuazú region), this movement attempted to establish a base of operations around the mining town of Teoponte, north of the capital of La Paz, and many of its members were massacred by the Bolivian army.

31. In particular Che paid tribute to the Guatemalan Luis Augusto Turcios Lima, the Colombian priest Camilo Torres, the Venezuelan Fabric Ojeda, and Peruvians Guillermo Lobaton and Luis de la Puente Uceda.

REFERENCES

Adda, Jacques (1996). *La mondalisation de l'économie.* 2 vols. Paris: Decouverte.

Aguilera, Eugenio; Hernández, Ana Laura; Rodríguez, Gustavo; Devereaux, Pablo Salazar (1994). "Interview with Subcommander Marcos." Editorial Collective for Autonomedia. *Zapatistas! Documents of the New Mexican Revolution.* Brooklyn, N.Y.: Autonomedia pp. 289–309.

Ahmad, Aijaz (1998). "The *Communist Manifesto* and the Problem of Universality." *Monthly Review,* vol. 50, no. 2, pp. 12–23.

Alcarón, Ricardo (1998). "Che Continues to Instill Fear in the Oppressors." *The Militant* (special issue celebrating the homecoming of Ernesto Che Guevara's reinforcement brigade to Cuba). New York: pp. 32–36.

Amin, Samir (1998). *Spectres of Capitalism: A Critique of Current Intellectual Fashions.* New York: Monthly Review Press.

Anderson, Jon Lee (1997). *Che Guevara: A Revolutionary Life.* New York: Grove.

Ashley, David (1997). *History without a Subject.* Boulder, Colo.: Westview.

Bauman, Zygmunt (1998). *Globalization: The Human Consequences.* New York: Columbia University Press.

Baxter, Kevin (1998). "Under the Volcano: Neoliberalism Finds Nicaragua." *The Nation,* April 6, pp. 21–24.

Berger, John (1998/1999). "Against the Great Defeat of the World." *Race & Class,* vol. 40, nos. 2/3, pp. 1–4.

Betto, Frei (1997). *Latin America,* vol. 29, no. 29, p. 5.

Blant, J. M. (1989). "Colonialism and the Rise of Capitalism." *Science and Society,* vol. 53, no. 3, pp. 260–296.

Boggs, Carl (1997). "The Great Retreat: Decline of the Public Sphere in Late Twentieth Century America." *Theory and Society,* vol. 26, pp. 741–780.

Brenner, Robert (1998a). "The Looming Crisis of World Capitalism: From Neoliberalism to Depression?" *Against the Current,* vol. 77 (November–December), pp. 22–26.

———— (1998b). "The Economics of Global Turbulence." *New Left Review,* vol. 229, pp. 1–138.

Brosio, Richard A. (1997). "The Complexly Constructed Citizen-Worker: Her/His Centrality to the Struggle for Radical Democratic Politics and Education." *Journal of Thought,* fall, pp. 9–26.

Buzgalin, Aleksandr (1998). "On the Future of Socialism in Russia." *Sociological Research,* vol. 37, no. 3, pp. 76–92.

Callinicos, Alex (1990). *Against Postmodernism: A Marxist Critique.* New York: St. Martin's.

———— (1992). "Race and Class." *International Socialism,* vol. 55, pp. 3–39.

———— (1993). *Race and Class.* London: Bookmarks.

Casagrande, June (1997). "Rising Like a Phoenix." Westside Weekly, *Los Angeles Times,* November 16, pp. 1, 9.

Castañeda, Jorge G. (1997). *Compañero: The Life and Death of Che Guevara.* New York: Knopf.

Castro, Fidel (1994). *Che: A Memoir.* Melbourne, Australia: Ocean Press.

———— (1998). "Speech by Fidel Castro in the City of Santa Clara, Oct. 17, 1997." *The Militant* (special issue celebrating the homecoming of Ernesto Che Guevara's reinforcement brigade to Cuba), pp. 29–31.

Ceceña, Ana Esther; and Barreda, Andres (1998). "Chiapas and the Global Restructuring of Capital." In John Holloway and Eloina Pelaez (eds.). *Zapatista! Reinventing Revolution in Mexico.* London, and Sterling, Va.: Pluto, pp. 39–63.

Chomsky, Noam (1995a). "Time Bombs." In Elaine Katzenberger (ed.). *First World, Ha Ha Ha! The Zapatista Challenge.* San Francisco: City Lights, pp. 175–182.

———— (1995b). "Introduction." In Jennifer Harbury, *Bridge of Courage: Life Stories of the Guatemalan Campañeros and Compañeras.* Monroe, Maine: Common Courage Press, pp. 2–29.

Churchill, Ward (1995). "A North American Indigenist View." In Elaine Katzenberger (ed.). *First World, Ha, Ha, Ha! The Zapatista Challenge.* San Francisco: City Lights, pp. 211–216.

Clarke, Simon (1999). "The Labour Debate." Unpublished paper presented at *The*

Labour Debate Seminar, February 24, Centre for Comparative Labour Studies, University of Warwick, Coventry, U.K.

Cockburn, Alexander (1997). "The Long March: Che Guevara, Enduring Icon." *Los Angeles Weekly, Weekly Literary Supplement,* November 28–December 4, p. 4.

Cockcroft, James D. (1998). *Mexico's Hope: An Encounter with Politics and History.* New York: Monthly Review Press.

Cole, Mike; and Hill, Dave (1995). "Games of Despair and Rhetorics of Resistance: Postmodernism, Education and Reaction." *British Journal of Sociology of Education,* vol. 16, no. 2, pp. 165–182.

Cole, Mike; Hill, Dave; and Rikowski, Glenn (1997). "Between Postmodernism and Nowhere: The Predicament of the Postmodernist." *British Journal of Educational Studies,* vol. 45, no. 2 (June), pp. 187–200.

Collier, George A. (1994). *Basta! Land and the Zapatista Rebellion in Chiapas.* Oakland, Calif.: The Institute for Food and Development Policy.

Combe, Victoria (1999). "Church Poster Shows Jesus as Che Guevara." *Electric Telegraph,* issue 1321, January 6. www.telegraph.co.uk

Cooper, Marc (1998). "Land of Illusions." Utne Reader (July–August), pp. 65–110.

Csikszentmihalyi, Mihaly (1990). *Flow: The Psychology of Optimal Experience.* New York: HarperCollins.

"Cuba to Remain Communist, Castro Vows at Latin Summit" (1997). *Los Angeles Times,* November 9, p. A4.

Cupull, Adys; and González, Froilán (1997). *A Brave Man.* Havana, Cuba: Editorial José Martí.

Dalton, Roque (1986). *Poemas Clandestinas.* East Haven, Conn.: Curbstone Press.

Darling, Juanita (1999). "Guatemalan Regime Blamed for War Atrocities." *Los Angeles Times,* February 26, pp. A1, A16.

Di Leonardo, Micaela (1998). *Exotics at Home: Anthropologies, Others, American Modernity.* Chicago and London: University of Chicago Press.

Dirlik, Arif (1997). *The Postcolonial Aura: Third World Criticism in the Age of Global Capitalism.* Boulder, Colo.: Westview.

Dorfman, Ariel (1999). "Che Guevara." *Time Magazine,* June 14, pp. 210, 212.

Dussel, Enrique (1993). "Eurocentrism and Modernity." *Boundary* 2, vol. 20, no. 3, pp. 65–77.

Ebert, Teresa L. (1996). *Ludic Feminism and After: Postmodernity, Desire and Labor in Late Capitalism.* Ann Arbor: University of Michigan Press.

Engelhard, Philippe P. (1993). *Principes d'une critique de l'économie politique.* Paris; Arléa.

Fairchild, Charles (1997). "The Sweatshops' Media Spin Doctors." *Against the Current,* vol. 12, no. 3, pp. 10–11.

Ferraro, Joseph (1992). *Freedom and Determination in History According to Marx and Engels.* New York: Monthly Review Press.

Fineman, Mark (1997). "30 Years after His Death, Cuba Honors Its Che." *Los Angeles Times,* Sunday, October 12, pp. A1, A11, A12.

Forbes, Jack (1995). "Native Intelligence: NAFTA is Unconstitutional." In Elaine Katzenberger (ed.). *First World, Ha Ha Ha! The Zapatista Challenge.* San Francisco: City Lights, pp. 183–192.

Forster, Cindy (1999). "Recovering the Memory of the Massacres." *Against the Current,* 15, no. 2 (May–June), p. 16.

Freire, Paulo (1994) *Pedagogy of Hope: Reliving Pedagogy of the Oppressed.* New York: Continuum.

———(1993). *Pedagogy of the Oppressed.* New York: Continuum.

Freire, Paulo; and Shor, Ira (1987). *A Pedagogy for Liberation: Dialogues on Transforming Education.* New York: Bergin and Garvey.

Fuentes, Carlos (1994). "Chiapas: Latin America's First Post-Communist Rebellion." *New Perspectives Quarterly,* vol. 11, no. 2, pp. 54–58.

Gabbard, David (1995). "NAFTA, GATT, and Goals 2000: Reading the Political Culture of Post-industrial America. *Taboo,* vol. 2 (fall), pp. 184–199.

Gall, Norman (1971). "The Legacy of Che Guevara." In Bruce Mazlish, Arthur D. Kaledin, and David B. Ralston (eds). *Revolution: A Reader.* New York: Macmillan, pp. 419–440.

García de León, Antonio (1995). "Galloping into the Future." In Elaine Katzenberger (ed.). *First World, Ha, Ha, Ha! The Zapatista Challenge.* San Francisco: City Lights, pp. 211–216.

Gee, James Paul; Hull, Glynda; and Lankshear, Colin (1996). *The New Work Order.* St. Leonard's, Australia: Allen and Unwin.

Giri, Ananta Kumar (1995). "The Dialectic between Globalization and Localization: Economic Restructuring, Women, and Strategies of Cultural Reproduction." *Dialectical Anthropology,* vol. 20, no. 2, pp. 193–216.

Giroux, Henry; and McLaren, Peter (1994). *Between Boarders: Pedagogy and the Politics of Cultural Studies.* New York and London: Routledge.

González, Mike (1997). "The Resurrections of Che Guevara." *International Socialism* (December), pp. 51–80.

Gordon, Lewis R. (1995). *Fanon and the Crisis of European Man: An Essay on Philosophy and the Human Sciences.* New York and London: Routledge.

Gott, Richard (1970). *Guerilla Movements in Latin America.* London: Nelson.

Grandin, Greg; and Goldman, Francisco (1999). "Bitter Fruit for Rigoberta." *The Nation,* vol. 268, no. 5 (February 8), pp. 25–28.

Gray, Chris Hables (1997). *Postmodern War: The New Politics of Conflict.* New York: Guildford.

Green, A. (1994). "Postmodernism and State Education." *Journal of Education Policy,* vol. 9, no. 1, pp. 67–83.

Greider, William (1997). "Saving the Global Economy." *The Nation.* vol. 265, no. 20, pp. 11–16.

Grossberg, Lawrence (1999). "Speculations and Articulations of Globalization." *Polygraph* 11, pp. 11–48.

Guevara, Ernesto. (1963). *Pasajes de la guerra revolucionaria.* La Habana: Ediciones Unión/Narraciones, UNEAC.

———(1967). *Che Guevara Speaks.* New York: Pathfinder Press.

———(1971). "Socialism and Man in Cuba." In Bruce Mazlish, Arthur D. Kaledin, and David B. Ralston (eds.). *Revolution: A Reader.* New York: Macmillan, pp. 410–419.

———(1985). *Guerrilla Warfare.* Lincoln and London: University of Nebraska Press.

———(1994a). *Bolivian Diary.* New York: Pathfinder.

———(1994b). *The Motorcycle Diaries.* London: Verso.

———(1999a). "Che Guevara Speaks at First Latin American Youth Congress in 1960." *The Militant,* vol. 63, no. 29, August 30, pp. 4–7.

———(1999b). *Pasajes de la guerra revolucionaria: Congo.* Italy: Grijalbo-Mondadori.

Guillén, Abraham (1973). *Philosophy of the Urban Guerrilla: The Revolutionary Writ-*

ings of Abraham Guillen. Translated and edited by Donald C. Hodges. New York: William Morrow and Company.

Hall, Stuart (1998). "The Great Moving Nowhere Show." *Marxism Today* (November–December), pp. 9–14.

Handy, Charles (1996). "What's It All For? Reinventing Capitalism for the Next Century." *RSA Journal*, vol. 154, no. 5475, pp. 33–40.

Hansberry, Lorraine (1994). "Les Blancs." *The Collected Last Plays: Les Blancs, The Drinking Gourd, What Use Are Flowers?* Edited, with critical backgrounds by Robert Nemiroff. New York: Vintage.

Harris, Richard (1970). *Death of a Revolutionary: Che Guevara's Last Mission.* New York: Norton.

——— (1998). "Reflections on Che Guevara's Legacy." *Latin American Perspectives*, vol. 25, no. 4, issue 101, pp. 19–32.

Harvey, Neil (1998). *The Chiapas Rebellion: The Struggle for Land and Democracy.* Durham and London: Duke University Press.

Hennessy, Rosemary (1993). *Materialist Feminism and the Politics of Discourse.* New York: Routledge.

Heredia, Blanca (1997). "Prosper or Perish? Development in the Age of Global Capital." *Current History: A Journal of Contemporary World Affairs* (November), pp. 383–88.

Hill, Dave; and Cole, Mike (1995). "Marxist State Theory and State Autonomy Theory: The Case of 'Race' Education in Initial Teacher Education." *Journal of Educational Policy*, vol. 10, no. 2, pp. 221–232.

Hill, Dave; McLaren, Peter; Cole, Mike; and Rikowski, Glenn (1999). *Postmodernism in Education: The Politics of Human Resistance.* London: The Tufnel Press.

Hobsbawm, Eric (1998). "The Death of Neo-Liberalism." *Marxism Today* (November–December), pp. 4–8.

Hodges, Donald (1973). "Introduction: The Social and Political Philosophy of Abraham Guillén." In *Philosophy of the Urban Guerrilla: The Revolutionary Writings of Abraham Guillén.* Translated and edited by Donald C. Hodges. New York: William Morrow and Company, pp. 1–55.

Holloway, John (1998). "Dignity's Revolt." In John Holloway and Eloina Peláez (eds.). *Zapatista! Reinventing Revolution in Mexico.* London and Sterling, Va.: Pluto, pp. 159–198.

Holloway, John; and Peláez, Eloina (1998). "Introduction: Reinventing Revolution." In John Holloway and Eloina Peláez (eds.). *Zapatista! Reinventing Revolution in Mexico.* London and Sterling, Va.: Pluto, pp. 1–18.

Kellner, Douglas (1989). *Che Guevara.* New York: Chelsea House.

Kincheloe, Joe (1999). *How Do We Tell the Workers?* Boulder, Colo.: Westview Press.

Kincheloe, Joe; and McLaren, Peter (1994). "Rethinking Critical Theory and Qualitative Research." In Y. Lincoln and N. Denzin (eds.). *Handbook of Qualitative Research.* Thousand Oaks, Calif., and London: Sage, pp. 138–157.

Kincheloe, Joe; and Steinberg, Shirley (1997). *Changing Multiculturalism.* Buckingham and Philadelphia: Open University Press.

Kissinger, Henry (1999). *Years of Renewal.* New York: Simon and Schuster.

Kornbluh, Peter (1999). "Kissinger and Pinochet." *The Nation,* 268, no. 12, March 29, p. 5.

Kovel, Joel (1997). "The Enemy of Nature." *Monthly Review,* vol. 49, no. 6, pp. 6–14.

Kun, Josh (1999). "Multiculturalism without People of Color: An Intervewiw with Guillermo Gómez-Peña." *Aztlán*, vol. 23, no. 1, Spring, pp. 187–199.

Kunzle, David (1997). *Che Guevara: Icon, Myth, and Message.* Los Angeles: University of California Fowler Museum of Cultural History.

La Botz, Dan (1996). "Rebellion and Militarization." *Against the Current,* vol. 11, no. 5, pp. 22–26.

Lankshear, Colin; and McLaren, Peter (1993). *Critical Literacy: Politics, Praxis, and the Postmodern.* Albany: State University of New York Press.

Larrain, Jorge (1996). "Stuart Hall and the Marxist Concept of Ideology." In David Morely and Kuan-Hsing Chen (eds.). *Stuart Hall: Critical Dialogues in Cultural Studies.* London and New York: Routledge, pp. 47–70.

Lather, Patti (1998). "Critical Pedagogies and Its Complicities: A Praxis of Stuck Places." *Educational Theory,* vol. 48, no. 4, pp. 487–497.

Lazarus, Neil (1998/1999). "Charting Globalization." *Race & Class,* vol. 40, nos. 2/3, pp. 91–109.

Lorenzano, Luis (1998). "Zapatismo: Recomposition of Labor, Radical Democracy and Revolutionary Project." In John Holloway and Eloina Peláez (eds.). *Zapatista! Reinventing Revolution in Mexico.* London and Sterling, Va.: Pluto, pp. 126–158.

Loveman, Brian; and Davies, Thomas M., Jr. (1985). "Preface." In *Che Guevara, Guerrilla Warfare.* Lincoln and London: University of Nebraska Press, pp. ix–xiv.

Löwy, Michael (1973). *The Marxism of Che Guevara: Philosophy, Economics, Revolutionary Warfare.* New York and London: Monthly Review Press.

——— (1997). "Che's Revolutionary Humanism." *Monthly Review,* vol. 49, no. 5 (October), pp. 1–7.

——— (1998). "Sources and Resources of Zapatism." *Monthly Review,* vol. 49 (March), pp. 1–4.

——— (1998a). "Globalization and Internationalism: How Up-to-Date Is the *Communist Manifesto?" Monthly Review,* vol. 50, no. 6 (November), pp. 16–24.

Marable, Manning (1999). "Race and Revolution in Cuba: African-American Perspectives." *Souls* 1, no. 2, pp. 6–17.

Marcos (Subcommander) (1994). "Chiapas: The Southeast in Two Winds." *Zapatistas! Documents of the New Mexican Revolution.* Brooklyn, N.Y.: (Edited by Autonomedia Collective) Autonomedia.

Markee, Patrick (1997). "Semper Fidel." *The Nation,* vol. 266, no. 1, pp. 25–29.

Martin, Hans-Peter; and Harald, Schumann (1997). *The Global Trap: Globalization and the Assault on Democracy and Prosperity.* London and New York: Zed.

Mazlish, Bruce; Kaledin, Arthur D.; and Ralston, David, B. (eds.) (1971). *Revolution: A Reader.* New York: Macmillan.

McChesney, Robert (1997). "The Global Media Giants." *Extra!,* vol. 10, no. 6, pp. 11–18.

McLaren, Peter (1995). *Critical Pedagogy and Predatory Culture.* London and New York: Routledge.

——— (1997a). *Revolutionary Multiculturalism: Pedagogies of Dissent for the New Millennium.* Boulder, Colo.: Westview.

——— (1997b). *Life in Schools: An Introduction to Critical Pedagogy in the Foundations of Education.* New York: Longman.

——— (1998). "Revolutionary Pedagogy in Post-revolutionary Times: Rethinking the Political Economy of Critical Education." *Educational Theory,* vol. 48, no. 4, pp. 431–462.

——— (1998a). "Beyond Phallogocentrism: Critical Pedagogy and Its Capital Sins: A Response to Donna LeCourt." *Strategies,* no. 11/12, pp. 34–55.

——— (1999a). *Schooling as a Ritual Performance.* 3rd ed. Lanham, Md.: Rowman & Littlefield.

——— (1999b). "Traumatizing Capital: Pedagogy, Politics and Praxis in the Global Marketplace." In Manuel Castells, Ramon Flecha, Paulo Freire, Henry Giroux, Donaldo Macedo, and Paul Willis (eds.). *New Perspectives in Education.* Lanham, Md.: Rowman & Littlefield, pp. 1–36.

McLaren, Peter; Fischman, Gustavo; Serra, Silvia; and Antelo, Estanislao (1998). "The Specters of Gramsci: Revolutionary Praxis and the Committed Intellectual." *Journal of Thought,* vol. 33, no. 3, pp. 9–42.

McLaren, Peter; and Lankshear, Colin (1994). *Politics of Liberation: Paths from Freire.* London and New York: Routledge.

McLaren, Peter; and Leonard, Peter (1993). *Paulo Freire: A Critical Encounter.* London and New York: Routledge.

McLaren, Peter; and Leonardo, Zeus (1998). "Dead Poet's Society: Deconstructing Surveillance Pedagogy." *Studies in the Literary Imagination,* vol. 31, no. 1, pp. 127–147.

Mészáros, István (1995). *Beyond Capital: Toward a Theory of Transition.* New York: Monthly Review Press.

Miller, Marjorie (1999a). "Church Ads Send Revolutionary Message." *Los Angeles Times,* January 7, pp. A1, A7.

——— (1999b). "Image of 'Che' as Jesus Stirs Up a Storm." *Miami Herald,* January 11, pp. A1, A7.

Naiman, Joanne (1996). "Left Feminism and the Return to Class." *Monthly Review,* vol. 48, no. 2, pp. 12–28.

National Commission for Democracy in Mexico "Fact Sheet: The Zapatista Army of National Liberation," n.d. National Commission for Democracy in Mexico, 5902 Monterey Rd., #194, Los Angeles, CA 90042. www.igc.org/ncdm.

Nugent, Daniel (1997). "Northern Intellectuals and the EZLN." In Ellen Meiksins Wood and John Bellamy Foster (eds.). *In Defense of History: Marxism and the Postmodern Agenda.* New York: Monthly Review Press, pp. 163–174.

"NYSE Chief Meets Rebel in Colombia." *Los Angeles Times,* Sunday, June 27, 1999, p. A20.

Ollman, Bertell (1998). "Why Dialectics? Why Now?" *Science and Society,* vol. 62, no. 3 (fall), pp. 339–357.

Oltuski, Enrique (1998). "Guevara: 'Human Beings Are No Longer Beasts of Burden.'" *The Militant* (special issue celebrating the homecoming of Ernesto Che Guevara's reinforcement brigade to Cuba), pp. 41–45.

Oppenheimer, Andres (1996). *Bordering on Chaos: Mexico's Roller-Coaster Journey toward Prosperity.* New York: Little, Brown.

Oropesa, Jesús Montané (1994). "Preface." In *Che: A Memoir,* Fidel Castro. Melbourne: Ocean Press, pp. 11–21.

Perera, Suvendrini (1998/1999). "The Level Playing Field: Hansonism, Globalisation, Racism." *Race and Class,* vol. 40, nos. 2/3, pp. 199–208.

Perrucci, Robert; and Wysong, Earl (1999). *The New Class Society.* Lanham, Md.: Rowman & Littlefield.

Petras, James (1997a). "Latin America: Thirty Years after Che." *Monthly Review,* vol. 49, no. 5 (October), pp. 8–21.

——— (1997b). "Latin America: The Resurgence of the Left." *New Left Review,* no. 223, pp. 17–47.

———— (1998). "Che Guevara and Contemporary Revolutionary Movements." *Latin American Perspectives,* vol. 25, no. 4, issue 101 (July), pp. 9–18.

Petras, James; and Morley, Morris (1992). *Latin America in the Time of Cholera: Electoral Politics Market Economies and Permanent Crisis.* New York and London: Routledge.

Petrich, Blanche (1996). "Likely, U.S. Troops Well Accepted if Mexican Government Is in Danger." *La Jornada,* August 31.

Poynton, Peter (1997). "Mexico: Indigeneous Uprisings: Never More a Mexico without Us!" *Race and Class,* vol. 39, no. 2 (October–December), pp. 65–73.

Ratner, Michael; and Smith, Michael (1997). *Che Guevara and the FBI: The U.S. Political Police Dossier on the Latin American Revolutionary.* Melbourne and New York: Ocean Press.

Resnick, Bill (1997). "Socialism or Nike? Just Do It!" *Against the Current,* vol. 12, no. 3, pp. 12–15.

Retamar, Roberto Fernández (1989). *Caliban and Other Essays.* Translated by Edward Bakes. Minneapolis: University of Minnesota Press.

Rikowski, Glenn (1997). "Left Alone: End Time for Marxist Educational Theory?" *British Journal of Sociology of Education,* vol. 17, no. 4, pp. 415–451.

Robinson, William I. (1996). "Globalisation: Nine Theses on our Epoch." *Race & Class,* vol. 38, no. 2, pp. 13–29.

———— (1998). "Beyond Nation-State Paradigms: Globalization, Sociology, and the Challenge of Transnational Studies." *Sociological Forum* 13, no. 4, pp. 561–594.

———— (1998/1999). "Latin American and Global Capitalism." *Race and Class,* vol. 40, nos. 2/3, pp. 111–131.

Rodríguez, Felix I.; and Weisman, John (1989). *Shadow Warrior: The CIA Hero of a Hundred Unknown Battles.* New York: Simon and Shuster.

Ronfeldt, David; Arquilla, John; Fuller, Graham; and Fuller, Melissa (1998). The Zapatista "Social Netwar" in Mexico. Santa Monica, Calif.: The Rand Corporation, MR/MR-994-A.

Root, Deborah (1996). *Cannibal Culture: Art, Appreciation and the Common Fiction of Difference.* Boulder, Colo.: Westview.

Ross, John (1999a). "The Zapatistas Are Back." *Los Angeles Weekly,* vol. 21, no. 17 (March 19–25), p. 24.

———— (1999b). "Breaking Ranks." *Los Angeles Weekly,* April 16–22, p. 170.

Rotella, Sebastian (1997). "In Latin America, Politics Become Eclectic." *Los Angeles Times,* December 19, 1997, p. A5.

Ruggiero, Greg (1998) "Introduction: The Word and the Silence." In Greg Ruggiero and Stuart Sahulka (eds.) *The Zapatistas: Zapatista Encuentro—Documents from the 1996 Encounter for Humanity and Against Neoliberalism.* New York: Seven Stories, pp. 6–10.

Ryan, Henry Butterfield (1998). *The Fall of Che Guevara: A Story of Soldiers, Spies, and Diplomats.* New York and Oxford: Oxford University Press.

Said, Edward W. (1996). *Representations of the Intellectual.* New York: Vintage.

Salmón, Gary Prado (1990). *The Defeat of Che Guevara: Military Response to Guerrilla Challenge in Bolivia.* Translated by John Deredita. New York and London: Praeger.

Sandison, David (1997). *Che Guevera.* New York: St. Martin's Griffin and Reed International Books.

Santamaría Gómez, Arturo (1994). "Zapatistas Deliver a Message from Deep Mexico." Z *Magazine*, vol. 7, no. 3, pp. 32–33.

Sanjinés, Javier (1986). "Beyond Testimonial Discourse: New Popular Trends in Bolivia." In Georg M. Gugelberger (ed.). *The Real Thing: Testimonial Discourse and Latin America*. Durham and London: Duke University Press, pp. 254–265.

San Juan, Jr., E. (1996). *Mediations: From a Filipino Perspective*. Pasig City, Philippines: Anvil.

——— (1998a). *Beyond Postcolonialism*. New York: St. Martin's.

——— (1998b). "The Limits of Postcolonial Criticism: The Discourse of Edward Said." *Against the Current*, vol. 77 (November–December), pp. 28–32.

——— (forthcoming). "Postcolonialism and Uneven Development." *Strategies*.

Schou, Nick (1998). "Mexico's Military Rolls Out." *Los Angeles Weekly*, vol. 20, no. 30 (June 19–25), pp. 22–23.

Sekine, Thomas T. (1999). "The Dialectic of Capital: An Unoist Interpretation." *Science & Society*, vol. 62, no. 3, Fall, pp. 434–445.

Silverstein, Ken (1995). "Wall Street Declares War on Zapatistas." *Covert Action Quarterly*, no. 52 (spring), pp. 42–45.

Sinay, Sergio (1997). *Che for Beginners*. New York: Writers and Readers Publishing.

Sinclair, Andrew (1998). *Che Guevara*. Gloucestershire: Sutton.

Sivanandan, A. (1998/1999). "Globalism and the Left." *Race & Class*, vol. 40, nos. 2/3, pp. 5–17.

Sleeter, Christine; and McLaren, Peter (eds.) (1995). *Multicultural Education and Critical Pedagogy*. Albany: State University of New York Press.

Smith, Michael; and Ratner, Michael (1997). "The Hidden History: Che Guevara and the CIA." *Covert Action Quarterly*, no. 62 (fall), pp. 38–44.

Smith, Paul (1988). *Discerning the Subject*. Minneapolis: University of Minnesota Press.

Soja, Edward (1997). *Thirdspace*. Cambridge, Mass.: Blackwell.

Spencer, Jayne, written communication to a draft of an essay on Che, 1999.

Spring, Joel (1998). *Education and the Rise of the Global Economy*. Mahwah: N.J.: Lawrence Erlbaum.

Stabile, Carole A. (1997). "Postmodernism, Feminism, and Marx: Notes from the Abyss." In Ellen Meiksins Wood and John Bellamy Foster (eds.). *In Defense of History*. New York: Monthly Review Press, pp. 134–148.

Stahler-Sholk, Richard (1998). "Massacre in Chiapas." *Latin American Perspectives*, vol. 25, no. 4, issue 101, pp. 63–75.

Stoll, David (1999). *Rigoberta Menchú and the Story of all Poor Guatemalans*. Boulder, Colo.: Westview.

Subcomandante Insurgente Marcos (1999). *The Story of Colors/La Historia de los Colores: A Bilingual Folktale from the Jungles of Chiapas*. Translated by Anne Bar Din. El Paso: Cinco Puntos Press.

Tablada, Carlos (1991). "The Creativity of Che's Economic Thought." *New International*, no. 8, pp. 67–96.

Taibo, Pancho Ignacio (1997). *Guevara: Also Known as Che*. Translated by Martin Michael Roberts. New York: St. Martin's.

Teeple, Gary (1995). *Globalization and the Decline of Social Reform*. Atlantic Highlands, N.J.: Humanities Press.

Terrero, Ariel (1998). "Interview with Orlando Borrego." *The Militant* (special issue celebrating the homecoming of Ernesto Che Guevara's reinforcement brigade to Cuba), pp. 37–40.

Tonelson, Alan (1997). "Globalization: The Great American Non-debate." *Current History: A Journal of Contemporary World Affairs* (November), pp. 353–359.

Villegas, Harry (1997). *Pombo: A Man of Che's Guerrilla.* New York and London: Pathfinder.

Viviana (1997). "U.S. Paper Companies Conspire to Squash Zapatistas." EARTH FIRST! (Summer).

Wainwright, Hilary (1994). *Arguments for a New Left: Answering the Free Market Right.* London and Cambridge, Mass.: Blackwell.

Wallach, Lori; and Storza, Michelle (1999). "NAFTA at 5." *The Nation,* vol. 268, no. 3, (January 25), p. 7.

Waters, Mary-Alice (1998). *Che Guevara and the Imperialist Reality.* New York: Pathfinder.

Waters, Mary-Alice; and Madrid, Luis (1997). "Che's Example Opened Up for Us a Broader Concept of Internationalism." *At the Side of Che Guevara: Interviews with Harry Villegas (Pombo).* New York: Pathfinder.

Weinberg, Bill (1998). "Mexico's Dirty Little War: US Implicated in Chiapas Massacre." *High Times* (July), no. 275, pp. 46–50.

Wenger, Morton (1991). "Decoding Postmodernism: The Despair of the Intellectuals and the Twilight of the Future." *Social Science Journal,* vol. 28, no. 3, pp. 391–407.

———— (1993/1994). "Idealism Redux: The Class-Historical Truth of Postmodernism." *Critical Sociology,* vol. 20, no. 1, pp. 53–78.

Wood, Ellen Meiksins (1995). *Democracy against Capitalism; Renewing Historical Materialism.* Cambridge: Cambridge University Press.

Young, Iris Marion (1990). *Justice and the Politics of Difference.* Princeton, N.J.: Princeton University Press.

Zeitlin, Maurice (1997). "Che and Me." In David Kunzle (ed.) *Che Guevara: Icon, Myth, and Message.* Los Angeles: UCLA Fowler Museum of Natural History.

Zimmerman, Marc (1986). "*Testimonio* in Guatemala: Payeras, Rigoberta, and Beyond." In George M. Gugelberger (ed.). *The Real Thing: Testimonial Discourse in Latin America.* Durham, N.C., and London: Duke University Press, pp. 101–129.

PART TWO

THE MAN WITH THE GRAY BEARD

What I have been proposing from my political convictions, my philosophical convictions, is a profound respect for the total autonomy of the educator. What I have been proposing is a profound respect for the cultural identity of students—a cultural identity that implies respect for the language of the other, the color of the other, the gender of the other, the class of the other, the sexual orientation of the other, the intellectual capacity of the other; that implies the ability to stimulate the creativity of the other. But these things take place in a social and historical context and not in pure air. These things take place in history and I, Paulo Freire, am not the owner of history.

—Paulo Freire, *"A Response"*

Paulo Freire at the Pedagogy of the Oppressed Conference,
Omaha, Nebraska, March 22, 1996 (courtesy of Peter McLaren)

Paulo Freire was one of the first internationally recognized educational thinkers who fully appreciated the relationship among education, politics, imperialism, and liberation. In fact, he clearly understood that they unavoidably abut to one another as well as flash off each other. He was also acutely aware that under the name of the 'free market,' democracy had retracted its commitment to social justice, and along with that retraction had imperiled its fundamental commitment to education.

With a "calm semblance, long gray hair and beard, medium height, slender body, eyes the color of honey" and a "strong, compassionate, profound communicating gaze and his always expressive gestures" (A. Freire and Macedo, 1998, p. 42), Paulo Freire appeared the archetypical philosopher and *eminence grise* of academic letters—sensitive, erudite, and exuding a quaint other-worldliness. Generally considered the inaugural protagonist of what has come to be known throughout education and the humanities as 'critical pedagogy,' Freire was able to effectively recast on a global basis the link between education and a radical politics of historical struggle, a mission that he expanded into a lifetime project. Long before his fatal heart attack on May 2, 1997, at the Albert Einstein Hospital in São Paulo, Freire had acquired a mythic stature among progressive educators, social workers, and theologians—as well as scholars and researchers from numerous disciplinary traditions—for fomenting interest in and dedication to the ways that education can serve as a vehicle for social and economic transformation. What is now termed 'a politics of liberation' is a topic of pivotal significance among educational activists throughout the globe, and one to which Freire has made important and pioneering contributions.

Paulo Reglus Neves Freire entered the world at 724 Enchantment Road on September 19th, 1921, in Recife, Pernambuco State, in the Northeast of Brazil (seven years before Che). The son of Joaquim Temístocles Freire and Edeltrudes Neves Freire, young Paulo grew up in a harmonious family atmosphere with three other siblings. Freire's mother (who died in 1978 and with whom Freire kept in close contact, even during his exile) was unarguably the most important figure in his emotional and intellectual development, but both parents can be credited with initiating him to the written word by reading to him storybooks and, in the case of his father, singing him to sleep at bedtime. As a child, Paulo was eager to communicate and first started to write about his life experiences with twigs from mango trees (A. Freire and Macedo, 1998). He attended the elementary school run by Eunice Vasconcelos, who over the years was to instill in Paulo a passion for the Portuguese language. In 1931, when Paulo was ten, his family moved to Jaboatâo, at the outskirts of the Pernambucan capital, eleven miles from Recife. The move was the result of the world economic crisis of 1929, which had greatly impacted the Northeast of Brazil, and Paulo's family did not enjoy the perquisites of belonging to an affluent family. Here, at thirteen, Paulo experienced his father's death. After school and on weekends he would spend time with children and teenagers from poor rural families and with children of laborers who lived in the hills or near the canals (Gadotti, 1994), sometimes playing games of pick-up soccer. Paulo finished his elementary school education and went through his first year of secondary schooling at the July 14 school, an extension of the Francês Chateaubriand School, where the final examinations took place. After his first year of secondary schooling, Paulo entered the Colégio Oswaldo Cruz in Recife, under the tutelage of mathematics professor, Luiz Soares. Aluízio Pessoa de Araújo, the father of Paulo's second wife, Ana Maria Araújo Freire, owned the Colégio Oswaldo Cruz and accepted Paulo as a scholarship student since Paulo's mother was not able to continue paying tuition. Aluízio played an important role in the education of the young Freire, channeling his interest in the direction of Christian humanism and nurturing his democratic spirit (A. Freire and Macedo, 1998). While still a high school student, Freire became a teacher of Portuguese (a fact that, coupled with his scrawny build, exempted him from serving in the Brazilian Expeditionary Force in Italy during World War II). While at the Colégio Oswaldo Cruz, Freire completed seven years of secondary school, including prelaw programs, and was accepted in 1943 into the secular School of Law of Recife, from which he graduated in 1947. By 1944, at the age of twenty-three, he had married elementary school teacher Elza Maria Costa Oliveira, five years his senior (whom Freire lovingly referred to as his "sweetheart"), who nurtured Paulo's early interest in literacy. Together they had five children: Maria Madalena, Maria Cristina, Maria de Fátima, Joaquim, and Lutgardes. The three daughters followed in their parents' footsteps and became educators. Following Eliza's death in 1986, Freire married in 1988 a graduate student and childhood friend, Ana Maria A. Hasche, whom Paulo endearingly called "Nita."[1] Nita became Paulo's loving life-force and he remained devoted to her until his death.

A courageous scholar, social activist, and cultural worker who was admired for his integrity and humility, Freire became internationally renowned for developing an anti-imperialist and anticapitalist literacy praxis employed by progressive educators throughout the world.[2]

After studying at the School of Law of Recife (1943–1947) and gaining some teaching experience in several educational institutions, Freire became a director at the Division of Education and Culture within the SESI (Social Service of Industry)—an agency created by the national Confederation of Industry. On August 1, 1947, he took a position as Assistant at the SESI–Pernambuco in the Division of Public Relations, Education, and Culture. That same year he received his law degree and was promoted to the position of Director of the Division of Education and Culture.[3] From December 1954 until October 1956, he held the post of Superintendent of the Division of Education and Culture. From 1956 until 1961, Freire traveled through a number of Brazilian states as a consultant for the Division of Research and Planning of the SESI.[4] Under the leadership of Raquel Castro, Freire helped to found the Capibaribe Institute, renowned to this day for its high-level scientific, ethical, and moral education (A. Freire and Macedo, 1998). In 1956, Freire was appointed a member of Recife's Educational Consulting Board, and in 1958 he was made Director of the Division of Culture and Recreation of the City of Recife's Department of Archives and Culture. During this time he had his first teaching experience in higher education as Professor of History and Philosophy of Education at the School of Fine Arts in Recife.

Paulo Freire completed his doctorate in 1959 with a thesis titled "Present-day Education in Brazil"; as a result he became a tenured professor (level 17) at the University of Recife's Faculty of Philosophy, Sciences, and Letters. In 1961 he was granted the certificate of "Livre-Docente" in History and Philosophy of Education at the Fine Arts School. That same year, he was invited by the Mayor of Recife to develop a literacy program for that city. As the newly appointed Director of the Extension Service of the University of Recife, Freire began to work with new methods in the teaching of adult literacy. His approach to literacy was greatly influenced by his activities in the Catholic Action Movement and by Catholic collectivism, Communidades Eclesiales de Base (Basic Church Communities), and by a close association with the Bishop of Recife, Dom Helder Camara, whom Pope John Paul II called a "brother of the poor" but whom Brazil's military dictators called a "subversive communist." ("If I may give food to the poor, they call me a saint," Camera once remarked. "If I ask why the poor do not have food, they call me a communist.") Freire was also one of the "Pioneer Council Members" of Pernambuco's State Council on Education, chosen by Governor Miguel Arraes. A founding member of the Movement for Popular Culture in Recife, Freire went on to influence the "bare feet can also learn how to read" campaign, which was supported by the popular administration of Mayor Djalma Maranhão.

In 1962, the town of Angicos, in Rio Grande do Norte, was witness to a remarkable event: Freire's literacy program helped 300 rural farm workers learn to read and write in forty-five days. By living communally with groups of peasants and workers, the literacy worker was able to help campesinos identify generative words according to their phonetic value, syllabic length, and social meaning and relevance to the workers. These words represented the everyday reality of the workers. Each word was associated with issues related to existential questions about life and the social factors that determined the economic conditions of everyday existence. Themes were then generated from these words (words such as 'wages' or 'government'), which were then codified and decodified by groups of workers and teachers who participated in groups known as 'cultural circles.' Reading and writing thus became grounded in the lived experiences of peasants and workers and resulted in a process of ideological struggle and revolutionary praxis—or what was to become famously known as Freirean *conscientização*. Workers and peasants were able to transform their 'culture of silence' and become collective agents of social and political change.[5] The success of this program—ironically supported by the U.S. Agency for International Development—marked the beginning of what was to become a legendary approach in literacy.

In 1963, Freire was invited by President João Goulart and by the recently inaugurated Minister of Education, Paulo de Tarso Santos, to rethink adult literacy on a national basis and to work with the National Literacy Program, the Movement for Basic Education. In 1964, 24,000 cultural circles were designed to assist two million illiterate workers. However, all of that was abruptly interrupted by a military coup (which was aided by the CIA as well as the AFL-CIO) that overthrew Goulart's democratically elected government. On March 31, 1964, thirteen of the fifteen members of the Council on Education renounced their terms. Freire was in Brasilia at the time with the National Literacy Program project and was dismissed from his position after Governor Miguel Arraes was arrested.

Freire was arrested and imprisoned by the military government for seventy days for his work in the National Literacy Program. Sensing an impeding threat to his life, Freire went into self-imposed exile upon his release from prison. According to one of Freire's biographers, Moacir Gadotti (also one of the founding members of the Partido dos Trabalhadores—Workers Party—and Freire's Chief of Cabinet in the administration of São Paulo's Municipal Secretariat of Education), the Brazilian military considered Freire to be "an international subversive," "a traitor to Christ and the Brazilian people," and accused him of developing a teaching method "similar to that of Stalin, Hitler, Perón, and Mussolini" (1994, pp. 34–35). He was furthermore accused of trying to turn Brazil into a "Bolshevik country" (Gadotti, 1994).

Moacir Gaddotti writes that Freire's imprisonment,

> which lasted seventy days, was sufficiently traumatic to teach him a number of things. In prison, the relationship between education and politics became even clearer to him and confirmed his thesis that social change would have to come from the masses and not from isolated individuals. On the subject of prison, he said that it was possible to learn and educate in the most diverse conditions: as a prisoner, he had something to learn from the experience, even though he might not like it.
>
> After his period in prison, Paulo Freire thought that in such a period of extremes and irrationality, it would be very risky to stay in the country. He said: "I have no vocation to be a hero. I even think that revolutions are made up of people that are living and one or two that are dead, not because the heroes wanted them." (1994, p. 37)

Of Freire's exile, Ana Maria Araújo Freire and Donaldo Macedo comment:

> Arrested twice in Recife, Paulo Freire was forced to come to Rio de Janeiro to testify in a military-police inquiry. Feeling threatened, he sought exile at the Bolivian

embassy and departed to that country in September, 1964. He was forty-three years old, and he carried with him the "sin" of having loved his people too much and having worked hard to politicize them so they would suffer less and participate in the country's decisions. He wanted to contribute to the building of consciousness on the part of the oppressed and to overcoming their centuries-old interdiction from society. (1998, pp. 20–21)

Freire's sixteen years of exile were tumultuous and productive:

- a short stay in Bolivia, where his health was affected by the high altitude of La Paz—not to mention the dangerous climate created by the military coup that took place shortly after his arrival;
- a five-year stay in Chile (November 1964 to April 1969) as an aide to the Instituto de Desarollo Agropecuario and to Chile's Ministry of Education, and as a UNESCO consultant with Chile's Instituto de Capacitación en Reforma Agraria;
- an appointment from April 1969 to February 1970 at Harvard University's Center of Educational and Developmental Studies [associated with the Center for Studies in Development and Social Change];
- a move to Geneva, Switzerland, in 1970 as consultant to the Office of Education of the World Council of Churches, where he developed literacy programs for Tanzania and Guinea-Bissau that focused on the re-Africanization of their countries;
- the development of literacy programs in some postrevolutionary former Portuguese colonies such as Angola and Mozambique[6];
- assisting the governments of Peru and Nicaragua with their literacy campaigns;
- the establishment of the Institute of Cultural Action in Geneva in 1971;
- a brief return to Chile after Salvador Allende was assassinated in 1973, working in the area of agrarian reform and provoking General Pinochet to declare Freire a subversive; as Maltese scholar Peter Mayo observes, "The power of the Brazilian educator's spirit was recognized, a long time ago, by none other than General Augusto Pinochet who, on seizing power through the 1973 coup, years after Freire had left Chile, paid the Brazilian the supreme compliment, declaring him a 'persona non grata'" (1997, p. 368).
- participation in literacy work in São Tomé and Príncipe from 1975 to 1979;
- a brief visit to Brazil under political amnesty in 1979; and a final return to Brazil in 1980 to teach at the Pontifícia Universidade Católica de São Paulo and the Universidade de Campinas in São Paulo state. Freire would go on to undertake literacy work in Australia, Italy, Angola, the Fiji Islands, and numerous other countries throughout the world.

Of his work in the World Council of Churches, Ana Maria Araújo Freire and Donaldo Macedo write:

> At the council's service, he "trod a path," as he likes to say, throughout Africa, Asia, Australia, and America, except for Brazil—for his sadness. In particular, he helped those countries that had conquered their political independence to systematize their plans in education. In Cape Verde, Angola, and Guinea-Bissau, he became known for that work, when those countries struggled in the sixties to free themselves of the remaining traces of the oppressor who had turned many of the black African bodies into white Portuguese heads overseas. Those peoples wanted and needed to free themselves from their "oppression-hosting conscience" to become citizens of their countries and of the world. (1998, p. 21)

Freire felt that the World Council of Churches was an important organization, particularly due to its involvement in African liberation movements. He moved to Geneva, the Council headquarters, in 1970.

Prior to his move to Geneva, he published the three major works for which he is best known: *Education as a Practice of Freedom,* which analyzed the role that education can play within the context of economic development and the struggle against colonialism; *Cultural Action for Freedom,* which explores the neocolonial relations between so-called First World and Third World countries, and where Freire contrasts theory to verbalism and action to activism; and *Pedagogy of the Oppressed,* which analyzes the dialectical relationship between domination and oppression in the context of the historical development of capitalist education.

Of considerable influence in Freire's life was his involvement in São Tomé and Príncipe as a militant educator, developing a literacy program that, by four years after it was initiated, achieved a success rate of 55 percent of all those who were enrolled and 72 percent of all those who finished the course (Gadotti, 1994).

Freire was a great admirer of Amilcar Cabral, a revolutionary leader who helped to liberate Guinea-Bissau from Portuguese domination in the 1960s.[7] Whereas Frantz Fanon had urged immediate armed intervention in Guinea-Bissau, Cabral had understood that the political education of the peasantry had to be achieved first or else the revolution would be short-lived. Cabral always stressed that the political struggle was paramount over the military struggle, and that the guerrillas were to assume the role of the servants of the people. Furthermore, he stressed education not only as a means to train doctors and nurses in order to lower the infant mortality rate, but also as a way to provide young people with a contextual understanding of their relationship to Portuguese colonialism and Western imperialism (Cohen, 1998). Cabral's theory of national liberation underscored a return to a history of the people through the recovery of specific African forms of subjectivity, a recovery staged as a popular cultural renaissance. According to E. San Juan (forthcoming), the chief pedagogical agency for Cabral was the party. The party wielded the weapon of theory and was the organized political expression of an emerging national popular culture. The Nation becomes, for Cabral, a form of revolutionary, collective subjectivity. Historical self-determination for the nation is based on its right to control the process of development of national productive forces.

In June 1979, the Brazilian government released the names of eight Brazilians who would continue to be denied a Brazilian passport; Freire's name was among them. However, with the help of Monsignor Paulo Evaristo Arns, Archbishop of São Paulo, Freire was able to return to Brazil in August 1979. After visiting Sao Paulo, Rio de Janeiro, and Recife, Freire accepted a teaching position at the Pontifícia Universidade Católica de São Paulo.[8]

In São Paulo, Freire had witnessed growing resistance to the military government, such as the 1979 strike by the metalworkers of São Bernardo (an industrial region of São Paulo); he joined the socialist democratic party, Partido dos Trabalhadores (Workers Party, or PT), which was formed in 1980. When the Workers Party won the 1989 municipal elections in São Paulo, Mayor Luiza Erundina appointed Freire Municipal Secretary of Education for São Paulo, a position he held until 1991. During his tenure as Secretary, Freire continued his radical agenda of literacy reform for the people of that city. Under Freire's guidance, the Secretariat of Education set up a literacy program for young people called MOVA-SP (Literacy Movement in the City of São Paulo) that contributed to strengthening popular movements and creating alliances between civil society and the state. Freire also created the Movimento de Reorientacão Curricular (Movement to Reorient the Curriculum), which attempted to create collective work through a decentralization of power, the fostering of school autonomy, and the reconstruction of the curriculum around critical community issues.[9]

Freire's work has a categorical focus—it is distinctly addressed to educators and literacy workers—but it is never confined just to that category, as it continues to be vigorously engaged by scholars in numerous disciplines: literary theory, composition, philosophy, ethnography, political science, sociology, teacher education, theology, and on and on. He has given the word "educator" a new meaning, broadly inflecting the term so that it arches across numerous disciplinary fields, embracing multiple perspectives: border intellectual, social activist, critical researcher, moral agent, insurgent Catholic worker, radical philosopher, political revolutionary. To a greater extent than any other educator of this century, Freire was able to develop a pedagogy of resistance to oppression. More than this, he lived what he taught. His life is the story of courage, hardship, perseverance, and an unyielding belief in the power of love.

FREIRE'S PHILOSOPHY OF EDUCATION:
A PEDAGOGICAL OPTION FOR THE POOR

Freire's life reveals the imprints of a life lived within the margins of power and prestige. Because his work centered on the issues of social and political change, Freire has always been considered controversial, especially by educational establishments in Europe and North America. Although he is recognized as one of the most significant philosophers of liberation and a pioneer in critical literacy and critical pedagogy, his work continues to be taken up mostly by educators working outside of the educational mainstream. The marginal status of Freire's followers is undoubtedly due to the fact that Freire firmly believed that educational change must be accompanied by significant transformations in the social and political structure in which education takes place. North America's leading Freirean educators—Donaldo Macedo, Henry Giroux, Ira Shor, Antonia Darder, Stanley Aronowitz, and Pepi Leistyana—are credited with making pathbreaking political interventions in numerous educational arenas but because their work, like Freire's, is highly controversial, their paths within academia have at times been rocky and mine-sown. Most educators find critical pedagogy politically untenable or hopelessly utopian. It is certainly a position that threatens the interests of those who are already served well by the dominant culture. This point can be vividly illustrated by the way in which Freire's work was taken up by the Harvard Graduate School of Education, only to be dropped precipitously following his death. Donaldo Macedo elaborates:

> On May 2, 1997, Paulo Freire died of heart failure. His death unveiled the hidden ideology that informs the conservative corporate empirical focus that shapes the Harvard Graduate School of Education, which reasserted itself when the school canceled the seminar on liberation pedagogy. Rather than affirming Freire's ideas and allowing the seminar to continue, Freire's death suggests that the Harvard Graduate School of Education's interest in his ideas and work was purely a matter of public relations. In other words, it is acceptable to embrace Freire as an icon for one semester to legitimize the Harvard Graduate School of Education's claim of openness, diversity, and democracy, but it is not acceptable to allow his ideas to become part of the general course offerings. Even though Freire has been considered the most important educator in the last half of this century, the Harvard Graduate School of Education does not offer a single course designed specifically to study Freire's theories and ideas. In recent years, a couple of junior, untenured professors who are highly influenced by Freire's ideas have included his work as a part of their reading lists for their course. However, one cannot comfortably study Freire as a part of the general course offerings. The irony is that while the Harvard Graduate School of Education is lukewarm toward Freire's theories and ideas, the Harvard Divinity School offers a course entitled "Education and Liberation" where Freire's work is the central focus. (Macedo, 1998, p. xiv)

Freire would have been the first to recognize that his work was often appropriated as a duplicitous, public relations move on the part of educational administrations. Clearly, it was the administration's way of responding—ingenuously—to the growing popularity of Freire among socially conscious students, especially students of color (Leistyna, 1999). Progressive radical students are eager to engage Freire's work because they see in Freire a way to tap their deepest yearnings for making a difference in the world through their vocations as teachers, social workers, and community activists—a difference that goes beyond mere cosmetic dimensions. Freire was respected as much by the most theoretical of progressive students and professors as he was by the most grass roots of students and social activists. Like Che, he had the reputation of being somebody who 'walked the walk.'

Freire believed that the ongoing production of the social world through dialogue occurs in a complex, dialectical interplay with the structural features of society such as its social relations of production, its cultural formations, and its institutional arrangements. As Freire so compellingly proclaimed in his *sui generis* monumental tome, *Pedagogy of the Oppressed,* more and more of the world's peoples are no longer feasting at the grand banquet of capitalism; they are spending ever more of their time under the table groveling and scrounging with the dogs, searching for scraps at the feet of the ruling elite. According to Freire, the capitalist social structure cannot be ignored when attempting to fathom the complex interplay among meaning making, history making, and the process of becoming literate. Throughout the process of becoming literate—a conjunctural process that Freire referred to as 'praxis'—meaning circulates, is acted upon, and is revised, resulting in political interpretation, sense making, and will formation. The outcome of this intersubjectivity (produced primarily through the codification and decodification process) is never fully predetermined:

> The codification/decodification process also represents an attempt at praxis, the means whereby learners are encouraged to re-experience the ordinary extraordinarily, through a process of critical distancing. . . . Most important of all, though, learners can be challenged to engage in praxis by a teacher whose pedagogy is directive (Freire is very explicit on this issue), in the sense that it is a pedagogy born out of a political choice the teacher makes, given that, for Freire, education can never be neutral. (Allman et al. 1998, p. 12)

According to Colin Lankshear, Freire's process of learning to read and write

> establishes literacy as a medium for expressing one's own intentions, creative potency, and (emerging) critical perspective, rather than serving as a vehicle for absorbing directives and myths imposed from without. And in providing access to

Paulo Freire at home in São Paulo, 1996 (courtesy of Ana Maria Araújo Freire)

wide-ranging information, theory, and other critical perspectives, literacy becomes
a means by which learners can continually expand and refine their own critical
awareness, and communicate this to others similarly intent on entering history
more fully and consciously. (1993, p. 114)

Freire's work has been identified with nearly a dozen different movements or
trends within education, yet Freire himself often actively resisted such identifications. For instance, his work is often equated with popular education, adult
education, educational change, and nonformal education, which are often
lumped together. According to Rosa María Torres:

He distanced himself from those who, often quoting his work, equated *popular
education* and *adult education, educational change* and *non-formal education:*
"Popular education cannot be confused with or restricted to adults. What
defines popular education is not the learners' age but the political option"
(1985). He emphatically denied having promoted the idea of non-directive education, where teachers and learners are considered equal and where the role of
the teacher is eliminated: "The educator who says that he or she is equal to his
or her learners is either a demagogue, lies or is incompetent. Education is

always directive, and this is already said in the *Pedagogy of the Oppressed"* (1985). (1998, p. 109; emphasis in original)

Freire emphatically did not relegate the role of the teacher to that of a 'guide on the side' or backstage 'facilitator' who moves forever sideways, slipping out of his or her responsibility to actively direct the pedagogical process. His was not a sidewinder pedagogy but rather cobra-like, moving back and forth and striking quickly when the students' conditioning was broken down enough so that alternative views could be presented. Perhaps the movement to which Freire's work is most closely associated is that of the 'active school' movement associated with John Dewey, Maria Montessori, and others. Here again Freire took pains to disassociate himself from these approaches yet at the same time refused to cast his own work as the monologic voice of authority. As Rosa María Torres says:

> Freire has been compared to and analyzed within the framework of the great ped-agogues and thinkers in education. Many associated him with the "active school" movement and some of its most prominent promoters (Dewey, Decroly, Montes-sori, Claparéde, Freinet). Others put Freire and Illich together when considering Illich's deschooling. Freire responded by differentiating himself from the "active school." . . . He also distanced himself from the deschooling approach, since Freire's proposal was never to deny or eliminate the school but rather to transform it. (1998, pp. 109–110)

Despite resisting affiliations with many of the schools of thought with which his work was compared, there is no question that Freire's work often did draw from a number of wide-ranging philosophical, theological, and social science tra-ditions. And though to a large extent his ideas were not completely original, what was striking about his perspective was the unique way in which he wove together ideas from different scholarly terrains. As Schugurensky notes:

> After reading *Pedagogy of the Oppressed,* it may be argued that, for the most part, Freire's theoretical contribution is not new or original. To some extent, this claim has its validity. In the writings of Freire we find, for instance, elements of Socratic maieutics, philosophical existentialism, phenomenology, Hegelianism, Marxism, progressive education and liberation theology. Together with Marx and the Bible are Sartre and Husserl, Mounier and Buber, Fanon and Memmi, Mao and Gue-vara, Althusser and Fromm, Hegel and Unamuno, Kosik and Furter, Chardin and Maritian, Marcuse and Cabral. Even though Freire was influenced by these and other authors, his merit was to combine their ideas into an original formulation. As Fausto Franco has pointed out, in reading Freire one may have the impression of listening to familiar sounds everywhere, but at the same time experiencing an over-all harmony of the whole that is new. (1998, pp. 19–20)

It would be inaccurate, however, to describe Freire's work merely as a "synthesis" of other people's ideas, because in many respects his ideas exceeded those developed by his predecessors and contemporaries. Ana Maria Araújo Freire and Donaldo Macedo describe the influence of other thinkers on Freire's work as follows:

> The influence in Paulo's own way of thinking—because he reinvented and surpassed in part or in the whole many of his masters—of Marxism cannot be denied, as well as that of existentialism, personalism, or phenomenology. These are present in his reading of the world: Marx, Lukács, Sartre, and Mounier, as well as Albert Memmi, Erich Fromm, Frantz Fanon, Merleau-Ponty, Antonio Gramsci, Karel Kosik, H. Marcuse, Agnes Heller, Simone Weill, and Amilcar Cabral.
>
> Freire never denied these influences, for he knew himself as living, working, and doing in given situations—which he did not create—and, therefore, suffering like every man and every woman—historical beings—the influences of his time's culture, and those before, even while knowing himself as a critic and creator. (1998, p. 39)

Henry Giroux identifies a parallel between Freire's exile and the borders that he subsequently crossed—to Bolivia, Chile, Africa, North America, Europe—and the theoretical and disciplinary borders that defined his work. Giroux notes that "for Freire, the task of being an intellectual has always been forged within the trope of homelessness: between different zones of theoretical and cultural differences; between the borders of non-European and European cultures" (1993, p. 179). Denominating Freire as a "border intellectual," Giroux argues that "Freire's writings embody a mode of discursive struggle and opposition that not only challenges the oppressive machinery of the state but is also sympathetic to the formation of new cultural subjects and movements engaged in the struggle over the modernist values of freedom, equality, and justice. In part, this explains Freire's interest for educators, feminists, and revolutionaries in Africa, Latin America and South Africa" (pp. 179–180). In the end, Giroux locates Freire's work as "a textual borderland where poetry slips into politics, and solidarity becomes a song for the present begun in the past while waiting to be heard in the future" (p. 186).

A staunch critic of neoliberalism, Freire perceived a major ideological tension to be situated in the ability of people to retain a concept of the political beyond a reified consumer identity constructed from the panoply of market logics and their demotic discourses. He further determined that the sociality and the discourses of daily life cannot—as many mainstream educators assert, even today—be *a priori* defined as excluding the realm of politics (McLaren, Leonard, and Gadotti, 1998).

According to Peter Mayo (1999), Freire emphasized the creation of an "organic relationship" (much like Gramsci's concept of the "organic intellectual") between educators and the class or group of people with whom they are working. Because educators can carry with them a "cultural capital" at odds with that of the learners, Freire urged educators to commit "class suicide" in order to integrate themselves with the masses and to become immersed in the culture of the popular classes (Mayo, 1999, p. 68).

Freire's own personal contact early in his life with Brazilian peasants profoundly shaped his assent to popular revolts against economic exploitation in Latin America, Africa, and elsewhere. Given the basic contradictions facing a social order encapsulated in the exploitation of the vast majority of Brazilian society, the task or mission of Freire centered on the transformation of the relations of the production of social wealth (together with their ideological-political levels). Yet such an attempt to establish a new social order underwritten by a just system of appropriation and distribution of social wealth was to relegate Freire to the ranks of educators considered to be subversive to the state. For Freire, the very protocols of literacy and the act of "coming to know" had to be themselves transformed in order to make a prominent place for issues of social justice and the struggle for emancipation. Freire taught that in order for the oppressed to materialize their self-activity as a revolutionary force, they must develop a collective consciousness of their own constitution or formation as a subaltern class, as well as an ethos of solidarity and interdependence (McLaren and Da Silva, 1993). For Freire, a pedagogy of critical literacy became the primary vehicle for the development of "critical consciousness" among the poor, leading to a process of exploration and creative effort that conjoin deep personal meanings and common purpose. Literacy, for Freire, became that common 'process' of participation open to all individuals. The problem of critical consciousness cannot be posed in abstraction from the significant historical contexts in which knowledge is produced, engaged, and appropriated.

Freire lamented the brute reality that witnessed the oppressed always living as the detachable appendages of other people's dreams and desires. It seemed to Freire that the dreams of the poor were always dreamt for them by distant others who were removed from the daily struggles of the working class and either were unable or unwilling to recognize the dreams that burned in the habitats of the hearts of the oppressed. Freire minces no words when he sketches the challenge that progressive pedagogy poses for Brazilian educators:

> The politico-pedagogical practice of progressive Brazilian educators takes place in a society challenged by economic globalization, hunger, poverty, traditionalism, modernity, and even postmodernity, authoritarianism, by democracy, by violence, by impunity, by cynicism, by apathy, by hopelessness, but also by hope. It is a society where the majority of voters reveal an undeniable inclination toward change. (1998b, p. 76)

Based on a recognition of the cultural underpinnings of folk traditions (which frequently offer their members magical solutions to the real contradictions of their social position) and on a recognition of the importance of the collective construction of knowledge, Freire's pedagogical project created a vivid new vocabulary of concern for the oppressed, and uncoiled a new and powerful political terminology that enabled the oppressed to analyze their location within the privileging hierarchy of capitalist society and to engage in attempts to dislocate themselves from existing cycles of social reproduction. As Marcia Moraes asserts, "The relevant aspect of Freire's pedagogy is its epistemological perspective within the process of creating knowledge; its relation to people's existential and cultural experiences; and its social dimension in the process of 'conscientization'" (1996, p. 105).

Freirean pedagogy was profoundly committed to honoring the experiences of the oppressed, though not necessarily taking such experiences at face value. And though the experiences of the oppressed served as a basis for interrogating the ideological dimensions of subjectivity and identity, Freire always respected them as important:

> It's impossible to talk of respect for students for the dignity that is in the process of coming to be, for the identities that are in the process of construction, without taking into consideration the conditions in which they are living and the importance of the knowledge derived from life experience, which they bring with them to school. I can in no way underestimate such knowledge. Or what is worse, ridicule it. (Freire, 1998a, p. 62)

Freire claims that we cannot know for certain the historical significance of a particular practice in advance, because every action is the product of its conjunctural position within a system of differences—in other words, within an ensemble of social relations and contradictions. The challenge is not only to recognize the historical limits placed on agents but also to realize that it is possible to push those limits and the conditions that constrain them. Agency, after all is more than one's insertion into a field of coded social practices that are organized within the contradictions of class, race, capital, and gender. The contradictions embodied in class social relations were paramount for Freire throughout his career.

In order to understand the 'theories' of Freire, one needs to recognize that they are refracted through the concepts that they employ—and implore us—to think with on a daily basis: imperialism, oppression, exploitation, liberation, authoritarianism, to name but a few. These concepts are themselves practices or interacting social forms. Freire lived his life through his theoretical practices. This is forcefully described by Ana Maria Araújo Freire and Donaldo Macedo:

> Freire was, no doubt, a sensitive, strong man and one of passionate feelings: his rejection of anything outside his ideological-political-ethical principles; the manner in which he spoke and wrote metaphorically through histories; his dietary

habits; his way of respecting the honor and good faith of men and women; and above all, his creative, revolutionary intelligence of a man unable to accept the injustice that historically has been imposed on a large part of the world's population. (1998, p. 41)

Freire very much lived his life embodying the principles about which he wrote and spoke. He fashioned his world from the concepts and systems of intelligibility that he held so dear to his heart. More specifically, he lived his life within the tension of problematizing these concepts as he encountered and engaged history through his everyday lived experiences. He knew that hegemony was leaky, that ideology does not determine subjectivity through the creation of an inescapable causal environment. His theory embodied a certain redemptive focus—that of liberation—and thus he did not allow himself to be constrained by theories whose propositional beliefs were of a different explanatory order and were informed by different constitutive assumptions, assumptions that could not help to explain the pain and suffering of the world in its totality. His theoretical world comprised a "narrative space" or discursive economy with its own catalogue of terms out of which he could fashion himself as a public intellectual and cultural worker—what he would call a "pilgrim of the obvious"—whose guiding interest was rooted in overcoming domination and exploitation through a revolutionary educational praxis. Such a narrative space must account for systematic oppression and as such must meet the methodological demands that could help to explain and overcome it. In the case of both Freire and Che, it could be said that their own subjectivities were fashioned—were dialectically constituted—out of the everyday theories that they employed to make sense out of their own experiences and those of others in a world of human suffering.

Literacy programs for disempowered peasants developed by Freire and his colleagues are now employed in countries all over the world. By linking the categories of history, politics, economics, and class to the concepts of culture and power, Freire managed to develop both a language of critique and a language of hope that work conjointly and dialectically and that have proven successful in helping generations of disenfranchised peoples to liberate themselves at a time in which the critical questions linked to these categories have been formalized out of existence by education officials. But it is important to realize that literacy, for Freire, was an introduction to a particular way of life, a way of living and caring for others. Critical literacy à la Freire is a revolutionary dialectics of interest and theory in which individuals can become self-conscious of their own self-formation in particular ways of life though an engagement in critical self-reflexivity.

Freire recognized that there is no way of representing the consciousness of the oppressed that escapes the founding assumptions of the culture and society in which the teacher or cultural worker is implicated (Freire, 1993, 1998a, 1998b). A central project of Freire's pedagogy was to transform through a revolutionary social praxis the "banking concept" of education, in which the teacher-expert deposits knowledge into the learner's memory bank in a mechanical fashion that suggests that content itself is autocritical. Freire speaks to this issue when he argues that

> a progressive educator must not experience the task of teaching in mechanical fashion. He or she must not merely transfer the profile of the concept of the object to learners. If I teach Portuguese, I must teach the use of accents, subject-verb agreement, the syntax of verbs, noun case, the use of pronouns, the personal infinitive. However, as I teach the Portuguese language, I must not postpone dealing with issues of language that relate to social class. I must not avoid the issue of *class* syntax, grammar, semantics, and spelling. Hoping that the teaching of content, in and of itself, will generate tomorrow a radical intelligence of reality is to take on a controlled position rather than a critical one. It means to fall for a magical comprehension of content, which attributes to it a criticizing power of its own: "The more we deposit content in the learners' heads, and the more diversified that content is, the more possible it will be for them to, sooner or later, experience a critical awakening, decide, and break away."
>
> Any back-alley neoliberal knows very well that such a view is absolute nonsense and that he or she would lend his or her support to any educational project where the "reading of the world" was irrelevant. (1998b, pp. 75–76)

Freire's *Pedagogy of the Oppressed* continues to serve as a lodestar for all those struggling to reach both the word and the world. In many ways, *Pedagogy of the Oppressed* is informed by a profound Hegelian-Marxist reading of social life. In fact, the master/slave dialectic constitutes the foundational narrative of the book and, for that matter, much of Freire's lifetime work. Describing Freire as "the exemplary organic intellectual of our time," Cornel West pronounced *Pedagogy of the Oppressed* as "a world-historical event for counter-hegemonic theorists and activists in search of new ways of linking social theory to narratives of human freedom" (1993, p. xiii). West added that Paulo Freire "dares to tread where even Marx refused to walk—on the terrain where the revolutionary love of struggling human beings sustains their faith in each other and keeps hope alive within themselves and in history" (p. xiv).

Freire attempted to create a social order in which the peasant who achieves conscientization and participates in creating a new social order does not merely end up oppressing those who have condemned him or her to a life of servitude. As Ana Maria Araújo Freire and Donaldo Macedo so eloquently convey, "The revolutionary thought by Freire does not presuppose an inversion of the oppressed-oppressor poles; rather, it intends to reinvent, in communion, a society where exploitation and the verticalization of power do not exist, where the disenfranchised segments of society are not excluded or interdicted from reading the world" (1998, p. 9).

This description of Freire's praxis is reflected in Freire's approach to becoming critically literate. In a brilliant reading of Freire's own 'method' of critical reading,

Abdul JanMohamed likens Freire's codification and decodification process to Ernesto Laclau's appropriation and rearticulation of Husserl's definition of "sedimentation" and "reactivation." JanMohamed argues that Freire's methodology is founded upon a notion of hegemony as a process that is never fully accomplished: "To the extent that the dominant society that disenfranchises the peasants is never a totally sutured and stable structure, it manages to sustain its coherence and power only by repressing the peasants who threaten it. Thus, for Freire to encourage them to study the conditions of their existence is implicitly to persuade them to study the power relations that define their current and future identities" (1994, p. 245).

JanMohamed sees Freire's literacy method as providing a distance in which a new type of subjectivity can emerge among the peasants, a new identity underwritten by an act of power. This new identity exists "at the point where their virtual powerlessness (in that they have little, if any, access to institutionalized power) intersects with the massive prohibitive power of various state and civil apparatuses, power that, it must be emphasized, is always underwritten by actual or potential use of coercive force" (JanMohamed, 1994, p. 245). Freire's approach to literacy encourages peasants to develop "clearer antagonisms" between themselves and the dominant group by creating borders—that is, by drawing boundaries between the dominant group and their nascent identities. Part of this process also involves a creation of nonidentity with one's own subject position by adopting another subject position from which to critique one's own position. According to JanMohamed, "such a procedure simultaneously requires disidentification and identification: it demands a shift away from the deeply cathected inertia of fixed, sedimented identities and toward an engagement in the process of reidentification" (p. 246). Of course this process also demands the formation of affiliations with other positions, defining equivalences, and constructing alliances. Faced with the internalization of hegemonic rules and regulations that cleaves the individual subject, Freire's method involves the ejection of the introjected subject positions of dominant groups. Such a move reactivates an examination of the dominant society and constitutes a shift in the form of agency, a movement from the social to the political.

JanMohamed also compares Freire's pedagogic site to Michel Foucault's notions of utopia/ heterotopia. Heterotopic sites are "countersites" that contest and invert real sites, and are linked to these sites in a relation of contradiction. They are constitutionally ambiguous sites that can work to increase hegemonic norms or oppose them, depending upon how they are utilized. Freire's method is described as inviting subjects to the task of reading the self—directly or indirectly—as a heterotopic border so that the subject can begin to "articulate his/her specular, antagonistic, transgressive potentiality" (JanMohamed, 1994, p. 248). Freire's literacy practices are designed to create border intellectuals (in Giroux's sense of the term), which transforms peasants into "archeologists of the site of their own social formation" (JanMohamed, 1994, p. 248). Here, the crossing of borders implies the reactivation of new borders:

> Hence in advocating that the peasants understand themselves as the "antithesis" of the dominant group and that their practices manifest antagonisms, Freire implies a simultaneous transgression of one border and the establishment of another. First, through the process of decodification as well as through the acquisition of literacy, that is, in the movement from semi-intransitive to naïve transitive consciousness, the peasants cross the border of their sedimented social existence, and then introduce, or, more accurately, "reactivate" the border between themselves and the dominant group. (p. 249)

Long before postmodernists brought us their version of 'identity politics,' Freire understood that the subjectivities of the oppressed are to be considered heterogeneous and ideologically pertuse, and that they cannot be represented extratextually, that is, outside of the discursive embeddedness of their own as well as the educator's own founding values and epistemological assumptions (McLaren and Leonard, 1993). In other words, education is never a neutral endeavor, never isolatable, but always trapped in the network of significations that make up the terrain of culture. Critical pedagogy is a struggle within this terrain, an archival-smashing terrain of agonistic exchanges or contradictions in which the concrete historical struggle over signification takes place within the sign and among signs (McLaren, 1997a). Such struggles attempt to win subjects over to certain representations and meanings that are discursively implicated in asymmetrical relations of power linked to race, class, gender, sexual orientation, and other systems of differences. Freire writes:

> In essence, my position has to be of a person who wants or refuses to change. I cannot deny or hide my posture, but I also cannot deny others the right to reject it. In the name of the respect I should have towards my students, I do not see why I should omit or hide my political stance by proclaiming a neutral position that does not exist. On the contrary, my role as a teacher is to assent the students' right to compare, to choose, to rupture, to decide.
>
> Recently, a young man who had begun his university studies told me, "I do not understand how you defend the rights of landless peasants who, in reality, are nothing but troublemakers." I respond that you do have some troublemakers among the landless peasants, but their struggle against oppression is both legitimate and ethical. The so-called troublemakers represent a form of resistance against those who aggressively oppose the agrarian reform. For me, the immortality and the lack of ethics rest with those who want to maintain an unjust order. (1998a, p. 68)

In his calibration of revolutionary praxis, Freire understood that as the oppressed take more control of their own history, they assimilate more rapidly into society, but on their own terms. Yet he was occasionally and sometimes resoundingly criticized for taking a populist stand and for not giving enough systematic emphasis in his work to the ways in which the dominant culture reproduces itself at the institutional and state levels. Schugurensky explains:

> Freire has been criticized . . . by vanguardist militants who argued that he tended to fall into a kind of populism that idealizes popular culture and forms of resistance. Addressing these issues, Freire cautioned [educators about] the two risks of elitism and basism, meaning that the rejection of popular knowledge was as dangerous as its exaltation or mystification. For him, education was communion: "I cannot think authentically unless others think. I cannot think for others, or without others." He also suggested that in order to establish a more dialogical relationship between teachers and learners, teachers should accept that they do not know everything and learners should recognize that they are not ignorant of everything. On a related issue, it has been also argued that although Freire's cultural analysis is illuminating, it is limited because he rarely ventured beyond the confines of popular culture, and thus did not incorporate an examination of the dominant culture into his approach. Freire's emphasis on the culture of the oppressed, then, could be enriched with a systematic and wide-ranging analysis of the hegemonic culture such as the one undertaken by Gramsci. (1998, p. 24)

Stanley Aronowitz (1993) notes that Freire in his later writings somewhat distanced himself from elements of his own revolutionary Marxist past, yet his was always an "open Marxism" best represented perhaps by the work of Antonio Gramsci. According to Aronowitz, Freire broke from an elitist conception of the intellectual as the vanguard for workers' and peasant movements to an emphasis on rediscovering the power of resistance to the state through new social movements. Such new social movements, argued Freire, must create alliances with the revolutionary parties. Aronowitz is adamant that Freire's later work—sometimes seen as a retreat from his earlier revolutionary pedagogy—does not represent a break from Freire's earlier Marxism, but rather indicates some shifts *within* this position. Aronowitz locates a major tension within Freire's work between his secular theology of liberation and the "open futurity" of his perspectives on pedagogy. This places Freire squarely against vanguards and populism and in favor of the struggle to build autonomous popular organizations. Aronowitz situates Freire as a libertarian in the tradition of Rosa Luxemburg and the anarchists in the sense that Freire stipulates the conditions for revolutionary initiative *from below*. Luxemburg, it may be recalled, hallowed spontaneity and spontaneous mass actions (Dunayeuskaya, 1982). Aronowitz (1993) goes so far as to describe Freire's position as "postmodern" and "postcolonialist" when referring to Freire's critique of "localism" and his challenging of the priority of class over other categories of oppression, resistance, and liberation—a position that marked his later work. Joe Kincheloe (1994) believes that a new synergism can be created by the fusion of Freirean ethics and postmodern analysis. While I agree that there are postmodern moments in Freire's work—moments that certainly enhance his work—the major thrust of his work remained that of class struggle, even into his later years.

Despite his failure to develop a systematic body of theoretical work that illustrates the ideological mechanisms and discursive and extradiscursive means by which the cultural dominant is reproduced, Freire warrants his reputation as a pre-eminent critical educationalist in the way that he was able to foreground the means by which *the pedagogical* (the localized pedagogical encounter between teacher and student) is implicated in *the political* (the social relations of production within the global capitalist economy). Whereas mainstream educators often decapitate the social context from the self and then cauterize the dialectical movement between them, Freire stresses the dialectical motion between the subject and object, the self and the social, and human agency and social structure.

Educators who work within a Freirean-inspired critical pedagogy are indebted to Freire's philosophical insights more than to his commentaries on teaching methodologies (Taylor, 1993). Freire's working vocabulary of philosophical concepts and his intercourse of vocabularies from theology to the social sciences enables the world of the oppressed to become visible, to inscribe itself as a text to be engaged and understood by the oppressed and nonoppressed alike. Freire's work does not reduce the world to a text but rather stipulates the conditions for the possibility of various competing and conflicting discourses, or ways of making sense out of lived experiences. Freire interrogates the catachresis of value by urging educators to identify the aporias within their own philosophies and epistemologies of teaching and daily life (Freire, 1998a; 1998b).

In all of Freire's teachings, the concept of truth becomes vitiatingly unwound as the truth becomes linked to one's emplacement in the reigning narratives about truth. Of course, Freire's own work can be used against itself in this regard, and interpreted as an epiphenomenon of the narratives that create the textual effects of his own work. In fact, Freire would most assuredly have encouraged readers to scrutinize his work by employing the same manner of ideology critique that he encouraged readers to employ while interrogating other texts.

FREIRE'S INFLUENCE ON NORTH AMERICAN CRITICAL PEDAGOGY

Discovering that pedagogy existed largely in pathological conditions, Freire magisterially ignored convention and sought to advance new approaches to teaching and learning, carefully avoiding those 'banking' varieties that separated mind from body, thought from action, and social critique from transformative praxis. Often accompanied by Deweyan (see Dewey, 1916) approaches to teaching and learning as well as those, like Habermas's (1979, 1987), that stress communicative competency and nondistorted forms of communication, critical ped-

agogy constitutes a set of practices that uncovers the ways in which the process
of schooling represses the contingency of its own selection of values and the
means through which educational goals are subtended by macrostructures of
power and privilege. For Freire, pedagogy has as much to do with the teachable
heart as the teachable mind, and as much to do with efforts to change the world
as it does with rethinking the categories that we use to analyze our current condition within history. In this way, Freire has pushed the debate over pedagogy
out of familiar, well-worn grooves. In essence, Freire's work is about hope:

> Without a vision for tomorrow, hope is impossible. The past does not generate
> hope, except for the time when one is reminded of rebellious, daring moments of
> fight. The past, understood as immobilization of what was, generates longing, even
> worse, *nostalgia*, which nullifies tomorrow. Almost always, concrete situations of
> oppression reduce the oppressed's historical time to an everlasting present of
> hopelessness and resignation. The oppressed grandchild repeats the suffering of
> their grandparent. (Freire, 1998b, p. 45; emphasis in original)

Yet for Freire, hope is not an interloper, some mysterious visitor that comes
to the rescue from the outside, from beyond the tangible territory of the daily
grind. Hope is internal to agency and constitutive of daily struggle, for without
hope, history would write us and would prevent us from writing history. Freire
is unflinching in his belief that

> [H]ope is something shared between teachers and students. The hope that we can
> learn together, teach together, be curiously impatient together, produce some-
> thing together, and resist together the obstacles that prevent the flowering of our
> joy. In truth, from the point of view of the human condition, hope is an essential
> component and not an intruder. It would be a serious contradiction of what we are
> if, aware of our unfinishedness, we were not disposed to participate in a constant
> movement of search, which in its very nature is an expression of hope. Hope is a
> natural, possible, and necessary impetus in the context of our unfinishedness.
> Hope is an indispensable seasoning in our human, historical experience. Without
> it, instead of history we would have pure determinism. History exists only where
> time is problematized and not simply a given. A future that is inexorable is a denial
> of history. (Freire, 1998a, p. 69)

Peter Mayo captures the essence of Freire's pedagogy of hope when he writes:

> The spirit of this remarkable figure . . . lives on. It is constantly felt by those, like
> myself, who often seek refuge and solace in his works, to recuperate that sense of
> hope and agency which can easily be lost as we are constantly assailed by the dom-
> inant hegemonic discourse of technical rationality and marketability. This sense of
> hope is communicated to us through the constant fusion of reason and emotion

which I consider to be one of the distinctive features of Paulo Freire's style as writer and speaker. (1997, p. 368)

As I mentioned in the introduction (pp. xx–xxi), Freire's work has unarguably been the driving force behind North American efforts at developing critical pedagogy. Freirean-inspired critical pedagogies in North America have grown out of a number of theoretical developments such as Latin American philosophies of liberation (McLaren and Leonard, 1993); critical literacy (Lankshear and McLaren, 1993; Macedo, 1994); critical literacy (Lankshear and McLaren, 1993; Macedo, 1994); the sociology of knowledge (Giroux and McLaren, 1989; Fine, 1991; McLaren, 1995); the Frankfurt school of critical theory (Giroux, 1983; McLaren and Giarelli, 1995); adult education (Hall, 1998); feminist theory (Weiler, 1988; Ellsworth, 1989; Lather, 1991; Gore, 1993); bilingual and bicultural education (Cummins, 1989; Darder, 1991; Moraes, 1996; Wink 1997); teacher education (McLaren, 1997a); and neo-Marxist cultural criticism (McLaren, 1997d). In more recent years it has been taken up by educators influenced by debates over postmodernism and post-structuralism (Giroux and McLaren, 1989; Aronowitz and Giroux, 1991; Kanpol, 1992; Kincheloe, 1993; McLaren, 1995); cultural studies (Kincheloe, 1993; Giroux and McLaren, 1994; Giroux, Lankshear, McLaren, and Peters 1997); and multiculturalism (Grant, 1977; McCarthy, 1988; Sleeter and McLaren, 1995; Kincheloe and Steinberg, 1997; McLaren, 1997d; Leistnya, 1999). For Freire, schools are places where, as part of civil society, spaces of uncoerced interaction can be created.

Yet even with such a divergent array of influences, at the level of classroom life, critical pedagogy is often erroneously perceived as synonymous with whole language instruction, adult literacy programs, and new 'constructivist' approaches to teaching and learning based on Vygotsky's work. Not all pedagogies that claim to be critical are necessarily Freirean but rather need to be judged in relation to the contextual specificity of their philosophy, their praxis, and their ethos of critical responsiveness with respect to bringing about a more just and humane social order. Lankshear and McLaren have summarized six learning principles from Freire's work, which are intended to provide educators with pivotal points of reference in the development of their pedagogical practices:

1. The world must be approached as an object to be understood and known by the efforts of learners themselves. Moreover, their acts of knowing are to be stimulated and grounded in their own being, experiences, needs, circumstances, and destinies.
2. The historical and cultural world must be approached as a created, transformable reality that, like humans themselves, is constantly in the process of being shaped and made by human deed in accordance with ideological representations of reality.

3. Learners must learn how to actively make connections between their own lived conditions and being and the making of reality that has occurred to date.

4. They must consider the possibility for "new makings" of reality, the new possibilities for *being* that emerge from new makings, and become committed to shaping a new enabling and regenerative history. New makings are a collective, shared, social enterprise in which the voices of all participants must be heard.

5. In the literacy phase learners come to see the importance of print for this shared project. By achieving print competence within the process of bringing their experience and meanings to bear on the world in active construction and reconstruction (of lived relations and practice), learners will actually *experience* their own potency in the very act of understanding what it means to be a human subject. In the postliteracy phase, the basis for action is print-assisted exploration of generative *themes*. Addressing the theme of "Western culture" as conceived by people like Hirsch and reified in prevailing curricula and pedagogies, and seeking to transcend this . . . involves exactly the kind of praxis Freire intends.

6. Learners must come to understand how the myths of dominant discourses are, precisely, myths which oppress and marginalize them—but which can be transcended through transformative action. (1993, pp. 43–44; emphasis in original)

Freire believed that the challenge of transforming schools should be directed at overcoming socioeconomic injustice linked to the political and economic structures of society. Thus, any attempt at school reform that claims to be inspired by Freire but that is only concerned with social patterns of representation, interpretation, or communication, and that does not connect these patterns to redistributive measures and structures that reinforce such patterns, exempts itself from the most important insights of Freire's work.

Freire's approach stipulates a trenchant understanding of patterns of distribution and redistribution in order to transform—and not just interpret—the underlying economic structures that produce relations of exploitation. Freire was also concerned with practicing a politics of diversity and self-affirmation—in short, a cultural politics—not as a mere end-in-itself but in relation to a larger politics of liberation and social justice. Consequently, a Freirean pedagogy of liberation is totalizing without being dominating in that it always attends dialectically to the specific or local "act of knowing" as a political process that takes place in the larger conflictural arena of capitalist relations of exploitation, an arena where large groups of people palpably and undeniably suffer needless privations and pain due to alienation and poverty. Thus, a pedagogy of the oppressed involves not only a redistribution of material resources but also a struggle over cultural meanings in relation to the multiple, social locations of students and teachers and their position within the global division of labor. Freire recognizes that ideology works at multiple levels and is a complex phenomenon. More than a *camera obscura* that masks the interests of the masses in the interests of the capitalist class, ideology is constitutive of knowledge production itself. Hence, one of the key foci of critical pedagogy is ideology critique. Joe Kincheloe views Freire's work as providing a "sharp political edge to postmodern analysis" that can "expose the insidious ways that oppression operates" (1994, p. 217). It is here that ideology critique refuses to enable the depoliticization of pedagogy, including recent postmodern variants.

Has Freire's name become a floating signifier to be attached adventitiously to any chosen referent within the multistranded terrain of progressive education? To a certain extent this has already happened. Liberal progressives are drawn to Freire's humanism; Marxists and neo-Marxists are drawn to his revolutionary praxis and his history of working with revolutionary political regimes; left liberals are drawn to his critical utopianism; and even conservatives begrudgingly respect his stress on ethics. No doubt his work will be domesticated by his followers—just as selected aspects of his corpus are appropriated uncritically and decontextualized from his larger political project of struggling for the realization of a truly socialist democracy—in order to make a more comfortable fit with various conflicting political agendas. Consequently, it is important to read Freire in the context of his entire corpus of works, from *Pedagogy of the Oppressed* to his recent reflection on this early work that he called *Pedagogy of Hope,* and ultimately to his *Pedagogy of Freedom.*

FREIREAN PEDAGOGY: ITS SHORTCOMINGS

Those who have an important stake in the meaning of Freire's life and work will continue to disagree over how his politics and pedagogy should be interpreted. The assertive generality of Freire's formulations of and pronouncements on pedagogy can be highly frustrating, in that they index important concerns but do not fully provide the necessary theoretical basis for positing more progressive and programmatic alternatives to the theories and perspectives that he is criticizing. For instance, few accounts are provided to help us understand how teachers are to move from critical thought to critical practice. Yet Freire's weakness is also a source of his strength and marks the durability of his thought. It is precisely his refusal to spell out in a "bag of tricks" fashion alternative solutions that enables his work to be re-invented in the contexts in which his readers find themselves, thereby enjoining a contextually specific translation across geographic, geopolitical, and cultural borders. It also grants to Freire's corpus of works a universal character, as they are able to retain their heuristic potency (much like the works of Marx) such that they can be conscripted by educators to criticize and to counterpoint pedagogical practices worldwide. In fact, Freire urged his readers to reinvent him in the context of their local struggles. What can be retained in every instance of this reinvention process is Freire's constant and unstoppable ethics of solidarity and an unrepentant utopi-

Paulo Freire, at a meeting of the Workers Party (Partido dos Trabalhadores)
in São Paulo during the campaign for the 1990 presidential elections;
Freire is seated next to candidate Luiz (Lula) Inácio da Silva
(courtesy of Ana Maria Araújo Freire)

anism. Freire writes that "the progressive educator must always be moving out on
his or her own, continually reinventing me and reinventing what it means to be
democratic in his or her own specific cultural and historical context" (1997a, p. 308).

Some have assigned to Freire's work the Archimedian conceit of the idealist
utopian view of society. But such a criticism risks overlooking the practical utility of
Freirean pedagogy, especially when one considers the success of the literacy campaigns that rely heavily on his work. Freire seized on the occult presence of seeds
of redemption at the center of a world gone mad. Yet his politics of liberation resists
subsumption under a codified set of universal principles; rather, it animates a set of
ethical imperatives that together serve as a precipitate of our answering the call of
the Other who is suffering from a heavy heart and an empty stomach. Such imperatives do not mark a naive utopian faith in the future; rather, they presage a form
of active, irreverent, and uncompromising hope in the possibilities of the present.

The legacy of racism left by the New World European oppressor—that Blacks
and Latino/as are simply a species of inferior invertebrates—was harshly condemned but never systematically analyzed by Freire. And though Freire was a
vociferous critic of racism and sexism, he did not, as Kathleen Weiler (1996)
points out, sufficiently problematize his conceptualization of liberation and the
oppressed in terms of his own male experience.

From the perspective of North American critical pedagogy, Freire's politics of liberation partakes of its own political inertia consequent in the limited range of narratives out of which he constructs his praxis of hope and transformation. For instance, Freire failed to articulate fully his position on Christianity (Elias, 1994) and the male bias in his literacy method (Taylor, 1993). Freire rarely addressed the ways that oppression on the basis of ethnicity, class, and sexual orientation are intermingled. As a number of North American critics have pointed out, Freire failed to fully engage the issue of white male privilege (Ladson-Billings, 1997) or the interest and agency of African Americans apart from a wider movement of emancipatory practices (Murrell, 1997). And when Freire did address this issue he often retreated into mystical abstractions, thereby discounting the deep significance of patriarchy as a practice of oppression (Weiler, 1996). Yet these lacunae should in no way diminish the genius, courage, and compassion of Freire's work. In Freire's later writings one can see an increasing interest in the themes of feminism and racial justice:

> His exposure to feminist writers and others focusing on race relations helped in the development of a non-essentialist post-colonial politics. This approach does not confront one form of oppression to the total exclusion of others, and it does not negate the fact that, as humans, we are "incomplete beings" . . . characterized by multiple and often contradictory identities. His constant willingness to learn from such writers as the numerous feminists who criticized his earlier work on the grounds of gender obliviousness, led him to advocate a pedagogical politics characterized by "Unity in diversity, so that the various oppressed groups can become more effective in their collective struggle against all forms of oppression." (Allman et al., 1998, p. 14)

In Freire's later works, he attempted to highlight the relational aspects of group identity and to avoid valorizing the subject as an autonomous or independent agent detached from any external Other or regime of discourse. Freire took pains not to romanticize cultural identity by giving it an 'essential,' internal coherence or symbolic pattern because he was aware that not everything in the archives of a culture is worth defending. This conclusion was unflinchingly drawn in this summarizing statement:

> First of all, I think that all cultures have their own identity, a reason for being, and they should undoubtedly struggle to preserve it. This does not mean that cultures don't carry within themselves weak dimensions. This reminds me of Amilcar Cabral, the famous African leader who used to talk about the weaknesses of cultures. One of the weaknesses that I found in Brazil, just to cite an example, is the "machismo." Machismo is part of our culture, but that doesn't mean that we should preserve it. So, I think that cultures should struggle to reinforce what is already valid and to promote what needs to be validated—especially that which has yet to be recognized—and obviously, understand and eradicate what is negative. (cited in Leistyna, 1999, p. 51)

Although Freire was careful to incorporate race, class, and gender dimensions into his later work, recognizing that they continually abut with each other in the realm of social life, at the same time he did not believe that all of social life could be explained by the holy trinity of race, class, and gender. As he pointed out:

> But to the extent that race, class, and gender are emphasized in the struggle for liberty—whether in this society or others and for historical, social, cultural, and economic motives—we must avoid succumbing to the temptation to reduce the entire struggle to one of these fundamental aspects.
> Gender cannot explain everything. Neither can race, nor class. (1998c, p. 85)

Well aware of the limitations of Freire's early writings in the area of gender and race, bell hooks nonetheless affirms the central importance of his work in her own struggle as an African American organic intellectual:

> There has never been a moment when reading Freire that I have not remained aware of not only the sexism of the language but the way he (like other progressive Third World political leaders, intellectuals, critical thinkers such as Fanon, Memmi, etc.) constructs a phallocentric paradigm of liberation—wherein freedom and the experience of patriarchal manhood are always linked as though they are one and the same. For me this is always a source of anguish for it represents a blind spot in the vision of men who have profound insight. And yet, I never wish to see a critique of this blind spot overshadow anyone's (and feminists in particular) capacity to learn from the insights. (1993, p. 148)

It is suggestive of the power and promise of Freire's work for hooks to acknowledge with unvarnished candor (and I dare say with courage) that Freire's writings have been much more compellingly central in her own work than the writings of many bourgeois white feminists:

> Freire's work (and that of many other teachers) affirmed my right as a subject in resistance to define my reality. His writing gave me a way to place the politics of racism in the United States in a global context wherein I could see my fate linked with that of colonized black people everywhere struggling to decolonize, to transform society. More than in the work of many white bourgeois feminist thinkers, there was always in Paulo's work recognition of the subject position of those most disenfranchised, those who suffer the gravest weight of oppressive forces (with the exception of his not acknowledging always the specific gendered realities of oppression and exploitation). This was a standpoint which affirmed my own desire to work from a lived understanding of the lives of poor black women. (1993, p. 151)

The modality of theoretical envisioning deployed by Freire is decidedly modernist, but as I have argued elsewhere (McLaren, 1997c), some trappings of postmodernist discourses are immanent—yet barely registered—in Freire's peripatetic articulation of human agency. This changes somewhat in his later writings, when he seemed sympathetic to some 'resistance postmodernist' positions such as those of Aronowitz and Giroux (1991). Like Aronowitz and Giroux, Kincheloe (1994), and others, Freire recognized that some social theory identified as 'postmodern' runs the serious risk of ignoring the brute reality that working people the world over share a common subjection to capitalist exploitation. The violent realities of the global economy are often dissipated within postmodern social theories (McLaren, 1997a). On the other hand, pedagogies of liberation such as Freire's, for the most part underwritten by modernist Marxian discourses, often seriously ignore issues of race, gender, and sexual orientation. Freire was aware of these omissions (Freire, 1997b, 1998a, 1998b) and had begun to address them with a passionate conviction in his most recent work.

Despite the fact that deconstructionists such as Stuart Parker (1997) have revealed much of the work of the critical educational tradition (exemplified by the work of Freire) to be located within modernist assumptions of teacher autonomy—assumptions that essentially serve as "devices of enchantment" that can be deconstructed as discursive fictions—Freire's work holds vital importance. Freire's contribution remains signal not for its methodology of literacy alone but in the final instance for its ability to create a pedagogy of practical consciousness that presages critical action (Taylor, 1993). Freire's primary achievement remains that of his work as the 'Pilgrim of the Obvious,' a term he often used to describe his pedagogical role. The shortcomings of Freire's work constitute more than minor rhetorical fallout, to be sure, but as many of Freire's aforementioned critics also acknowledge, these lapses should not detract from Freire's central importance as a foundational education thinker, a philosopher who ranks among the most important educators of this century or any other.

Ultimately, what is important to recognize in the shifts in Freire's position in his later writings is that, though he greatly deepened his engagement with issues of race and class, he also emphasized the crisis within global capitalism. This is a point underscored by Antonia Darder, who writes that it

> is a real tribute to Freire, that in *Pedagogy of the Heart* (or *Under the Shade of the Mango Tree*—its original title), written shortly before his death, Freire demonstrated signs of change and deepening in his thinking about many of these issues. For example, the language in the book finally reflected an inclusiveness of women when making general references, which had been missing in his earlier writings. He spoke to the issue of capitalism more boldly than ever before and considered the nature of globalization and its meaning for radical educators. He also addressed issues of diversity and racism . . . and more forcefully than ever, he spoke of the necessity of moving beyond our . . . differences so that we might forge an effective attack against the wiles of advanced capitalism in the world. (1998, p. 31)

Enduring imbalances in the 'globalitarian world'—the worldwide problem of overcapacity, the random destruction of the ecosystem by unregulated markets accompanying the new bargain-basement capitalism, the imposition of exchange values upon all productions of value, the creation of a uniform culture of pure consumption or Wal-Martization of global culture, the vampirism of Western carpetbaggers sucking the lifeblood from the open veins of South America, opportunistic politicians, assaults on diasporic cultures, and new waves of xenophobia—have brought about a serious political inertia within the United States Left in general, and the educational Left in particular. The logic of privatization and free trade—where social labor is the means and measure of value and surplus social labor lies at the heart of profit—now shapes the very fabric of our lifeworld. Neoliberal education merely reimposes the commodity status of labor power by treating students as human capital for the new global marketplace.

RACE, OR CLASS, OR GENDER, OR ALL TOGETHER

The issue of whether a culturalist or an economist perspective prevails today in critical pedagogy is a nagging one, but essentially presents us with a false dichotomy. Individuals and groups live class relations through difference (that is, through raced and gendered experiences), and live difference through class relations. Identity, difference, and class are mutually informing relations. Class relations embody all kinds of differences that have been historically organized and structurally determined by imperialist and colonialist economies of privilege. The issue should not be: Critical race theory is superior to critical pedagogy or vice versa. The more important question is: How are differences mediated through the social contradictions of class formations, and vice versa? This suggests that we examine the institutional and structural aspects of difference as they have been produced historically out of the contradictions of capitalist social practices. We can do this only if we examine how the production of gendered and racialized identities are shaped by the totality of social relations of production. That is, how can we read off in a dialectical manner particular formations and expressions of difference against the overarching and complex organization, networks, and mutually informing relationships that at different levels and in different modalities constitute global capitalist relations?

The logic of transnational capitalism now flagrantly guides educational policy and practice to such an extent that one could say without exaggeration that education has been reduced to a subsector of the economy. Freire's work is indispensable to the progressive evolution of educational thought, to the extent that the future of education is intimately connected to the ability of students and teachers to become more critically self-reflective in analyzing ways in which their own gendered, racialized, and sexualized experiences have been inscribed by enchaining discursive practices and material social relations that support powerful elite groups at the expense of the majority of the population. Of course, the continuing advancement of critical pedagogy and Freirean praxis cannot be divorced from the crisis of the late bourgeois world, whose greatest symptom includes the logic of consumption as a regulating democratic ideal. Freire was always a revolutionary and as such never abandoned the dream of a radical trans-formation of the capitalist world. In his magisterial *Pedagogy of Hope,* he writes:

> My rebellion against every kind of discrimination, from the most explicit and cry-ing to the most covert and hypocritical, which is no less offensive and immoral, has been with me from my childhood. Since as far back as I can remember, I have reacted almost instinctively against any word, deed, or sign or racial discrimina-tion, or, for that matter, discrimination against the poor, which quite a bit later, I came to define as class discrimination. (1994, p. 144)

As Freire's future hagiographers and *luchadores* wrestle in the educational arena over what represents the "real" Freire and his legacy, Freire's work will continue to be felt in the lives of those who knew him and who loved him. Just as important, his work will continue to influence generations of educators, schol-ars, and activists around the world.

Freire acknowledges that decolonization is a project that knows no endpoint, no final closure. It is a lifetime struggle that requires counterintuitive insight, honesty, compassion, and a willingness to brush one's personal history against the grain of "naive consciousness" or commonsense understanding. After engag-ing the legacy of revolutionary struggles of the oppressed that has been bequeathed to us by Freire, it remains impossible to conceive of pedagogical practice evacuated of social critique. Freire has left stratified deposits of peda-gogical insight upon which the future development of progressive education can—and must—be built. There is still reason to hope for a cooperative peda-gogical venture among those who support a Freirian, class-based, pedagogical struggle, feminist pedagogy, or a pedagogy informed by queer theory and poli-tics, that may lead to a revival of serious educational thinking in which the cate-gory of liberation may continue to have and to make meaning. The internation-alization of the market and its border-crossing dimensions strongly suggests that in order to halt the continuing assaults of the market on human subjectivity, cul-tural workers must create active alliances across national borders. McLaren and Da Silva stress that any struggle to create revolutionary subjectivity must include redemptive remembering, or "a critical engagement of and resistance to the dominative society—a society that possesses a crippling potential to disable the oppressed to a supplicatory attitude that is placatory toward regimes of domi-nation" (1993, p. 76).

THE POWER OF LOVE

What sets Freire apart from most other leftist educators in this era of cynical reason, and joins him in spirit with Che, is his unashamed stress on the importance and power of love. Love, he claims, is the most crucial characteristic of dialogue and the constitutive force animating all pedagogies of liberation:

> Dialogue cannot exist, however, in the absence of a profound love for the world and for people. The naming of the world, which is an act of creation and re-creation, is not possible if it is not infused with love. Love is at the same time the foundation of dialogue and dialogue itself. It is thus necessarily the task of responsible Subjects and cannot exist in a relation of domination. Domination reveals the pathology of love: sadism in the dominator and masochism in the dominated. Because love is an act of courage, not of fear, love is commitment to others. No matter where the oppressed are found, the act of love is commitment to their cause—the cause of liberation. And this commitment, because it is loving, is dialogical. As an act of bravery, love cannot be sentimental: as an act of freedom, it must not serve as a pretext for manipulation. It must generate other acts of freedom; otherwise, it is not love. Only by abolishing the situation of oppression is it possible to restore the love which that situation made impossible. If I do not love the world—if I do not love life—if I do not love people—I cannot enter into dialogue. (1993a, pp. 70–71)

Love, for Freire, always stipulates a political project, since a love for humankind that remains disconnected from a liberatory politics does a profound disservice to its object. A love that does not liberate feeds off its object like worms off a corpse. Its narcissism destroys the Other by turning the Other into itself; it transforms the Other into inert matter that it uses to fertilize its own image. Here the act of love becomes the act of self-love, as the subject becomes its own object, consuming itself in an orgy of necrophilia. It is possible to love only by virtue of the reciprocal presence of others. Whereas authentic love opens up the self to the Other, narcissistic love culminates in a self-dissolving spiral by refusing the Other (through consuming the Other) who stands at the door of self-understanding. Only when the Other is encountered behind the door can the self find its authentic eyes, ears, and voice in the act of dialogic, reciprocal understanding. Love both embodies struggle and pushes it beyond its source. In Freirean terms, revolutionary love is always pointed in the direction of commitment and fidelity to a global project of emancipation. In this respect, Freire's concept of love coincides with that of Che. The commitment of revolutionary love is sustained by preventing nihilism and despair from imposing their own life-denying inevitability in times of social strife and cultural turmoil. Anchored in narratives of transgression and dissent, love becomes the foundation of hope. In this way, love can never be reduced to personal declarations or pronouncements but exists always in asymmetrical relations of anxiety and resolve, interdependence and singularity. Love, in this Freirean sense, becomes the oxygen of revolution, nourishing the blood of historical memory. It is through reciprocal dialogue that love is able to serve as a form of testimony to those who have struggled and suffered before us, and whose spirit of struggle has survived efforts to extinguish it and remove it from the archives of human achievement. Refusing to embrace the Orphic lyre, the crown of thorns, or the automatic rifle, Freirean pedagogy faces the intractable forces of capitalistic domination with a bittersweet optimism. Freire understood that while we often abandon hope, we are never abandoned by hope. This is because hope is forever engraved in the human heart and inspires us to reach beyond the carnal limits of our species being.

In *Pedagogy of the Oppressed*, Freire denominates Che Guevara as the epitome of revolutionary praxis and makes clear his immitigable admiration for the Cuban revolution. His comments on how Fidel and the Cuban guerrillas developed an unshakable dialogical bond with the people, which increased during the process of revolutionary action, are celebratory:

> This sharing in no way diminishes the spirit of struggle, courage, capacity for love, or daring required of the revolutionary leaders. Fidel Castro and his comrades (whom many at the time termed "irresponsible adventurers"), an eminently dialogical leadership group, identified with the people who endured the brutal violence of the Batista dictatorship. This adherence was not easy; it required bravery on the part of the leaders to love the people sufficiently to be willing to sacrifice themselves for them. It required courageous witness by the leaders to recommence after each disaster, moved by undying hope in a future victory which (because forged together with the people) would belong not to the leaders alone, but to the leaders and the people—or to the people including the leaders. (1993a, pp. 145–146)

Freire describes how the 'dominated consciousness' is dual, ambiguous, and full of fear and mistrust. He notes how, in Che's diary about the struggle in Bolivia, Che refers several times to the lack of peasant participation and their fear and inefficiency. For Freire, this is a clear case of the internalization of the oppressor within the dominated consciousness of the peasants. Freire remarks that dialogical theory requires that the leader create the conditions for the oppressed to unveil the world for themselves, which is the mark of authentic praxis. Yet at the same time, Freire credits Che with correctly mistrusting that aspect of the oppressed that "houses" the oppressor within. He writes:

> This adherence coincides with trust the people begin to place in themselves and in the revolutionary leaders, as the former perceive the dedication and authentic-

*Paulo Freire, Peter McLaren, and Augusto Boal at a seminar at the Rose The-
ater, Omaha, Nebraska, March 23, 1996* (courtesy of Marta Baltodano)

ity of the latter. The trust of the people in the leaders reflects the confidence of the
leaders in the people.

This confidence should not, however, be naïve. The leaders must believe in the
potentialities of the people, whom they cannot treat as mere objects of their own
action; they must believe that the people are capable of participating in the pursuit of liberation. But they must always mistrust the ambiguity of oppressed
people, mistrust the oppressor "housed" in the latter. Accordingly, when Guevara
exhorts the revolutionary to be always mistrustful, he is not disregarding the fundamental condition of the theory of dialogical action. He is merely being a realist.
(1993a, p. 150)

According to Freire, Che understood correctly why guerrillas may suddenly
or eventually desert the struggle: because the oppressor within them is stronger
than they are, and because they exist in a state of ambiguity.

As long as the oppressor "within" the oppressed is stronger than they themselves
are, their natural fear of freedom may lead them to denounce the revolutionary
leaders instead! The leaders cannot be credulous, but must be alert for these possibilities. Guevara's *Episodes* confirms these risks: not only desertions, but even
betrayal of the cause. At times in this document, while recognizing the necessity

of punishing the deserter in order to preserve the cohesion and discipline of the group, Guevara also recognizes certain factors which explain the desertion. One of them, perhaps the most important, is the deserter's ambiguity. (1993a, pp. 150–151)

And finally, Freire is equally appreciative of Che's love for the people, a love that became the seedbed of each individual's revolutionary praxis:

It was, then, in dialogue with the peasants that Guevara's revolutionary praxis became definitive. What Guevara did not say, perhaps due to humility, is that it was his own humility and capacity to love that made possible his communion with the people. And this indisputably dialogical communion became cooperation. Note that Guevara (who did not climb the Sierra Maestra with Fidel and his comrades as a frustrated youth in search of adventure) recognizes that his "communion with the people ceased to be a mere theory, to become an integral part of [himself]." He stresses how from the moment of the communion the peasant became "forgers" of his guerrillas' "revolutionary ideology." (1993a, pp. 151–152)

A serious difference between Freire and Che was their perspective on violence. According to Ana Maria Araújo Freire and Donaldo Macedo, Freire

never spoke, nor was he ever an advocate, of violence or of the taking of power through the force of arms. He was always, from a young age, reflecting on education and engaging in political action mediated by an educational practice that can be transformative. He fought and had been fighting for a more just and less perverse society, a truly democratic one, one where there are no repressors against the oppressed, where all can have a voice and a chance. (1998, p. 21)

It is important to note that though Freire personally abhorred violence, it did not stop him from being a great admirer of Che. [This point was confirmed during a conversation this writer had with Ana Maria Araújo Freire ("Nita") on an airplane traveling from São Paulo to Porto Alegre.] I very much see a resemblance between Freire's position on violence and struggle and that of Martin Luther King and Cesar Chavez (the 'Mexican Gandhi'). Che's position is obviously closer to that of Malcolm X. King, Chavez, and Malcolm were all fearless warriors and men of great dignity, intelligence, and sensitivity. The tension between violence and nonviolence has remained undiminished throughout modern history and this book does not attempt to exercise a reconciliation.

As distinct from the Guevarean agent, the Freirean agent works silently but steadfastly in the margins of culture and the interstices of collapsing public sectors, away from the power-charged arenas of public spectacles of accusation and blame regarding what is wrong with our schools. Freirean educators do not conceive of their work as an antidote to today's sociocultural ills and the declining level of ambition with respect to contemporary society's commitment to democracy. Rather, their efforts are patiently directed at creating counterhegemonic sites of political struggle, radically alternative epistemological frameworks, and adversarial interpretations and cultural practices, as well as advocacy domains for disenfranchised groups.

Freirean pedagogy is important for contemporary educators to revisit, to build upon, and to reinvent in the contextual specificity of today's sociopolitical world, as we pass through the fragile portal of the new millennium. Freire's work needs to be engaged and put into practice at a deeper level than the falsely intimate emptiness that often passes for 'dialogical' encounters among liberal teachers and their students, who are carefully seated in dialogue circles and encouraged to emote.

A limited praxis—a praxis that does not take into account the totality of social relations—only reproduces the given social order and its dialectical contradictions in their inversion. Revolutionary or critical praxis must both *critique* the resulting ideological explanations and *transform* those relations that constitute the social contradictions. Freire writes that the "revolution loves and creates life; and in order to create life it may be obliged to prevent some men from circumscribing life" (1993a, p. 152). A revolutionary pedagogy reveals what Freire means by a liberation that moves from the liberal humanist notion of "traditional democratic freedom" to that of freeing oneself and others from the relation of the dialectical contradiction.

Freire is clear that education and cultural processes aimed at liberation do not succeed by freeing people from their chains, but by preparing them collectively to free themselves. This is dialectically facilitated when conversation is replaced by a dialogical praxis. Like Freire, we need to restore to liberation its rightful place as the central project of education. Ana Maria Araújo Freire and Donaldo Macedo write:

> Proud and happy, modest and conscious of his position in the world, Paulo Freire lived his life with faith, with humility and with contained happiness. With curiosity, serenity, and a desire for transformation, he lived, learning with the oppressed and fighting to overcome relationships of oppression. Living through the tensions and the conflicts of the world, but hopeful in its necessary changes, he lived. Impatiently patient, he fought his whole life for a more democratic world. (1998, p. 40)

The Secret Museum of the Human Race displays a mysterious painting in its Gallery of Great Teachers. In this painting San Ernesto de la Higuera and Paulo Freire are standing at the opposite sides of the abyss of human suffering. Suspended across its jagged mouth, their hands arch toward each other, their fingers straining to touch. Beneath them the exploited and the oppressed disappear into the darkness. There is no evidence of nine circles of damnation, only one vast pit into which all of humanity is consigned, and Virgil, the poet-guide, is nowhere to be found. Throughout the steady decline, there is no rhyming or free verse, no singing, only the furious sound of machine-gun fire, machetes chopping into human bone, flesh being torn asunder, and the deathly screams of men, women, and children recoiling from the iron fists of the *judiciales*, stained with the blood of innocents. Over this dark pit these two hands form a bridge of hope, one that can be maintained only through the unification of particular struggles: feminist, indigenist, environmental, ethnic, and class. Across the fathomless emptiness created by greed and the unquenchable thirst for power, women, men, and children can walk with dignity and in peace across the bridge and into the unknown.

These are the two hands of the revolution. One is the hand of the martyr: rough-edged, bold, powerful and erotic; the other is the hand of the educator: steadying, confident, sensitive, yet tender to the touch. One beckons us to struggle against impossible odds and toward impossible ends; the other directs our gaze to what has been lost and instills hope that it can be recovered anew with each succeeding generation.

Che and Freire realized that it is not necessary to travel to the bleak favelas of Rio, the majesty of Cuba's Sierra Maestra, or the dense thickets of La Higuera, Bolivia, to find such an abyss. It begins its formation in the push and pull of the human heart. The day that the *corazón* of humanity becomes filled with the collective love of its people, the abyss will disappear, and the bridge across it will no longer be necessary. Even museums will cease to exist.

NOTES

1. Freire had been Nita's elementary school teacher at the Colégio Oswaldo Cruz, and they had met again in the master's program at the Pontifícia Universidade Católica de São Paulo. Both were widowed at the time.

2. It was his ten-year involvement with the Industry Council's Social Service Organization in the Regional Department of Pernambuco and subsequently his General Superintendency of that division and his participation in the Movement for Popular Culture of Recife that helped to motivate him to devote his energies to the area of adult literacy.

3. He abandoned his vocation as a lawyer shortly after his first case (when he opened a small office to practice litigation and was approached by a creditor who wanted to confiscate the instruments from a dentist struggling to keep his practice alive) in order to study the relationships among pupils, teachers, and parents in working-class communities in the Northeast of Brazil.

4. The SESI is an employers union where Freire learned to understand the consciousness of working-class people. As educational director of the SESI, he co-ordinated the work of teachers with the children, as well as worked with their families (Gadotti, 1994).

5. Freire's literacy method grew out of the Movement for Popular Culture in Recife that had set up "cultural circles" (discussion groups with nonliterates) by the end of the

1950s. Freire believed that the oppressed could learn to read provided that reading was not imposed upon them in an authoritarian manner and that the process of reading validated their own lived experiences. After all, adults could speak an extraordinarily rich and complex language but lacked the graphical skills to write their ideas down. Freire understood that alienated and oppressed people are not heard by the dominant members of their society. The "culture of silence" that we created by the dominant culture did not mean that the oppressed could not respond to their own reality but that such a response often lacked a critical dimension.

In the "circulo de cultura" educators and learners employed codifications to engage in dialogue about the social, cultural and material conditions that impacted their lives on a daily basis. In the cultural circle, the peer group played a crucial role by providing the theoretical context for reflection and by transforming interpretations of reality from the production of 'everyday commonsense' to a more critical knowledge.

Freire and his colleagues spent considerable time in cultural circle settings with people from the local communities, making a list of the words used, the expressions, the informal jargon, and the characteristic mannerisms that accompanied certain phrases in order to gain an understanding of the 'cultural capital' of the people. Such topics as nationalism, development, democracy, and illiteracy were introduced through the use of slides or pictures, followed by a dialogue. The words "codified" the ways of life and the lived experiences of the local community members. Codifications included photographs, drawings, or even words, since they were all representations that permitted extended dialogue and an analysis of the concrete reality represented. Codifications mediated between the everyday lived experiences of the people and the theorizing that took place related to the context of everyday life. Codifications also mediated between the educators and learners who were actively engaged in co-constructing the meanings of their daily existence. In this way, Freire's approach to literacy brushed against the grain of mainstream literacy methods that required individuals to learn the words and ideas from books or materials that were produced by those in power. To learn to read from a primer meant that learners must accept the experiences inscribed in the primer as more important than their own. Freire was able to identify generative themes that permeated the experiences of those who believed the current conditions of their existence—such as poverty and illiteracy—were due to fate, or to chance, or to their own constitutive inferiority, yet who desired so much to become literate. Freire recognized that oppressed learners had internalized profoundly negative images of themselves (images created and imposed by the oppressor) and felt incapable of taking an active participation in their own affairs.

The generative themes that Freire was able to elicit from his time spent with the oppressed were codifications of complex experiences that had a great deal of social meaning and political significance for the group and were likely to generate considerable discussion and analysis. They were selected because they derived from the contextual specificity of the history and circumstances of the learners, but they were also chosen for their syllabic length and with the goal of presenting all the phonemes of the Portuguese language. Freire's 'method' (Freire's work can't be reduced to a method strictly speaking, since it is more of a political philosophy) consisted of an investigative stage of finding the words and generative themes of a group in terms of their social class relevance and meaning for that group. Generative themes were often codified into generative words—more specifically, tri-syllabic words that could be broken down into syllabic parts and used to "generate" other words (Brown, 1987). Freire and his culture circles practiced a form of decodification that broke up a codification into its constituent elements so that the learners began to perceive relationships between elements of the codification and other experiences in their day-to-day lives. Such decodification took place through dialogue, in which familiar, everyday experiences were made strange and the strange or unknown process of generating critical knowledge was made familiar.

Freire followed the creation of generative themes with the process of thematization, where generative themes were codified and decodified and replaced by a critical social vision. New generative themes were then discovered and instructors were able to breakdown and identify phonetic groups at this stage. This was followed by problematization (the antithesis of problem-solving) that consisted of codifying reality into symbols that could generate critical consciousness. During the problematization stage, the group within the cultural circle examined the limits and possibilities of the existential situations that emerged from the previous stage. Critical consciousness demanded a rejection of passivity and the practice of dialogue. Critical consciousness was brought about not through an individual or intellectual effort, but through conscientization or identifying contradictions in one's lived experience, and understanding and overcoming dominant myths, traditions, and ideologies in order to reach new levels of awareness of being an "object" in a world where only "subjects" have the means to determine the direction of their lives. The process of conscientization involved becoming a "subject" with other oppressed subjects and taking part in humanizing the world through collective struggle and praxis. Conscientization involved experiencing oppressive reality as a process that can be overcome through transformative praxis. Such a praxis (a cycle of action-reflection-action) involved overcoming through concrete actions and group effort those obstacles to the process of becoming human (Gadotti, 1994). Freire's approach to literacy created the conditions for the oppressed to liberate themselves and, in the process, liberate their oppressors. See the excellent summary of Freirean literacy methodology by Cynthia Brown (1987).

6. This program was motivated by the work of Frantz Fanon, a re-engagement with the works of Marx, and personal sympathy for Amilcar Cabral's Movimento Popular Libertação de Angola (Popular Movement for the Liberation of Angola), Frente de Libertação de Moçcambique (Mozambique Liberation Front), and Partido Africans para Independência da Guinea-Bissau e Cabo Verde (African Independence Party for the Liberation of Guinea and the Cape Verde Islands).

7. Ninety-nine percent of the population numbering 600,000 were illiterate, and there were only fourteen university graduates in the entire country (Cohen, 1998). Cabral realized that the peasantry had to be organized effectively as participants—and not merely as observers—in the armed military struggle that began in 1962. Cabral had visited all the ethnic groups in every section of the colony, talked to the elders (*homens grandes*), and learned, analyzed, and assessed their various economic systems, customs, and traditions (Cohen, 1998). He realized that the peasants had to understand the need for a revolution, and to do this he trained revolutionary political workers to mobilize and politicize all the peasant groups. Hundreds of meetings and discussions with the village elders and peasants transpired, and Cabral's workers facilitated discussion on all matters relevant to the liberation struggle (Cohen, 1998).

8. He returned to Europe briefly to make arrangements for his permanent voyage back to Brazil in 1980.

9. The week after his death on May 2, 1997, Freire was scheduled to attend a ceremony in Cuba, where Fidel Castro was to present him with a major award for this contribution to education. According to his friends, this was to be the most important award of Freire's life.

REFERENCES

Allman, Paula; with Mayo, Peter; Cavanagh, Chris; Heng, Chan Lean; and Haddad, Sergio (1998). "Introduction: '. . . The Creation of a World in Which It Will Be Easier to Love.'" *Convergence,* vol. 31, nos. 1 and 2, pp. 9–16.

Aronowitz, Stanley (1993). "Paulo Freire's Radical Democratic Humanism." In Peter McLaren and Peter Leonard (eds.). *Paulo Freire: A Critical Encounter.* London and New York: Routledge, pp. 8–24.

Aronowitz, Stanley; and Giroux, Henry (1991). *Postmodern Education.* Minneapolis: University of Minnesota Press.

Brown, Cynthia (1987). "Literacy in 30 Hours: Paulo Freire's Process in Northeast Brazil." In Ira Shor (ed.). *Freire for the Classroom: A Sourcebook for Liberatory Teaching.* Portsmouth, N.H.: Boynton/Cook, pp. 215–231.

Cohen, Sylvester (1998). "Amilcar Cabral: An Extraction from the Literature." *Monthly Review,* vol. 50, no. 7 (December), pp. 39–47.

Cummins, Jim (1989). *Empowering Minority Students.* Sacramento: California Association for Bilingual Education.

Darder, Antonia (1991). *Culture and Power in the Classroom: A Critical Foundation for Bicultural Education.* Westport, Conn.: Bergin and Garvey.

——— (1998). "Teaching as an Act of Love." *Reclaiming Our Voices.* Los Angeles: California Association of Bilingual Education, pp. 25–41.

Dewey, John (1916). *Democracy and Education.* New York: Macmillan.

Dunayeuskaya, Raya (1982). *Rosa Luxemburg, Women's Liberation, and Marx's Philosophy of Revolution.* Atlantic Highlands: N.J.: Humanities Press; and Sussex: Harvester.

Elias, John (1994). *Paulo Freire: Pedagogue of Revolution.* Melbourne, Fla.: Krieger.

Ellsworth, Elizabeth (1989). "Why Doesn't This Feel Empowering? Working through the Repressive Myths of Critical Pedagogy." *Harvard Educational Review,* vol. 59, no. 5, pp. 297–324.

Fine, Michelle (1991). *Framing Dropouts.* Albany: State University of New York Press.

Freire, Ana Maria Araújo; and Macedo, Donaldo (1998). "Introduction." In Ana Maria Araújo Freire and Donaldo Macedo (eds.). *The Paulo Freire Reader.* New York: Continuum, pp. 1–44.

Freire, Paulo (1967). Educacão como Prática da Liberdade (Education as a Practice of Freedom). Rio de Janeiro: Paz e Terra.

——— (1970). *Cultural Action for Freedom.* Harmondsworth, U.K.: Penguin.

——— (1973). *Education for Critical Consciousness.* New York: Seabury.

——— (1978). *Pedagogy in Process: The Letters to Guinea-Bissau.* New York: Seabury.

——— (1985). *The Politics of Education: Culture, Power, and Liberation.* South Hadley, Mass.: Bergin and Garvey.

——— (1993a). *Pedagogy of the Oppressed.* New York: Continuum.

——— (1993b). *Pedagogy of the City.* New York: Continuum.

——— (1994). *Pedagogy of Hope: Reliving Pedagogy of the Oppressed.* New York: Continuum.

——— (1996). *Letters to Christina; Reflections on My Life and Work.* New York: Routledge.

——— (1997a). "A Response." In Paulo Freire with James W. Fraser, Donaldo Macedo, Tanya McKinnon, and William T. Stokes (eds.). *Mentoring the Mentor: A Critical Dialogue with Paulo Freire.* New York: Peter Lang, pp. 303–329.

——— (1997b). *Teachers as Cultural Workers: Letters to Those Who Dare to Teach.*

Translated by Donaldo Macedo, Dale Koike, and Alexandre Oliviera. Boulder, Colo.:
Westview.

———(1998a). *Pedagogy of Freedom: Ethics, Democracy, and Civic Courage.* Boulder,
Colo., and New York: Rowman and Littlefield.

———(1998b). *Pedagogy of the Heart.* New York: Continuum.

———(1998c). *Politics and Education.* Translated by Pia Lindquist Wong. Los Angeles:
UCLA Latin American Center Publications.

Freire, Paulo; with Faundez, A. (1989). *Learning to Question: A Pedagogy of Liberation.*
New York: Continuum.

Freire, Paulo; and Macedo, Donaldo (1987). *Literacy: Reading the Word and the World.*
South Hadley, Mass.: Bergin and Garvey.

Freire, Paulo; with Escobar, Miguel; Fernandez, Alfredo L.; and Guerarr-Niebla,
Gilberto (1994). *Paulo Freire on Higher Education: A Dialogue at the National University of Mexico.* Albany: State University of New York Press.

Gadotti, Moacir (1994). *Reading Paulo Freire: His Life and Work.* Albany: State University of New York Press.

Giroux, Henry (1983). *Theory and Resistance in Education: A Pedagogy for the Opposition.* South Hadley, Mass.: Bergin and Garvey.

———(1993). "Paulo Freire and the Politics of Postcolonialism." In Peter McLaren and
Peter Leonard (eds). *Paulo Freire: A Critical Encounter.* London and New York:
Routledge, pp. 177–188.

Giroux, Henry; and McLaren, Peter (eds.) (1989). *Critical Pedagogy, the State, and Cultural Struggle.* Albany: State University of New York Press.

———(1994). *Between Borders: Pedagogy and the Politics of Cultural Studies.* New
York and London: Routledge.

Giroux, Henry; Lankshear, Colin; McLaren, Peter; and Peters, Michael (1997). *Counternarratives: Cultural Studies and Critical Pedagogies in Postmodern Spaces.* London and New York: Routledge.

Gore, Jennifer (1993). *The Struggle for Pedagogies: Critical and Feminist Discourses as
Regimes of Truth.* New York: Routledge.

Grant, Carl (1977). *Multicultural Education: Commitments, Issues, and Applications.*
Washington, D.C.: Association for Supervision and Curriculum Development.

Habermas, Jurgen (1979). *Communication and the Evolution of Society.* Translated by
T. McCarthy. Boston, Mass.: Beacon.

———(1987). *The Theory of Communicative Action.* Vol. 2. *Lifeworld and System: A
Critique of Functionalist Reason.* Translated by T. McCarthy. Boston, Mass.: Beacon.

Hall, B. (1998). "'Please Don't Bother the Canaries': Paulo Freire and the International
Council for Adult Education." *Convergence,* vol. 31, nos. 1 and 2, pp. 95–103.

hooks, bell (1993). "bell hooks Speaking about Paulo Freire—The Man, His Work." In
Peter McLaren and Peter Leonard (eds.). *Paulo Freire: A Critical Encounter.* London and New York: Routledge, pp. 146–154.

JanMohamed, Abdul R. (1994). "Some Implications of Paulo Freire's Border Pedagogy."
In Henry A. Giroux and Peter McLaren (eds.). *Between Borders: Pedagogy and the
Politics of Cultural Studies.* New York and London: Routledge, pp. 242–252.

Kanpol, Barry (1992). *Towards a Theory and Practice of Teacher Cultural Politics: Continuing the Postmodern Debate.* Norwood, N.J.: Ablex.

Kincheloe, Joe (1993). *Toward a Critical Politics of Teacher Thinking: Mapping the Postmodern.* South Hadley, Mass.: Bergin and Garvey.

Kincheloe, Joe (1994). "Afterword." In Peter McLaren and Colin Lankshear (eds.). *Politics of Liberation: Paths from Freire.* London and New York: Routledge, pp. 216–218.

Kincheloe, Joe; and Steinberg, Shirley (1997). *Changing Multiculturalism.* Buckingham and Philadelphia: Open University Press.

Ladson-Billings, Gloria (1997). "I Know Why This Doesn't Feel Empowering: A Critical *Race* Analysis of Critical Pedagogy." In Paulo Freire, James W. Fraser, Donaldo Macedo, Tanya McKinnon, and William T. Stokes (eds.). *Mentoring the Mentor.* New York: Peter Lang, pp. 127–141.

Lankshear, Colin (1993). "Functional Literacy from a Freirean Point of View." In Peter McLaren and Peter Leonard, (eds.). *Paulo Freire: A Critical Encounter.* London and New York: Routledge, pp. 90–118.

Lankshear, Colin; and McLaren, Peter (eds.) (1993). "Introduction." In Colin Lankshear and Peter McLaren (eds.). *Critical Literacy: Politics, Praxis, and the Postmodern.* Albany: State University of New York Press, pp. 1–56.

Lather, Patti (1991). *Getting Smart: Feminist Research and Pedagogy within the Postmodern.* New York and London: Routledge, p. 88.

Leistyna, Pepi (1999). *Presence of Mind: Education and the Politics of Deception.* Boulder, Colo.: Westview.

Macedo, Donaldo (1994). *Literacies of Power.* Boulder, Colo.: Westview.

———(1998). "Foreword." In Paulo Freire, *Pedagogy of Freedom.* Lanham, Md.: Rowman & Littlefield, pp. xi–xxxii.

Mayo, Peter (1999). *Gramsci, Freire and Adult Education: Possibilities for Transformative Action.* London and New York: Zed Books.

———(1997). "Tribute to Paulo Freire (1921–1997)." *International Journal of Lifelong Education,* vol. 16, no. 5, pp. 365–370.

McCarthy, Cameron (1988). "Rethinking Liberal and Radical Perspectives on Racial Inequality in Schooling: Making the Case for Nonsynchrony." *Harvard Educational Review* 58 (3), pp. 265–279.

McLaren, Peter (1995). *Critical Pedagogy and Predatory Culture.* New York and London: Routledge.

———(1997a). *Life in Schools: An Introduction to Critical Pedagogy in the Social Foundations of Education.* White Plains, N.Y.: Longman.

———(1997b). "La Lucha Continua: Freire, Boal and the Challenge of History. To My Brothers and Sisters in Struggle." *Researcher,* vol. 1, no. 2, pp. 5–10.

———(1997c). "Freirean Pedagogy: The Challenge of Postmodernism and the Politics of Race." In Paulo Freire, James W. Fraser, Donaldo Macedo, Tanya McKinnon, and William T. Stokes (eds.). *Mentoring the Mentor.* New York: Peter Lang, pp. 99–125.

———(1997d). *Revolutionary Multiculturalism: Pedagogies of Dissent for the New Millenium.* Boulder, Colo.: Westview.

McLaren, Peter; and Da Silva, Tomaz Tadeu (1993). "Decentering Pedagogy: Critical Literacy, Resistance, and the Politics of Meaning." In Peter McLaren and Peter Leonard (eds.). *Paulo Freire: A Critical Encounter.* London and New York: Routledge, pp. 47–89.

McLaren, Peter; and Giarelli, Jim (eds.). (1995). *Critical Theory and Educational Research.* Albany: State University of New York Press.

McLaren, Peter; and Lankshear, Colin (eds.) (1994). *Politics of Liberation: Paths from Freire.* New York and London: Routledge.

McLaren, Peter; and Leonard, Peter (eds.). (1993). *Paulo Freire: A Critical Encounter.* New York and London, Routledge.

McLaren, Peter; Leonard, Peter; and Gadotti, Moacir (1998). *Paulo Freire: Poder, Desejo e Memórias da Libertação.* Porto Alegre: Artes Médicas Sul LTDA.

Moraes, Marcia (1996). *Bilingual Education: A Dialogue with the Bakhtin Circle.* Albany: State University of New York Press.

Murrell, Jr., Peter (1997). "Digging Again the Family Wells: A Freirean Literacy Framework as Emancipatory Pedagogy for African American Children." In Paulo Freire, James W. Fraser, Donaldo Macedo, Tanya McKinnon, and William T. Stokes (eds.). *Mentoring the Mentor.* New York: Peter Lang, pp. 19–58.

Parker, Stuart (1997). *Reflective Teaching in the Postmodern World: A Manifesto for Education in Postmodernity.* Buckingham and Philadelphia: Open University Press.

San Juan, E. (forthcoming). "Postcolonialism and Uneven Development." *Strategies.*

Schugurensky, Daniel (1998). "The Legacy of Paulo Freire: A Critical Review of His Contributions." *Convergence,* vol. 31, nos. 1 and 2, pp. 17–38.

Sleeter, Christine; and Grant, Carl (1988). *Making Choices for Multicultural Education: Five Approaches to Race, Class, and Gender.* Columbus: Merill.

Sleeter, Christine; and McLaren, Peter (eds.) (1995). *Multicultural Education and Critical Pedagogy.* Albany: State University of New York Press.

Taylor, Paul (1993). *The Texts of Paulo Freire.* Buckingham and Philadelphia: Open University Press.

Torres, Rosa María (1998). "The Million Paulo Freires." *Convergence,* vol. 31, nos. 1 and 2, pp. 107–116.

Weiler, Kathleen (1988). *Women Teaching for Change: Gender, Class and Power.* South Hadley, Mass.: Bergin and Garvey.

———— (1996). Myths of Paulo Freire. *Educational Theory,* vol. 46, no. 3, pp. 353–371.

West, Cornel (1993). "Preface." In Peter McLaren, and Peter Leonard (eds.). *Paulo Freire: A Critical Encounter.* New York and London: Routledge, pp. xiii–xiv.

Wink, Joan (1997). *Critical Pedagogy: Notes from the Real World.* White Plains, N.Y.: Longman.

PART THREE

A PEDAGOGY FOR THE REVOLUTION OF OUR TIME

Colonization can only disfigure the colonizer. It places him before an alternative having equally disastrous results; daily injustice accepted for his benefit on the one hand and necessary, but never consummated, self-sacrifice on the other. That is the situation with the colonizer who individually decays if he accepts, and repudiates himself if he refuses to accept.

— Albert Memmi, *The Colonizer and the Colonized*

In August 1964, at a ceremony awarding communist certificates to the best workers of the Ministry of Industry, Che, with his fine human sensibility, cited a few paragraphs from a book by the poet León Felipe:
"But man is a hard-working and stupid child, who has turned work into tiresome toil, he has turned the drumstick into a hoe, and instead of tapping out a song of joy on the land, he began to dig. . . ."
The poet continued:
"I want to say that no one has been able to dig to the rhythm of the sun, and that no one has yet cut a stalk of corn with love and grace."
Che stated in reply:
"That's why I wanted to quote those lines. Because today we could tell that great desperate poet to come to Cuba to see how man, after passing through all the stages of capitalist alienation, and after being considered a beast of burden harnessed to the yoke of the exploiter has rediscovered his course, has found his way back. Today in our Cuba, work takes on new meaning every day. It is done with new joy."
And we say as in the song: Che, you are the poet.

— Enrique Oltuski (1998)

If we workers take notion, we can stop all speeding trains
Every ship upon the ocean we can tie with mighty chains
Every wheel in the creation, every mine and every mill
Fleets and armies of all nations will at our command stand still.

— Joe Hill, unpublished pamphlet

Why should educators bother to engage with the legacies of Che Guevara and Paulo Freire, especially now that the 'end of history' has been declared? Especially, too, when broadside condemnations of Marxism abound uncontested? And why now, at a time when the marketplace has transformed itself into a *deus ex machina* ordained to rescue humankind from economic disaster and when voguish theories imported from France and Germany can abundantly supply North American radicals with veritable plantations of no-risk, no-fault, knock-off rebellion? Why should North American educators take seriously two men who were propelled to international fame for their devotion to the downtrodden of South America and Africa? One reason is that capitalism's Faustian urge to dominate the globe has generated a global ecological crisis. Another obvious, but no less important, reason is that the economic comfort enjoyed by North Americans is directly linked to the poverty of our South American brothers and sisters. As Elvia Alvarado proclaims in *Don't Be Afraid Gringo,* "It's hard to think of change taking place in Central America without there first being changes in the United States. As we say in Honduras, 'Sin el perro, no hay rabia'—without the dog, there wouldn't be rabies'" (1987, p. 144). Still yet another reason is that Che and Freire have given us a pedagogical course of action (not to be confused with a blueprint) for making bold steps to redress locally and globally current asymmetrical relations of power and privilege.

But no one can deny that the climate for such an undertaking is not favorable. The advance of critical pedagogy within the current historical juncture appears to have reached an unresolvable impasse, at least within the United States. Stanley Aronowitz captures the ethos of these current "dark times":

> These are dark times for education innovation and its protagonists. In schools and universities "reactionaries" (as Paulo Freire calls them) have all but overwhelmed the "progressives." Their agenda to construe the very concept of education as training dominates schooling in public universities and is steadily gaining ground in private institutions as well. During the last decade, schools that insisted on their difference committed an unholy violation of the new common sense that the highest mission and overriding purpose of schooling was to prepare students, at different levels, to take their places in the corporate order. The banking or transmission theory of school knowledge, which Freire identified more than thirty years ago as the culprit standing in the way of critical consciousness, has returned with a vengeance. (Aronowitz, 1998, p. 4)

Given the current times we live in, critical pedagogy needs to reflexively engage its own premises, to challenge its own decidability, and to be self-conscious of its own constructed character. Surely critical pedagogy must not only continue to be critical of its own status as a commodity, it must also remain critical of its own presumed role as the metatruth of educational criticism. The language of critical pedagogy, after all, is also a social system that inscribes subjects. Critical pedagogy in this regard will always be Other to itself, will always be at odds with itself.

It's important to recognize that *now* is the time to brush hard against the grain of teaching until the full range of revolutionary pedagogical options are made available in the public schools of the nation, realizing that none of these options is panacean and that all of them will require sustained theoretical and political engagement. Part of this task is exegetical: to recognize and research the distinctions among teaching, pedagogy, critical pedagogy, and revolutionary pedagogy. Part of the task is ethical: to make liberation and the abolition of human suffering the goal of the educative enterprise itself. Part of the task is political: to create a democratic socialist society in which democracy will be called upon daily to live up to its promise.

Teaching is a process of organizing and integrating knowledge for the purpose of communicating this knowledge or awareness to students through an exchange of understanding in prespecified contexts and teacher/learner environments. *Pedagogy* is distinct from teaching in that it situates the teacher/learner encounter in a wider context of historical and sociopolitical forces in which the 'act of knowing' recognizes and takes into account the differentiated politics of 'reception' surrounding the object of knowledge by the students. *Critical pedagogy* constitutes a dialectical and dialogical process that instantiates a reciprocal exchange between teachers and students—an exchange that engages in the task of reframing, refunctioning, and reposing the question of understanding itself, bringing into dialectical relief the structural and relational dimensions of knowledge and its hydra-headed power/knowledge dimensions. *Revolutionary pedagogy* goes further still. It puts power/knowledge relations on a collision course with their own internal contradictions; such a powerful and often unbearable collision gives birth not to an epistemological resolution at a higher level but rather to a provisional glimpse of a new society freed from the bondage of the past, a vision in which the past reverberates in the present, standing at once outside the world and beside the world, in a place of insight where the subject recognizes she is in a world and subject to it, yet moving through it with the power to name it extopically so that hidden meanings can be revealed in the accidental contingencies of the everyday. Revolutionary pedagogy creates a narrative space set against the naturalized flow of the everyday, against the daily poetics of agency, encounter, and conflict, in which subjectivity is constantly dissolved and reconstructed—that is, in which subjectivity turns-back-on-itself, giving rise both to an affirmation of the world through naming it, and an opposition to the world through unmasking and undoing the practices of concealment that are latent in the process of naming itself.

Che and Freire both recognized that categorizing the world is always a violent act in that it inevitably naturalizes dangerous hierarchies. The revolutionary educator always wounds the ordinary so that it can be seen not as something that is permanently sealed but as a space of wild fluids, of shifting boundaries. The revolutionary educator engages the world reflexively, dedicated to the praxis of transforming knowledge through epistemological critique. Epistemological critique involves more than unpacking representations but also exploring the how and why of their historical production. Revolutionary educators do not merely track the hemorrhaging of signifiers into other signifiers but also explore how these signifiers are concealed within larger organizational formations, institutional arrangements, and concrete and contradictory social relations. For revolutionary educators, knowledge exceeds its semiotic end products; it travels intertextually within demarcated systems of intelligibility. Critical knowledge is understood as persistently open, disclosive, incomplete and open-ended. In this way it remains cautious in the presence of reified social relations and epistemological distortions that occlude both the social ontology of knowledge and its processual journey from 'fact' to 'value.' In other words, critical epistemological practice not only examines the content of knowledge but also its method of production. It seeks to understand how ideological constructions are encoded and administered, how metonymic and synecdochical gestures are performed so as to obscure relations of domination and oppression, how the interpretive and interpellative frameworks by which we organize our sentiments construct ruling stereotypes and how the governing categories of our everyday discourse render invisible and obscure real social relations of exploitation (see Bannerji, 1995).

Larry Grossberg has fashioned a contemporary understanding of agency that complements my analysis. Grossberg argues, rightly so, that agency is more than the power to act, it is also "about access to particular places—places at which particular kinds of actions, producing particular kinds of effects, are possible— places at which one can intercede and influence the various 'forces' and vectors that are shaping the world" (1999, p. 32).

According to Grossberg, agency refers to structured mobilities and what he calls a "lived geography of practices." It refers to sites where individuals and groups "install" their "selves" into practices. These include places of temporary stability and the organization of the dispersed spaces between them that both construct and constrain peoples' possibilities at any moment. Grossberg writes that

> A lived geography defines a constant transformation of places into spaces, and spaces into places, the constant shuttling between the dispersed system of stabilities within which people live out their everyday lives. It defines the sites which people can occupy, the investments people can make in them, and the planes along which people can connect and transform them so as to construct a consistent, livable space for themselves. Not everyone has access to the same maps, and even within a specific map, not everyone has the same access to the same places, nor

can everyone travel along the same vectors traversing space. Not all spaces are equal or equally accessible, and the question of the relations of space and place are always implicated in relations of power and control. Further, such maps are themselves distributed and always contested, inseparable from the relations of power and control. (1999, p. 33)

The struggle, as I see it, from the standpoint of revolutionary pedagogy, is to construct sites—provisional sites—in which new structured mobilities and tendential lines of forces can be made to suture identity to the larger problematic of social justice. In other words, students and cultural workers need to attach themselves to modalities of belonging fashioned out of new economies of subjectivities and difference. This requires breaking the imaginary power of commodified identities within capitalism as well as the forces and relations that both produce and are products of capitalism.

In their best moments, the pedagogies of Freire and Che exemplify the characteristics of revolutionary pedagogy. While both pedagogical approaches place a profound emphasis on critical literacy and are underwritten by an explicit political project, it is not surprising to find that Freire's project is more systematic, more coherent, more dialogical, and more self-reflexive than that of Che. Che's pedagogy was more intuitive, but what made Che so remarkable was that this intuition was profoundly counterintuitive. Yet the political project that unites both Che and Freire speaks to mutual concerns.[1] It should be emphasized, too, that Che's pedagogy is most asssuredly dialectical in nature and grounded in the lived experiences of the oppressed becoming transformed into the "new man" through acquiring a revolutionary consciousness while at the same time 'living the life' (what we might colloquially refer to as 'walking the walk') of the revolutionary. This meant for Che, as it did for Freire, that education needs to take on an extra-ivory-tower, public-sphere role in contemporary revolutionary movements and in politics in general. However, it was not imperative for Che that everyone become a *guerrillero* or *guerrillera*. But it was manifestly important that everyone develop a revolutionary consciousness and engage in actions that directly contribute to the furthering of the revolution.

For Che, the "new man" is not merely a zombified agent who has been whisked to critical consciousness by the winds of revolutionary indoctrination and the repeated declamations of ideologues from Politburo to pulpit. The *point d' appui* of critical pedagogy for both these figures was the development of a dialectical grasp of history and of the contradictions of human labor under capitalism; for those of us working in education, this means recognizing and transforming those contradictions that create asymmetries of power in the manufacturing of relations of race, gender, class, and sexuality. Clearly, these revolutionaries did not equate political liberation with the exposure of dominative social practices as a *trompe-l'oeil*, nor did they consider it sufficient to bewail the trials and tribulations of the dispossessed; they were both unwaveringly committed to transforming those social practices that lay at the root of human exploitation and misery.

Che's project of revolutionary life avoided the repressive desublimation of the totalitarian 'leader' who enjoins his followers to transgress everyday moral rules in the name of some higher good; he did not insist that fellow fighters enjoy what they do. The rules that governed guerrilla life produced a psychic economy of privation and sacrifice that was only survivable when it became affectively invested in a profound desire to overcome the systematic abuses of tyranny and exploitation. To be a guerrilla fighter was not to engage in a stylized revolt against the cohesive, seamless, and sanitized bourgeois self. Nor was it an effort to push subversion into the ethereal realm of the sublime. Rather, to be a guerrilla fighter was, for Che, to stalk state-sponsored terror and defeat it at every turn. It was to create the initial momentum for the popular revolution that would follow in its wake.

In the theater of battle, Che did not have time to create the conditions for peasants to achieve conscientization before he tried to conscript them into his guerrilla project. Nevertheless, he never threatened to use force against—or to cajole or insult—those who were unable to or refused to join him. And to his credit, he never tried to entice them with monetary rewards. Rather, he appealed to their sense of justice, and in entering into discussions with them enjoined them to follow his group of fighters for the good of the collectivity of the toilers of the world.

Freire's pedagogy was fertilized more in the domain of critical dialogism than was Che's, and his vision of the new society was decidedly more open ended. The revolutionary character of Freire's approach is lucidly reflected in Bertell Ollman's recent description of what constitutes a 'dialectical understanding' of everyday life. Because he believes that the current stage of capitalism is characterized by far greater complexity and much faster change and interaction than at any time in human history, Ollman argues that a dialectical understanding of social life is "more indispensable now than ever before" (1998, p. 342). Ollman articulates a dialectical method that he breaks down into six successive moments. The *ontological moment* has to do with the infinite number of mutually dependent processes that make up the totality or structured whole of social life. The *epistemological moment* deals with how to organize thinking in order to understand such a world, abstracting out the main patterns of change and interaction. The *moment of inquiry* appropriates the patterns of these internal relationships in order to further the project of investigation. The *moment of intellectual reconstruction or self-clarification* puts together the results of such an investigation for oneself. The *moment of exposition* entails describing to a particular audience the dialectical grasp of the facts by taking into account how others think. Finally, the *moment of praxis* uses the clarification of the facts of social life to act consciously in and on the world, changing it while simultaneously deepening one's understanding of it. These dialectical acts, which are traversed repeatedly over time, bear a striking similarity to the pedagogy of Paulo Freire. Adumbrating Freire's radical theory of knowledge, powered by a process of dialectical thinking, Paula Allman and her colleagues write:

> Freire's dialectical thinking, all dialectical thinking for that matter, treats history as a process. This is a key pre-condition that enabled Freire to convey a radical theory of what it means to be a human being (a radical ontology) and a radical theory of knowledge (a radical epistemology). Whether they recognize it or not, most people have ontological and epistemological theories or at least assumptions. Freire's ontological theory is radical because it critiques what it has meant thus far to be a human being and also offers the philosophy of what we could become. Therefore it is not only a theory of being but also a theory of becoming. His theory of knowledge is equally radical/dialectical. Accordingly, no person is an 'empty vessel' or devoid of knowledge. Many people have valuable experiential knowledge; all of us have opinions and beliefs; others have greater or lesser degrees of extant—i.e. already existing—knowledge and may even hold qualifications that signify their "possession" of that knowledge. However, in Freirean education the affirmation or acquisition of these types of knowledge is not the end objective of learning but rather the beginning of the dialogical/problem-posing approach to learning. (Allman et al. 1998, p. 11)

The concept of dialectics is, of course, an abstraction intended to help explain the messy and sinewy web of concrete social life and to offer a way of overcoming its contradictions. Admittedly, however, it is difficult to overcome the contradictions of lived experience, even for somebody as politically erudite and sensitive as Freire. Schugurensky remarks that

> Freire's analysis is based on Hegelian dialectics, in which unity is understood as a constant tension of theses, antitheses and syntheses, and change is the resolution of the conflict between two opposites. Theoretically, a dialectical approach overcomes dualism and false dichotomies, but to what extent Freire was able to accomplish this is still open to debate. Similarly, Freire's tendency to use bipolar strategies has led some disciples to advocate a monolithic rejection of banking education, colonialism, capitalist development and so forth. The complexity of the real world makes such a position difficult to sustain, as it was even for Freire himself. (1998, pp. 24–25)

Freirean pedagogy is a story about the struggle for critical consciousness read against the powerful dialectical contradictions of capitalism that exist between productive labor and capital and between production and exchange and their historical linkage and development. Though to a large extent the guiding narratives of critical pedagogy concern the politics of interpreting revolutionary theory, they also constitute an immensely personal story of the journey of teachers toward critical consciousness. Regardless of the personal, epistemological, onto-logical, and moral paths that we choose to take as educators, at some point we have to come face-to-face with the naked reality of capitalist social relations in both local and global contexts. We cannot ignore these relations, and if we are to engage in a revolutionary educational praxis, we need to do more than rail against the suffering and tribulations of the oppressed and instead seek ways of transforming them.

Freire's comments on neoliberalism are apposite:

> I would like to call attention to an implication present in a veiled manner within neoliberal discourse. When they speak about the death of history, of ideologies, of utopia, and about the disappearance of social classes, they make me certain that they defend a posterior sort of fatalism. It is as if they regret not having stated the *domestication* of the future sooner. The mechanists of Marxist origin *deproblema-tized* the future and reduced it to a premade, preknown time; those who now defend the end of history welcome the "new time," the time of "definitive victory" for capitalism, as a future that was late in coming, but that is finally here. They wipe out sixty years of human achievement with a sponge, considering it an error of his-tory finally corrected. According to such discourse, having reached the levels it has, as it created the social classes of modern society, the capitalist system would have a greater purpose than the one Marx attributed to the working class: being the undertaker of the dominant class. As it constituted itself, the capitalist system was doomed to end with history itself. (1998b, p. 47; emphasis in original)

It is important to note that while Freire lamented the authoritarianism and dogmatism that often accompanied socialist regimes, he believed—and indeed struggled for—a form of democratic socialism. Freire did not believe that Stal-inism had informed the Marxian project of creating 'real existing socialism.' This is clear when he writes:

> [S]ince I do not believe Stalinist authoritarianism is part of the nature of social-ism, I have no reason to admit that a truly democratic socialism is an impossi-ble proposition.
>
> I refuse to accept that the presence of authoritarianism within socialism is due to some ontological incompatibility between human beings and the essence of socialism. That would be the same as saying: "So averse is human nature to the fun-damental virtues of socialism that only under coercion would it be possible to make it work." That which human ontology rejects, on the contrary, is authoritarianism, regardless of what attributes it may receive. (1998b, p. 49)

Even though socialism, in numerous instances, transformed democracy into sites of disablement and made a mockery of socialism's original dedication to social justice, and even though it now has been declared toxic to the postmodern landscape and reviled as an unwanted interloper from the past—just like a dusty, washed-up, homeless intruder who approaches you on your way to your cappuccino stand, demanding that you pay attention to his unshaven face and running eyes—Freire not only held out for, but actively worked to create, a socialist alternative to what he perceived to be the inevitable conditions brought about by global capitalism. Like Che, Freire was driven to socialism not only by its utopian possibilities—it critical and not naïve utopian dreams—but also by the brute reality of capitalist social relations. As Freire comments:

> I feel utterly at peace with the interpretation that the wane of "realistic socialism" does not mean, on one side, that socialism has shown itself to be intrinsically inviable; on the other, that capitalism has now stepped forward in its excellence once and for all.
>
> What excellence is this, that manages to "coexist with more than a billion inhabitants of the developing world who live in poverty," not to say misery? Not to mention the all but indifference with which it coexists with "pockets of poverty" and misery in its own, developed body. What excellence is this, that sleeps in peace while numberless men and women make their home in the street, and says it is their own fault that they are on the street? What excellence is this, that struggles so little, if it struggles at all, with discrimination for reason of sex, class, or race, as if to reject someone different, humiliate her, offend him, hold her in contempt, exploit her. . . . What excellence is this, that tepidly registers the millions of children who come into the world and do not remain, or not for long, or if they are more resistant, manage to stay a while, then take their leave of the world? (1994, p. 94)

The linchpin of revolutionary pedagogy, from the perspectives of both Freire and Che, is Marx's theory of consciousness/praxis, which maps the movement of their pedagogical problematic onto the terrain of a Marxist humanism. Revolutionary pedagogy signals both an epistemological and ontological revolution in the way that we think about 'knowledge' and 'being' and the relationship between them. Emphasizing the importance of a critical/dialectical praxis that is infused with an alternative educational approach—one that can be applied in both formal and informal contexts—revolutionary pedagogy reveals how praxis needs to employ both cultural action and cultural revolution. Freire and Che share with Marx the idea that our human potential is directly linked to human relationships in naturally occurring circumstances—that is, in lived experiences. For Che and for Freire, the philosophy of praxis represents the apogee of achievement and possesses a scientific, nonideological, and dialectical coherence. The philosophy of praxis is a radical educational praxis, a method of analysis and a conception of the world that involves a dialectical comprehension of reality and a dialogical unity with the people. It involves making coherent the principles and problems of the masses in their practical activity.

In some ways, Freire's 'problem-posing' as distinct from 'solution-giving' pedogogy comes closer to Holloway's post-Marxist description of the Zapatista struggle as insurgency with no guarantees—meaning no predefined utopia or blueprint for a new society. It is a struggle that creates collective memory to disarm the professional political class through poetry and word-play, to politicize the language of society, to abandon the *deus ex machina* concept of the vanguard party, and to struggle against the negation of dignity. And though Freire's pedagogical work reflects the concern of the Zapatistas for the political education of civil society, he never abandons the concept of class struggle. There is no doubt that Holloway's depiction of the Zapatistas' mission as the struggle against the denial of dignity is a fecund one, rich in metaphorical possibility. But at the same time as it enables the Zapatistas to call attention to exploitation in *all* of its forms, it also enfeebles the struggle for overcoming exploitation in *some* of its forms by diffusing the concept of exploitation into the more subjective concept of domination. Do we want individuals to identify with the refrain 'We are all Zapatistas!' because we are sympathetic to the chilling discomfort of university students whose parents won't buy them a BMW or a condo in Beverly Hills? Of course, this is a far cry from the Zapatistas' view of struggle as *la palabra de los armados de verdad y feugo* (the word of those who are armed with truth and fire). To be armed by truth is important, and to echo that truth across the five continents through Zapatista solidarity networks (via a Deleuzian rhizomatic as distinct from a *foquista guerrillero* organization) is surely important. But along with achieving the goal of humanity recognizing itself and its true nature, there is the danger of revolutionary praxis neutralizing itself by means of reformism. Can an (anti)politics of the nonpolitical that "walks asking" and that involves "humor, stories, dance, openness to new ideas and a willingness to admit mistakes" (Holloway and Peláez, 1998, p. 1–18) be sufficient to contest capital in all of its invidious and multipronged formations? I think it is unlikely. I believe that the Zapatistas realize this, too, which is why they have so far resisted the idea of transforming themselves into a political party. Like Che and Freire, the Zapatistas recognize that revolutionary praxis must be two-pronged and must transform consciousness as well as social structures. Were they content to achieve only the former, there is the possibility that their project would be diffused into reformism; yet their attentiveness to the latter assures—for the time being, at least—a similar fidelity to the revolutionary praxis that underwrites the projects of both Che and Freire.

Critical pedagogy has implications for rethinking and recreating democracy through the development of a collective or communal concept of rights and responsibilities and for putting technology into the service of integrating or reintegrating the political with the economic realms of collective decision making and popular democratic governance. Contemporary critical pedagogy needs to rescue Freire's work from the reformists who wish to limit his legacy to its contribution to consciousness-raising. Reformists are often victims of a subjectivism that occurs when people verbally denounce social injustice but leave intact the existing structures of society. Freire's approach only makes sense when read in the context of Marx's negative concept of ideology and the epistemological and ontological shifts that his approach requires. Revolutionary praxis in this sense is only limited by a corrupted will, an interminable obtuseness, a poverty of the imagination that loses faith in all essences, and by allowing the oppressor "within" to overtake the subject in the back alley of history.

Freire and Che were unwavering in their view that education and cultural processes aimed at liberation do not succeed by freeing people from their chains, but by preparing them collectively to free themselves. Freire was more systematic in his approach and was able to work out the formal and informal conditions for this pedagogical encounter to occur successfully. For Freire, liberation was always facilitated through dialectical movement, when conversation is replaced by a dialogical praxis, coupled to a great opening up of the subject to the Other. Whereas conversation or discussion mainly focuses on *what* we think and assists subjects in articulating their interpretation of reality against other interpretations (in this regard it resembles a form of "managed communication of monologues"), dialogue involves the critical investigation of knowledge—not only with respect to what subjects think but also to *why* subjects think what they do. Trust—a very important aspect of dialogue—does not pre-exist dialogical engagement among subjects but instead is created within the act of dialogue itself, *"haciendo el camino al andar"* (making the road as we walk). But as we make this road by walking, we need to seize the territory out of which the path of history is formed, even as we acknowledge history's contingency, its conjunctural characteristics, and its infinite unknowability. Such a carving out of the path of history—a history that has been made, that will be made, and that is in the process of being made—was understood by Che and Freire within an uncompromising materialist conception of history. Che and Freire argued that we must detach ourselves from the delusory idea that we are agents of capital. We are not. We have *become* agents of capital, but this need not be our inevitable condition.

Within a materialist conception of history, we do not witness history occurring in a nonideological space purged of social relations, where the integument of culture is ripped open and difference sucked out. Human actors do not make history in a cultural interregnum or a sterile chamber disinfected of the social. Nor are they subject to the whims of mysterious, other-worldly forces predestined by a metaphysical plan of redemption. Rather, history is conditioned by the nature of labor and its international division. It is conditioned, too, by the stage of development of the productive forces and the manifold conflicts and contradictions associated with the established social relations of production. Historical materialism, then, takes bold yet careful notice of the totality of the productive forces and relations that shape social actors, with an understanding that every new social order carries its own negation within itself. This is why Marx wrote that "the tradition of all the dead generations weighs like a nightmare on the brain of the living" (1950, p. 225). Historical materialism is not propelled by casuistical, theoretical contortions intended to beget every interpretation anew, under the auspices of some Great Decoder. Far from it. Historical materialism is not a Grand Synthesizer of competing ideas and practices but rather an attempt to connect political strategy with an historical understanding of everyday lived experience. Joseph Ferraro writes:

> Historical materialism, by virtue of its emphasis on human productive practices and historical specificity, holds out the prospect of perceiving the present as history. Human beings can know the human world, despite its complexity, because they have made it. . . . A *materialist conception of history* unites ontology, epistemology, and history around a single premise of "struggle." Once asked by a reporter "What is?" Marx replied without hesitation, "Struggle." (1992, p. 35; emphasis in original)

Within the materialist history of class struggle, Freire saw two kinds of education: cultural action and cultural revolution. Cultural action takes place as an oppositional movement against the ruling elite. Cultural revolution takes place after the political and social revolution have been victorious. Freire writes:

> There is one revolutionary kind of education before and another after the revolution has been established. At the beginning, it can't be made inside the power bases as these power bases will silence everything, but it should take place inside popular social movements like unions and nonpopulist popular political parties. And it is through the educators that the traitor pedagogues make their conversion from one side to another, their class suicide. When the revolutionary cry is in power, then revolutionary education will take on another dimension: what was before an education to contest and challenge becomes a systematized education, recreating, helping the reinvention of society. In the previous phase, it helped the call to overthrow a power which was hostile to the masses; now on the side of the masses, education becomes an extraordinary instrument to help build a new society and a new man. (cited in Gadotti, 1994, p. 63)

Here, Freire's phrase "new man" echoes that of Che. It also reflects Freire's concept of revolutionary praxis, in which the denunciation of existence in sedimented society is followed by an annunciation of an alternative set of possibilities—with the announced new reality always already present in the act of denunciation and annunciation (JanMohamed, 1994). Denunciation and annunciation in this sense constitute what Freire calls an "historic commitment." According to JanMohamed, "what Freire seems to imply here is that the temporality entailed in the establishment of a 'fully' achieved new reality must be distinguished from its inaugural moment, which as such is qualitatively different from the temporality that follows" (1994, p. 250).

Revolutionary struggle as a form of border-crossing praxis is aimed at problematizing experience that has been informed by structures of sedimented historical conflict; it carries within its acts of denunciation and annuciation the seedbed of new spaces of heterotopic possibility. From inaugural moments of victory, a more sustained and widespread struggle must be born.

Admittedly, liberation tracks a realm that historical materialism cannot precisely delineate but that needs multiple perspectives to illuminate it. Che and Freire recognized that their theories did not explain all aspects of liberation, but they did recognize that their work made a necessary and fundamental link between human agency and social structure—a link that psychodynamic and Cartesian theories failed to make. What they understood about social life was precisely its dialectical character and its ability to commodify human relations.

Marx's theory of commodity fetishism reveals how the value-relation of commodities realized in their prices of exchange is really a social relation between individuals that, in their eyes, appears to be a relation between things—that is, a natural force beyond the precincts of human control. Social relations appear in a phantasmagoric (*phantastische*) form, and from this form the product of social labor is reified and appears as a thing. Exchange value encodes the practical relations between people, but it does so as if these relations were somehow not historically produced but rather transhistorical relations between things. In the first volume of *Capital*, Marx argues that the relations connecting the labor of one individual with the rest of society appear as they really are: material relations between persons, and social relations between things. Here it is important to note that the particular commodity is the product of private labor, whereas the money commodity is the embodiment of social labor. It is only through the production and sale of the products of labor as commodities that the concrete labors of individuals are brought into relation with one another. Social relations only become fetishized and seen as a relation between things when one commodity (money) is fashioned to serve as a universal equivalent. Slavoj Žižek argues that we need to remember the lesson of the Marxist dialectic of fetishization: "The 'reification' of relations between people (the fact that they assume the form of phantasmagorical 'relations between things') is always redoubled by the apparently opposite process, by the false personalisation ('psychologisation') of what are effectively objective social processes" (1998, p. 160).

PRINCIPLES OF LEADERSHIP FOR REVOLUTIONARY STRUGGLE

What do the examples of the lives and thoughts of Che and Freire have to offer educators in the United States? The fact that the U.S. government helped to hunt down Che in Bolivia and execute him indicates the scale of the threat that Che presented to U.S. interests and values. Che threw into critical relief the so-called untouchable virtues of capitalism and revealed how democracies such as the United States work in clandestine ways through acts of imperialism to destabilize regimes whose resources and leaders it couldn't control. Both Che and Freire were able to reveal the messy underside of democracy, and to expose the crucial links between exploitation and misery in Latin American countries and the interests and practices of the U.S. capitalist class. Today in the United States, African American and Latin youth are almost as likely to end up in the prison system as they are in universities. And when you examine the growing disparity between the rich and the poor in the United States, a powerful case can be made that class and race warfare is being waged by the rich against the poor and powerless in this country.,

Richard Alarcón remarks how crucial the example of Che has become for these contemporary times of subtle ideological assaults:

> Because of the fact that the inevitable changes in our society and the brutal impe-
> rialist offensive introduce new—and sometimes more subtle and serpentine—ele-
> ments in the ideological struggle, Che is indispensable for us. We must take his
> ideas and turn them into a vital guide for workers, students, professors, and the
> entire people. At a time when the poison of selfish individualism threatens us from
> the inside, when some people are giving in or vacillating, we must reproduce his
> unblemished example in the conduct of the vanguard and extend it throughout
> society. We must create solidarity as a norm of everyday life. (1998, p. 35)

As it stands, the major purpose of education is to make the world safe for global capitalism. Education's tropism toward entrepreneurialism—that is, privatization, magnet schools, and vouchers plans—is just one indication of the ballast that corporate-driven curricula provide for capitalist social relations. A revolutionary pedagogy informed by Guevarian- and Freirean-inspired leadership qualities would place the liberation from race, class, and gender oppression as the key goal for education for the new millennium. Education—as well as imperialist practices against other countries—so conceived would be dedicated to creating a citizenry dedicated to social justice and to the reinvention of social life based on democratic socialist ideals. Educational leadership could then not only challenge the vaporous abstractions that constitute the moral authority of United States domestic and foreign policy but also be purposively linked to the development of a coalition of new revolutionary movements that would work conjointly with students, teachers, and administrators to create a civil society responsive to all of its citizens, echoing the *zapatudo* "!Ya Basta!" (Of course, the question of universalizing socialist democracy is not without its difficulties, not least of which are the important debates surrounding rationalism and internationalism.)

A revolutionary pedagogy resists those immaculate discourses and repre-sentations of U.S. history, culture, and politics that too often make their way into the classrooms of the nation. Such representations fail to accommodate the opaque and contradictory social forces and relations that inform U.S. cul-ture and society, and in so doing they ignore the heterogeneity of insurgent struggles that have challenged—and continue to challenge—its imperial world view and practices. A revolutionary pedagogy names and gives voice to those nonparticipants in the colonial encounter who refuse to work as adjuncts for global capitalism's consumerist ideology. Furthermore, revolutionary educa-tors refuse the role that global capitalism has assigned for them: to become the supplicants of corporate America and to work at the behest of the corporate bottom line. Revolutionary pedagogy argues for nonabstract and nonhomoge-nous forms of universalism that do not oppose postmodern particularism but rather are attentive to the dialectical relationship between local and global struggles for emancipation. Revolutionary educators contest the growing assaults on protections for the poor, for women, and for people of color—such as the attacks on affirmative action, immigration, and language rights that we have witnessed in California over recent years—attacks that have become well-nigh irresistible for politicians and education officials only too willing to genuflect at the corporate altar sanctified by reactionary conservative ideology (and theology).

A revolutionary pedagogy challenges the ideological assumptions that underlie both conservative and progressive schooling. It attempts to refashion a politics in which market reality yields to the larger universal values of social-ist democracy that both Che and Freire so forcefully advocated. While busi-ness leaders continue to serve as functionaries and cheerleaders for privatiza-tion, and as capitalism continues to crash all around us, collapsing under the weight of its own contradictions, the ideas and ideals of Che and Freire consti-tute bold and heretical strokes in the ongoing struggle of fashioning human free-dom out of the debris of collapsed dreams. The greater the in-built contradic-tions of capital are exposed, the more the spirits of Che and Freire will shine forth in their full effulgence.

To develop a revolutionary pedagogy premised on historical materialism in the homeland of pragmatism is indeed a daunting task. Those critical educators who object to revolutionary pedagogy (because 'socialism' still remains one ide-ology among many) appear resigned to accepting capitalism as the 'best of all possible worlds.' Given this attitude, critical pedagogy, as it remains trapped within bourgeois pedagogical practices, abandons its struggle against the capi-talist state, preferring instead to interrogate the schisms within capitalism's ide-ological state apparatuses. Consequently, anti-capitalist struggle is replaced by an attack on bourgeois ideology. But simply to replace bourgeois ideology with proletarian ideology, as laudable as this effort is, certainly falls short of a Gue-

varian or Freirean revolutionary praxis. While some new efforts at deconstruction and post-structuralism can indeed help us to reassess our ability to grasp the
world and to understand those aspects of our thought embedded most deeply in
our use of language, to understand how fiction and truth can and do overlap, how
'play' limits meaning as well as enables it, and how readings are always inter-
connected and integrated (MacDonald, 1999), such approaches too often dismiss Marxism as an onto-teleological mistake. We need to move beyond those
"epistemological breaks" provided by deconstruction and post-structuralism,
beyond "the give-and-take between foundationalists and contextualists" (Scott,
1999). David Scott is on the right track when he advocates that another "candidate" be folded into the discussion, and that this candidate must address the
"prospective political forms of community" and engage in a reproblematization
of citizen and community (1999, p. 142). Genealogy and deconstruction are
indispensable practices related to the interdependence of identity/difference
and questions of ethics but in themselves are insufficient to sustain a theory of
politics, let alone a praxis of possibility, in the creation of a socialist alternative.
In saying this, I am not arguing for educators to simply reembrace Freire and
Che as a gesture toward—at least in the case of political *veteranos* such as
myself—salvaging a politics of familiarity, but rather suggesting a repositioning
of the question of the political and the pedagogical that includes, but moves
beyond, questions of epistemology and ethicality toward a concern with rethinking human possibility in materialist terms.

While we may not find the spirit of Che and Freire among the ranks of the
avant-garde here in Los Angeles—hidden among the nomadic amalgamation
of students, artists, musicians, and hangers-on congregating outside of The
Viper Room, or the underage club-hoppers cruising the Plaza or La Luz de
Jesus (where visitors can browse art shows such as "Tortures and Torments of
the Christian Martyrs," or an exhibition curated by Adam Parfrey that features
artwork by mass murderers such as Charles Manson and John Wayne Gacy), or
the punkers outside the Whiskey a-Go-Go wearing T-shirts emblazoned with
"the nature of your oppression is the aesthetic of my rebellion"—we do find a
growing realization among numerous youth sectors that capitalism has over-
dosed. New possibilities abound for coalitions to be forged among the avant-
garde, workers, students, unions, Zapatista brigades, and national and international social movements that are appearing on a daily basis. This is not an
endorsement of social movementism over Marxist proletariat struggle but a
recognition that we need to support signs of collective rebellion wherever they
spring up. The time has come to challenge collectively, for the purpose of struggling toward a socialist future, the ideological hegemonizations of the state, the
swindle of hope propagated by the managerial class, and the silencing of het-
erogeneities by right-wing political and religious fundamentalists. While many
cultural workers appear resplendent in their indifference to assume a class

identity or to sustain class interests, many other people— young and old—have reached their breaking-point and are starting to look to alternative political philosophies and practices, such as those proposed by Che and Freire.

Whereas post-structuralists legitimate their politics primarily on the basis of experience, Che and Freire link such "experience" to an objective economic analysis and historical materialist view of consciousness that does not divorce the "subject" from the messy terrain of the social. Freirean and Guevarian pedagogy stipulates as its aim the transformation of the means of production into the means of emancipation. While post-structuralist criticism can often tragically expose the illusion of democracy and the ruse of capitalist progress, in the end such a species of *faux* radicalism is functionally advantageous to ruling class interests and, by reactivating existing power relations, biased in favor of capitalist stability. For Freire and Che, social relations are always historical-materialist relations arising from the specific conditions under which surplus labor is extracted from the direct producers. Guevarian and Freirean pedagogy point beyond a liberal humanist harmonization of the social order fractured by capital's internal contradictions. Far from serving as a mechanism for social stability, it is fundamentally agonistic. It fights not only for changes within the classroom and institutional context of the school but also supports a transformation in the objective conditions in which students and their parents labor. A revolutionary pedagogy fights for macroeconomic policies favoring full employment and guaranteed support in the public sector for public schools, global labor rights, sustainable development, environmental protections, and the growth of popular movements for social and economic change.

The short-sightedness, mendacity, and bloodless corporate-backed policies for educational reform in this current age of cynical reason cannot be overestimated. It is important that revolutionary educators resist those pundits who would police the poles of debate on education and disabuse educators of the notion that real educational reform requires social transformation, not merely reformation. Both Freire and Che exulted in restoring to the role of the teacher not that of the demiurge of the revolution but that of the revolutionary social agent committed both to a grasp of the contiguity of power and knowledge and to the necessity of social transformation, a position that mainstream pedagogy disablingly ignores. Such a transformation must occur from below—from the power seized by the hands of the *terrae filius*—for the interests and needs of the working class must become the motor of any new revolutionary project. And as the Zapatistas have taught us, the revolution of our time must not only stress the possibilities of Internet insurgency and the articulation of national and local networks designed to build transborder coalitions with NGOs, but also must learn from and build upon the politics and practices of indigeneity.

Che Guevara, circa 1960, Havana (Roberto & Osvaldo Salas/Liaison Agency)

The experiences of indigenous peoples must not be appropriated by Euro-American criticalists in an attempt to essentialize or prescriptively hold prisoner the meaning of subaltern alterity/difference. Neither should these experiences be epistemologically privileged by investing them with an iconicity that lifts their systems of intelligibility to out-of-reach pristine heights that always already exceed Western analytic categories. The repository of lived experiences of which the indigenous agent is the bearer is not immune to critique, even as we acknowledge the violence with which indigenous voices have been displaced by imperialism, patriarchy, and colonialism. Indigenous agents must speak their own realities with their own voices and not be prevented from naming their own experiences, even as we acknowledge that such experiences do not possess an epistemological transparency. These acts of naming must not be rerouted through overdetermined patriarchal Western narratives in order to acquire legitimacy in the larger narrative of liberation. They must, however, be given ethical priority. Indigenous peoples have the right to speak their own truth with-out seeking permission to narrate from those who would continue to oppress them. Not only must the voices of indigenous agents be sounded, but also they must be granted the opportunity to be heard without their voices being bent into

Paulo Freire in Brazil, 1997 (courtesy of Ana Maria Araújo Freire)

the decibels most harmonious to Western ears by imperializing systems of regulation and the gross postulates of the colonial attitude. In creating the "new
agent" of socialism, the preferential option is to listen to the voices that are
sounded from the standpoint of the oppressed. However, in undertaking such a
project it is important to maintain an internationalist focus so that meaning-mak-
ing is not embedded only in the militant particularism and interpretations of
geographically delimited communities, and conscientization is not something
that is confined to the context of a community-situated praxis with its idiographic
singularity. Critical theory, after all, depends upon certain universalizing refer-
ential systems (Honneth, 1995). Revolutionary praxis must equally be insistent
upon totalizing understandings—that is, upon understandings of the totality of
social forces and relations, both in local and global contexts (McLaren, 1995,
1997) while at the same time encouraging relationships to noncontingent, supra-
individual cultural forms (Alexander, 1995). The point here is that a pedagogy
of liberation must be a pedagogy in which location is taken into account but in
which generalization also plays an important role. As Freire argues:

> Take, for example, a classroom in the United States, where the object of knowl-
> edge is multiculturalism. Let's say we have a diverse group of participants—a
> Kenyan, a Dutch, a Norwegian, and so on—and each one of them would look at
> the issue from the point of view of their location, their culture. What we aim at is
> to reach a knowledge that generalizes. That is, while it is very important to use your

location as a point of reference to know your world in more depth, and to also use this point of reference to relate to other locations in the world, the challenge is always to transcend without losing touch of that place. By overemphasizing your immediate location without reflection or understanding of other perspectives of the world, you will invariably fall into a form of *essentialism*. (cited in Leistyna, 1999, p. 50; emphasis in original)

"Unity in diversity"—a key phrase in Freire's later writings—means that all oppressed groups should come together in an effort to struggle against inequality in all of its odious manifestations. The implications in this effort are internationalist in scope and designed to promote a coalitional alliance in which one mode of collective organizing does not trump all others. But it is important to remember that though, for Freire, "unity in diversity" opened up genuine political fusion in broad, international alliances, it did not require struggle to be uniform. Freire implicitly recognized struggle as an embodied materiality that constituted multiple bonds of belonging but also conflicting positions within the collectivity. For Freire and Che, revolutionary praxis aggregates political agency—including its differences—into one collective unit without ignoring those differences. Identity is not a precipitate oozing from the collective, but rather is that which informs or enables the collective—that is, it links individuals ontologically to the collective in such a way that the experience of the self does not pre-empt engagement with otherness.

Freire's struggle was not a monistic one that strove for a common culture, but was anchored instead in a common ground of suffering and hope that pointed provisionally toward utopia. Such a utopia was always more contingent than categorical, always more relationally conceived than dogmatically produced. In the final instance, the inspiration for revolutionary pedagogy must be cultivated from a shared history of struggle, a struggle that is the constant companion and outcome of acting in and on the world, a struggle conjugated with hope, infused with revolutionary love, and dignified by a great exertion of the ethical imagination and human will and its infusion into the struggle for social justice.[2]

One of the most important contributions of Che and Freire was the emphasis they placed on praxis. For both Che and Freire, the dialectic must be disencumbered by metaphysics and grounded in the concrete materiality of human struggle. In the process of becoming fully human, everyday life must be informed by a theory and practice relationship that truly alters ideas and experience within a larger revolutionary dialectic. Paraphrasing Marx, this dialectic operates from each according to her abilities, to each according to her needs, within a context in which the free development of each is the precondition for the free development of all. Raya Dunayevskaya captures this relationship:

[W]ithout a philosophy of revolution activism spends itself in mere anti-imperialism and anti-capitalism, without ever revealing what it is *for*. We have been made to see anew that, just as the movement from practice disclosed a break in the Absolute Idea that required both a new relationship of practice to theory, and a new unity of practice and theory, so that new unity is but a *beginning:* Absolute Idea as New Beginning. . . . Absolute negativity manifests its pivotal role in the Idea precisely because it is both totality (summation) and new beginning, which each generation must first work out for itself. . . . Only live human beings can recreate the revolutionary dialectic forever anew. And these live human beings must do so in theory as well as in practice. It is not a question only of meeting the challenge from practice, but of being able to meet the challenge from the self-development of the Idea, and of deepening theory to the point where it reaches Marx's concept of the philosophy of "revolution in permanence." (1982, pp. 194–195; emphasis in original)

In the wake of Moses Lake in Washington, Pearl in Mississippi, Jonesboro in Arkansas, Springfield in Oregon and Littleton in Colorado, alienation brought about by the fetishization of the global lifeworld continues to swirl angrily about us. We are faced with pandemics of crime and drugs, armies of alienated workers, and the severing of communal bonds. Under the cover of a multicultural democracy, capitalism provides us with race, class, and gender enclaves but divides us in ways that prevent the building of local and global solidarities. As Assata Shakur proclaims:

So in the States what's happening now with the multiculturalism, everybody's talking about, "I'm part Egyptian and part whatever." And I appreciate people discovering that about themselves and discovering aspects of who they are. But that is not political activity. The police are not going to ask you as they shoot you down, "Oh, are you part whatever?" The census is not going to change the district 'cause you are one-fifth Cherokee or whatever.

I think that we have to take a new look at what globalization means in terms of gender issues, in terms of race issues, and to rethink very seriously the kinds of not only structures that we deal with in terms of building social justice but the kinds of lives we live and the kinds of examples we're settling for those people who follow us. Because unless we make our lives as people who are dedicated to social change attractive so people are attracted to it, they feel good, they feel warm, they feel a sense of community, we're going to lose a majority of our youth. Because I think that in our style of political work, political activism has left a lot to be desired. I think a lot of people struggled for a lot of years without forming some kind of family or creating warm relationships. I think this has meaning. [Without this] I think we haven't discovered a new way of humanity. (1999, p. 99)

Young people searching for "a new way of humanity" have the examples of Freire and Che to ponder, to inspire and to emulate. For United States youth faced with an eviscerated public sphere, an absence of communal forms and relations, and the constriction of an empty self cobbled out of the scraps and debris of a consumer-based economy, Che's and Freire's example of collective solidarity offers a striking alternative. Whereas youth in the United States fill the void in their pertuse identities with incendiary fantasies of revenge, rampant violence and unabated sex (not to mention dreams of vast wealth and extreme levels of power) the revolutionary self inscribed in the ideas and practices of Che and Freire offers a new model of political and pedagogical agency.

At the moment of our birth we receive a ticket to Death. No reservations are necessary and our destination is assured. What remains open to fortune is what we choose to do along the way. Che and Freire both understood that we can rail against our fate but we cannot injure eternity. They chose not to mourn destiny but to celebrate the journey of life. To celebrate life always demands sacrificing our ontological security because, as Che and Freire both knew, it is impossible to celebrate life under conditions that do not obtain for all, that did not allow all others to enjoy the fruits of their struggle and labor. As long as others suffer, celebration is empty. But when collective struggle triumphs, that is—and continues to be—a cause for joy. Few figures as vivid as Che Guevara and Paulo Freire have ever crossed the stage of human history. It surely is tragic that their generation did not awaken at their call, but more tragic still is the possibility that future generations will choose not to heed their message nor follow their bold example. We will never see the likes of them again.

Dear *compañeros* and *compañeras,* ours is the epoch of hope and dreams. There are still challenges ahead on the unbeaten path of revolutionary struggle and it is up to us to meet them. The challenge ahead is to reclaim the pedagogical praxis of the revolutionary and to summon the world-historical actions of the victims of capital, remembering that the pedagogy of revolution cannot be sacrificed to the fashionable apostasy of today's education pundits, who, in this postsecular, heterophilic culture of the dead end, would all too willingly domesticate the political reach of vision and ontological vocation that Che and Freire so steadfastly struggled to keep alive—which was the transformation of the capitalist world system, and through that struggle, the transformation of the human heart.

¡Hasta la Victoria Siempre! Che and Paulo, *No los vamos a oldivar!*

NOTES

1. This exegesis of the pedagogy of Che and Freire is admittedly partial. It is impossible for any author (especially in this case, one from *el norte*) to fully redeem the current object under analysis. There is always an extraliterary remainder, given the differently constituted transnational positionalities of the author and his (or her) object of analysis. Is there not always a hidden verso to the recto of analysis? That this work is undertaken as a hermeneutics of solidarity does not mean that it completely escapes the fetishization of the object as abject other. A certain mechanics of representation preconditions the tropological and rhetorical registers I have used. My attempt to restore to the subaltern a position of central historical agency through a reengagement with the figures of Che and

Freire is openly stalked by modernity. Yet my refusal to abandon "totality" is not to create an impassable limit but to locate the unsayable as a redemptive site of engagement. Such an exotopic site of epistemic breakdown—while arching toward collective struggle—is prone to internal collapse, negating the very possibility of a horizontal politics of coalition. Yet paradoxically such a project is necessary in order to fashion a pedagogical project where *praxis* is not held hostage to undecidability. In my conjunctural engagement with Che and Freire, I have undoubtedly occluded some relations of exploitation hidden in the act of discursive elaboration itself and implemented unknowingly a neo-colonial vertical political matrix in my avowed project of horizontalist solidarity formation and coalition building (see Moreiras, 1996; Williams, 1996). The pedagogical agent must continue to press forward while at the same time being self-reflexive about the contradictions and aporias in his or her own political project.

2. Recently the Escola de Samba Leandro de Itaquera in São Paulo, Brazil, developed a samba performance for the 1999 carnival. Called "Por Paulo Freire: Educação, um Salto para Liberdade," the samba now makes it possible for all to read, sing, and dance Paulo Freire.

Acorda meu Brasil	Wake up Brasil
Desperta pra Felicidade	Arise to Happiness
Eu quero amor, eu quero amar	I want love, I want to love } refrain
Em liberdade	In freedom
E hoje!	And today?
Hoje a Leandro tão bonita, faz o seu papel	Today beautiful Leandro asks permission
Pede licença, e mostra	To play its part and show
A realidade nua e crua	The naked, raw conditions
No quadro negro, a nossa luta continua	On the blackboard, our struggle continues
A minha escola da um salto pro futuro	My school takes a leap into the future
E vem pra guerra de caneta na mão	And comes to the war with pen in hand
Vermelho e branco pede educação	The red and white asks for education
Sem preconceito e discriminação	Without prejudice and discrimination
Divina luz inspirou	Inspired by divine light
Cantamos numa só voz	We sing with one voice: } repeat
E Paulo Freire, está presente em nós	Paulo Freire is here by our choice
Moço	Young man,
Não abro mão dos meus direitos	I do not let go of my rights
Eu também tenho o meu conceito	I also have faith in my insights:
No universo da criação	In the created universe

Mentes são dotades de virtude e poder	Minds are imbued with virtue and power
Basta abrir as portas verá florescer	Just open the doors you'll see them flower
O mundo, onde a magia forma os ideais	The world, where magic shapes ideals
E o saber, não se difere por camadas sociais	And knowledge, is not divided by social class
É hora de reflexão	Let reflection play its part
E consciência em cada coração Um clarão reluz, mundança	And make conscious every heart Relight the flame of change
Salve a juventude, criança	All hail the youth, the child
Na fé que incendeia	Let faith illuminate the creation } repeat
Futuro feliz, nação brasileira	A happy future for our Brazilian nation.

English translation by Peter Lownds.

REFERENCES

Alcarón, Ricardo (1998). "Che Continues to Instill Fear in the Oppressors." *The Militant* (Special issue celebrating the homecoming of Ernesto Che Guevara's reinforcement brigade to Cuba), pp. 32–36.

Alexander, Jeffrey (1995). *Fin-de-siècle Social Theory: Relativism, Reduction, and the Problem of Reason.* London: Verso.

Allman, Paula; with Mayo, Peter; Cavanagh, Chris; Heng, Chan Lean; and Haddad, Sergio (1998). "Introduction: '. . . The Creation of a World in Which It Will Be Easier to Love.'" *Convergence*, vol. 31, nos. 1 and 2, pp. 9–16.

Alvarado, Elvia (1987). *Don't Be Afraid Gringo: A Honduran Woman Speaks from the Heart.* Translated and edited by Medea Benjamin. New York: HarperCollins.

Aronowitz, Stanley (1998). "Introduction." In Paulo Freire, *Pedagogy of Freedom: Ethics, Democracy, and Civic Courage.* Lanham, Md.: Rowman & Littlefield, pp. 1–19.

Bannerji, Himani (1995). *Thinking Through.* Toronto: Women's Press.

Dunayevskaya, Raya (1982). *Rosa Luxemburg, Women's Liberation, and Marx's Philosophy of Revolution.* Atlantic Highlands, N.J.: Humanities Press; and Sussex, England: Harvester Press.

Ferraro, Joseph (1992). *Freedom and Determination in History According to Marx and Engels.* New York: Monthly Review Press.

Freire, Ana Maria Araújo; and Macedo, Donaldo (1998). "Introduction." In Ana Maria Araújo Freire and Donaldo Macedo (eds.), *The Paulo Freire Reader.* New York: Continuum, pp. 1–44.

Freire, Paulo (1998b) *Pedagogy of the Heart.* New York: Continuum.

——— (1994). *Pedagogy of Hope: Reliving Pedagogy of the Oppressed.* New York: Continuum.

Gadotti, Moacir (1994). *Reading Paulo Freire: His Life and Work.* Albany, N.Y.: State University of New York Press.

Grossberg, Lawrence (1999). "Speculations and Articulations of Globalization." *Polygraph* 11, pp. 11–48.

Holloway, John; and Peláez, Eloina (1998). "Introduction: Reinventing Revolution." In John Holloway and Eloina Peláez (eds.). *Zapatista! Reinventing Revolution in Mexico.* London and Sterling, Va.: Pluto Press, pp. 1–18.

Honneth, Axel (1995). *The Struggle for Recognition: The Moral Grammar of Social Conflicts.* Cambridge: Polity.

JanMohamed, Abdul R. (1994). "Some Implications of Paulo Freire's Border Pedagogy." In Henry A. Giroux and Peter McLaren (eds.). *Between Borders: Pedagogy and the Politics of Cultural Studies.* New York and London: Routledge, pp. 242–252.

Leistyna, Pepi (1999). *Presence of Mind: Education and the Politics of Deception.* Boulder, Colo.: Westview.

MacDonald, Eleanor (1999). "Deconstruction's Promise: Derrida's Rethinking of Marxism." *Science & Society,* vol. 63, no. 2, pp. 145–172.

Marx, Karl (1950). "The Eighteenth Brumaire of Louis Bonaparte." In *Karl Marx and Frederich Engels: Selected Works,* vol. 1. Moscow: Foreign Languages Publishing.

——— (1983). *Capital.* Vol. 1, London: Lawrence and Wishard.

McLaren, Peter (1995). *Critical Pedagogy and Predatory Culture: Oppositional Politics in a Postmodern Era.* London and New York: Routledge.

——— (1997). *Revolutionary Multiculturalism: Pedagogies of Dissent for the New Millennium.* Boulder, Colo.: Westview.

Memmi, Albert (1965). *The Colonizer and the Colonized.* Boston: Beacon.

Moreiras, Alberto (1996). "The Aura of Testimonio." In George M. Gugelberger (ed.). *The Real Thing: Testimonial Discourse in Latin America.* Durham N.C., and London: Duke University Press, pp. 192–224.

Ollman, Bertell (1998). "Why Dialectics? Why Now?" *Science and Society,* vol. 62, no. 3, fall, pp. 339–357.

Oltuski, Enrique (1998). "Guevara: 'Human Beings Are No Longer the Beasts of Burden.'" *Militant* (Special issue celebrating the homecoming of Ernesto Che Guevara's reinforcement brigade to Cuba), pp. 41–45.

Schugurensky, Daniel (1998). "The Legacy of Paulo Freire: A Critical Review of His Contributions." *Convergence,* vol. 31, nos. 1 and 2, pp. 17–38.

Scott, David (1999). *Refashioning Futures: Criticism after Postcoloniality.* Princeton, N.J.: Princeton University Press.

Shakur, Assata (1999). "Assata Shakur: 'The Continuity of Struggle.'" *Souls,* Vol. 1, No. 2, pp. 93–100.

Williams, Gareth (1996). "The Fantasies of Cultural Exchange in Latin American Subaltern Studies." In George M. Gugelberger (ed.). *The Real Thing: Testimonial Discourse in Latin America.* Durham, N.C., and London: Duke University Press, pp. 225–253.

Žižek, Slavoj (1998). "Risk Society and Its Discontents." *Historical Materialism,* no. 2, pp. 143–164.

INDEX

Movimento de Reorientacão Curricular, 147

NAFTA. *See* North American Free Trade Agreement
Naiman, Joanne, 128n26
Nasser, Gamal, 94
nationalism, cultural, 64
nation-state, 85, 86; allegiance to, 107–8; Che's view of, 92
Neary, Mike, xxv
Nechayev, Sergei, 125n10
neoliberalism, 20, 26, 33; Freire criticism of, 152, 190; Marxism in, 99
Nicaragua, 44, 124n8
nonviolence, 113–14
Noriega, Manuel, 62
North American Free Trade Agreement (NAFTA), 25, 37; effect on Mexico, 47–48
Nugent, Daniel, 51

Odria, Manuel, 45
OECD. *See* Organization for Economic Cooperation and Development
oil, 54
Ollman, Bertell, 188
ontology, xi, 189
Oppenheimer, Andres, 49
oppression, 154; bases of, 166; freeing self from, 175; internalizing oppressor, 172–74; inversion of, 156; pedagogy for resistance to, 147
Organization for Economic Cooperation and Development (OECD), 25, 26
Ortega, Daniel, 40
Osinaga, Susana, 5
Ovando Candía, Alfredo, 4, 6
overcapacity, 23, 169
overconsumption, 99
overproduction, 23
Owen-Jones, Peter, 11

Panoso, Carlos Pérez, 3, 121n1
Pantoja, Orlando (Antonio, Olo), 6
paranoia, 30–31

Paravicini, José Arce, 10
Paredo, Inti, 71, 114, 127n21
Parker, Stuart, 168
Partido Democrático Popular Revolucionario (PDPR), 52
Party of the Poor (PDLP), 52
patriarchy, 166
PDLP. *See* Party of the Poor
PDPR. *See* Partido Democrático Popular Revolucionario
peasants, 157–58, 172, 174, 188
pedagogy, xxvi, 185; critical (*see* critical pedagogy); Guevarian/Freirean, 198–99; liberation (*see* liberation pedagogy); political nature of, 164; politics and, 160; revolutionary (*see* revolutionary pedagogy). *See also* education
Pedagogy of Freedom, 164
Pedagogy of Hope, 164, 170
Pedagogy of the Oppressed, xx, 146, 156, 172
performative identity, 92
Perrucci, Robert, 34
Peru, 45
Pessoa de Araújo, Aluízio, 142
Petras, James, 14, 42, 51; on armed struggle, 114; on Che's view of globalization, 106, 107, 108; on contemporary political action, 111; on Mexico, 56
Pinochet, Augusto, 27, 28, 53, 145
political activism, 102
political change, education and, 148
political parties, 110
political praxis, xix
political styles, 51
politics: in daily life, 152; historical context of, 83; pedagogy and, 160; performative, 103
Polyani, Michael, 22
polyarchy, 36–37
Ponce, Anibal, 73
Popular Movement for the Liberation of Angola (MPLA), 80
postcolonial theory, 92
postmodernism, xxiv–xxv; critiques of, 36; culture of, 88; education and, 89,

ABOUT THE AUTHOR

Peter McLaren is known worldwide for his educational activism and scholarly writings on critical pedagogy, critical literacy, the sociology and anthropology of education, cultural studies, critical ethnography, and Marxist theory. Formerly Renowned Scholar-in-Residence and Director of the Center for Education and Cultural Studies, Miami University of Ohio, McLaren is now a professor at the Graduate School of Education and Information Studies, University of California, Los Angeles. His scholarship and political activism take him throughout Latin America, the Caribbean, Europe, the Middle East, and Southeast Asia.

McLaren's most recent books include *Revolutionary Multiculturalism: Pedagogies of Dissent for the New Millennium* (Routledge); *Critical Pedagogy and Predatory Culture: Oppositional Politics in a Postmodern Era* (Westview); *Schooling as a Ritual Performance: Toward a Political Economy of Educational Symbols and Gestures,* 3d ed. (Rowman & Littlefield); and *Life in Schools,* 3d ed. (Longman). His works have been translated into twelve languages.